THREE BYZANTI

Three Byzantine Saints

*Contemporary Biographies translated
from the Greek*

by

Elizabeth Dawes

and

Norman H. Baynes

ST. VLADIMIR'S SEMINARY PRESS
Crestwood, New York 10707
1977

First Published 1948
This edition published 1977
by St. Vladimir's Seminary Press
Crestwood, NY 10707

ISBN 0-913836-44-3

CONTENTS

NOTE TO THE REPRINT

N. H. Baynes himself much regretted that in pruning his Introduction to Theodore of Sykeon at short notice he inadvertently omitted to retain the reference to Theophilus Joannou, Μνημεῖα ἁγιολογικά, Venice, 1884, pp. 361–495, where the text of Theodore's *Life* is to be found.

Had he lived he would almost certainly have wished to see some revision of the work, particularly of the Notes to the text. Apart from the correction of a few minor misprints, it has not however been possible to make any changes. But for supplementary information and bibliography readers are referred to such works as the *Bibliotheca Hagiographica Graeca*, 3rd ed., 3 vols., Brussels, 1957, H.-G. Beck, *Kirche und theologische Literatur im byzantinischen Reich*, Munich, 1959, *Lexikon für Theologie und Kirche*, Freiburg, 1957–67 and the more recent fascicules of the French ecclesiastical encyclopedias.

In general Dr. Dawes first made a translation, and that translation we have discussed together many times. Our aim throughout has been to produce to the best of our ability a faithful version of the Greek texts. Dr. Dawes living in Weybridge had not access to a library and therefore asked me to be responsible for the Introductions and the Notes. The Notes make no pretensions to learning; they are intended simply to answer questions which might naturally arise in the mind of a reader.

N. H. B.

INTRODUCTION

THESE simple biographies of three Byzantine saints should speak for themselves: they need no lengthy preface or elaborate annotation. A brief introduction will suffice.

During the period of persecution the virtues of the Christian champions of the faith had been recorded in the Acts of the Martyrs, of those who had borne the supreme witness to their Lord in the surrender of their life. But when persecution had ceased in the fourth century it was by his life and not by his death that the Christian established his loyalty to his Master, and the record of the conflict with evil and the passionate struggle towards perfection created a new type of literature. So far as we know, it was Athanasius, Patriarch of Alexandria, who in his life of Antony, 'the first monk', originated the model for this new literary form. He chose as his theme the ascent of the saint from strength to strength in his pilgrimage towards the ultimate goal — the vision of God. And this development in the spiritual life of the Christian 'athlete' determined the traditional shape of the biography of the Byzantine saint.

To enter into the thought-world of the Byzantine ascetic one must always be conscious of the biblical background which forms its presupposition. From the first Christianity has been an other-worldly faith: in this present world the Christian had no abiding city, he was a sojourner awaiting the coming of One Who should make all things new. The Christian had been assured (John xii. 31, xiv. 30) that the ruler of this world was the Prince of Evil who had no part in Christ. In this life with its besetting cares the ascetic heard his Master's words — 'If thou wouldst be perfect' — as they were read in church, and the passion for a fuller discipleship carried the day. It is the glory of the early Church that it never succumbed to the temptation to restrict salvation to the learned — the Christian gnostic; the gate for the simple — the 'little ones' of the Gospel — even with the Alexandrian thinkers always remained open. The Church of the third century thus came to develop a double morality: there was one

ix

ethical standard for the ordinary Christian living his life in the world and another standard for those who 'saying good-bye' to the world sought the high goal of perfection. For that life the Christian had to go into 'training' (askesis), he became an 'ascetic', and it was to the ascetic that the common folk of the Byzantine world looked with wonder and admiration. The battle waged by the ascetic is a struggle on a double front — against his own body and against the forces of the demons. It is sometimes said that 'the animal instincts are morally neutral', but it was not thus that the Christian saint regarded the body: he was constantly reminded of the strength of the lusts of the body and of its sadistic passions. The body was an enemy which only the sternest contest could subdue. Paul had said, 'I give my body a black eye and reduce it to slavery', and this was the aim which inspired the Byzantine ascetic. The biographer of St. Luke the Stylite appropriates the language of Paul: the task of the saint was 'the strangling of the body'. The good fight might last for many a long year, but in the end victory was possible, the body would be forced to surrender and to come to terms with the soul. Thereafter for the saint the body ceased to have a moral significance, it was no longer a source of temptation.

'Unto you', Christ had said to His chosen disciples, 'unto you it is given to know the mystery of the kingdom of God', and it was initiation into that mystery that the Byzantine ascetic sought. Antony immured himself in a deserted fort; after twenty years when those who were determined to see the holy man had broken down the door of his retreat, Antony came forth 'as from some secret shrine, initiated into the mysteries and indwelt by God', and straightway the divine grace manifested itself in miracles of healing. The author of the biography of St. Luke writing in the tenth century uses the same language of the moment when the saint left the cave in which he had been confined and then similarly obtains from God a special gift — the gift of perfect endurance.

But even though the saint might win the battle over the body, the attacks of the demons did not cease — they lasted until death, for the pride of the demons did not permit them to confess that their efforts were fruitless. But the saint had won through to a new confidence: he knew that with God's aid the demons were powerless to harm — he could laugh them to scorn.

Further, if we are to realize the significance of these records of the achievements of Byzantine saints we must seek to understand something of what these 'holy men' meant for the folk of their own day. To the East Roman Christ had become the Pantokrator, the all-powerful Sovereign, throned in glory. The figure of the Christ as it was represented in the mosaics of Byzantine churches was so majestic and remote that common folk felt that they needed a mediator who would represent them in the courts of Heaven. The humanity of the Saviour tended to be obscured by the splendour of the Second Person of the Trinity. The religion of the Byzantine world is thus a religion of mediation, but it is to the ascetic saint rather than to the priest that the East Roman turns. When you feel that death is near it is to the saint on his pillar that you look for a letter which shall grant you absolution from past sins; the saint, even without your asking, may send you such a letter. The saint has liberty of access, freedom of speech in the heavenly places. He can perform the task of acting as ambassador for humble people.

And the saint's services are not confined to the other world, in this world, too, the saint is a very present help in time of trouble. He can defend those who are without influence against the injustice of the powerful: he can even admonish emperors. The only thing which an emperor can take from an ascetic is his life, and if his life were taken, he would as a martyr be but the more dangerous, and emperors were unwilling to run that risk. The ascetic saint was not only the people's champion against injustice, he was the source of a healing power more potent than that of any doctor. Through his conflict with evil and victory over the demons he had been granted the grace of healing — the power to fulfil the apostolic commission to heal the sick and to cast out demons. The Byzantine could claim divine authority for his belief in these miracles of healing. Jesus had promised: 'he that believeth on me the works that I do shall he do also; and greater works than these shall he do, because I go unto the Father'. A Byzantine writer recording the miracles of Saints Cosmas and Damian — the saints who had vowed to take no gift however small from those whom they had healed — reminds the reader that nowhere are we told that Christ's shadow worked a miracle of healing, but we do know that men and women brought forth the sick into the streets and laid them on beds and couches that at the least the shadow of Peter as he passed by might fall on some of them and they were healed. 'If thou canst believe, all things are possible to him that believeth.' God's power was not straitened; if miracles had been performed in earlier days, a living God must still be active in the world which He had created. To deny that beneficent activity was to make Christ a liar.

And such an assurance was of daily significance when man was beset with uncounted demons on every side. It needs some imagination to recover a sense of the burden which this belief in the universal presence of the demons must have laid upon men. If we believed that the myriad bacilli about us were each and all inspired by a conscious will to injure man we might then gain a realization of the constant menace which broods over human life in the biographies of Byzantine saints. The sign of the Cross and the succour of the 'holy man', these were the East Roman's stand-by in a dangerous world. We can still catch the echo of the excitement and enthusiasm of the disciples as they returned from their first missionary journey: 'Lord, Lord', they cried, 'even the demons are subject to us in Thy name.' This subjection of the demons was the supreme test of the virtue of the Gospel which they had been commissioned to declare. Preaching that Gospel and driving out demons formed from the first but two sides of one and the same divine commission and both tasks are in our own day still undertaken by the Christian missionary.

The saint's healing could be carried to the sick by many different means: just as 'from Paul's body were brought unto the sick handkerchiefs or aprons, and the diseases departed from them', so the Byzantine saint would send the towel with which he had washed his hands, telling the sufferer to tear up the towel and make little crosses of it; when these had been nailed up on door and window in the name of the Trinity the demon would find entry barred. Or the saint would send a 'benediction' of consecrated bread and water, or the water in which he had washed his hands or a fragment of his leathern girdle. It might be the image of the pillar saint or a little holy dust from the foot of the pillar, it mattered not provided only that the 'power' of the saint was conveyed to the sufferer, the 'power' which was God's gift. Or in some cases healing came through sleeping in the church or oratory dedicated to the saint who appeared in dream to the faithful and either cured them or gave directions how they should be cured. This seeking of a miraculous cure through sleeping close by the relics of the saint — 'incubation' — is still practised in the churches of Southern Europe.

East Roman asceticism took many forms and we have sought to illustrate that diversity in the choice of biographies to be translated. St. John the Almsgiver was the Patriarch of Alexandria in a time of crisis during the early years of the seventh century; St. Theodore the Sykeote represents life amongst the peasantry of Anatolia at the end of the sixth century, while Daniel, the pillar saint, brought to the neighbourhood of Constantinople the peculiar form of the ascetic life which St. Simeon had devised for himself in Syria. Daniel, stationed on the European shore of the Bosphorus, is in close touch with the Patriarch, with successive emperors and with the people in the capital. In the present book we have not included any descriptions of life in the community of a monastery.

Byzantine literature is aristocratic: it centres in the life of Constantinople, while in language and style it is dominated by the traditions derived from the masterpieces of the classical period. It is through the biographies of East Roman saints that we can form some picture of the life of the province, some understanding of the thought-world of those humble folk who appear so rarely in the works of writers whose interests are urban, who are closely linked with the life of the imperial court.

If for you a world where miracles happen is hopelessly and irredeemably repellent, East Rome will remain a closed book. Moreover, you must not bring to the study of Byzantine asceticism a delicate and queasy stomach; you must banish from your mind the curious western notion that cleanliness is next to godliness. You must be prepared to accept the sanctity of dirt, the virtue of 'alousia', abstention from washing. The modern cult of the body must be for a while forgotten. But when you have liberated yourself from inherited prejudices, then you will be free to sympathize with the devotion which inspired these contemners of the body, who sought through penitential suffering to attain to peace of soul (ataraxia) and through that peace to union with God.

The background of miracle in these biographies is omnipresent; students may find of service some references to modern work on the subject:

R. HERZOG, *Die Wunderheilungen von Epidauros*. Leipzig, Dieterich, 1931.

J. TAMBORINO, *De antiquorum daemonismo* (=Religionsgeschichtliche Versuche und Vorarbeiten edd. R. Wünsch and L. Deubner, vol. 7, Heft 3). Giessen, Töpelmann, 1909.

L. DEUBNER, *De Incubatione*. Leipzig, Teubner, 1900.

F. J. DÖLGER, *Der Exorzismus im altchristlichen Taufritual* (=Studien zur Geschichte und Kultur des Altertums edd. E. Drerup, H. Grimme and J. P. Kirsch, vol. 3, Heft 1-2). Paderborn, Schöningh, 1909.

MARY HAMILTON, *Incubation or the Cure of Disease in pagan temples and Christian churches*. St. Andrews, Henderson, 1906, and *Greek Saints and their Festivals*. Edinburgh, Blackwood, 1910.

G. G. DAWSON, *Healing Pagan and Christian*. London, Society for Promoting Christian Knowledge, 1935.

T. K. OESTERREICH, *Possession Demoniacal and Other among primitive races, in Antiquity, the Middle Ages and modern times*. London, Kegan Paul, 1930.

E. R. MICKLEM, *Miracles and the New Psychology*. London, Milford, 1922 — in this book the evidence for demon possession as studied by missionaries is discussed.

ST. DANIEL THE STYLITE
A.D. 409-493

INTRODUCTION

THE Emperor Marcian died early in A.D. 457 and with him the Theodosian dynasty (to which he belonged through his marriage with Pulcheria) came to an end. His successor, Leo I, owed his throne to the influence of the all-powerful master of the soldiery, the Alan Aspar and his father Ardaburius. They doubtless thought that Leo would play the part of their puppet, but the new Emperor was not prepared to accept that rôle and the Life of Daniel shows us how the plots of Aspar to overthrow the Augustus of his making were defeated by Zeno the Isaurian. Leo sought through the support of the hardy mountaineers of Isauria to rid himself of the dominance of the German element in the imperial army. From the Life we learn for the first time of the reason for the disgrace of Aspar and are informed of the way in which Zeno became known to Leo. We can understand why it was that the Emperor desired to engage condottieri from Gaul, and it is not surprising that he was angered when Titus, their leader, chose to abandon the life of a soldier.

The two outstanding disasters of Leo's reign were the fire in the capital (September 465) which devastated whole quarters of Constantinople, and the failure of the naval expedition against the Vandals for which both the West and the East of the Empire joined forces. Concerning that defeat the Vita is discreetly silent, for Daniel's prophecy this time had but a partial fulfilment; but from the Vita we learn that a report had reached the Emperor that Gaiseric, the Vandal king, intended to attack Alexandria. For that intention the Life is our sole authority, but at a time when the Vandal fleet was laying waste the coastlands of Greece and massacring the population of the island of Zacynthus an assault on Egypt might naturally be feared. The costly preparations for the African expedition emptied the East Roman treasury, and it is little wonder that the Emperor's subjects complained of the brutality and oppression of the imperial tax-collectors.

In 468 Leo married his daughter Ariadne to Zeno and the child of that marriage (born in 469), who was given the name of Leo, was declared Augustus in the autumn of 473 and became sole emperor on the death of Leo I in February 474. For the child-emperor Zeno acted as regent until with the consent of Leo's widow Verina he was himself created his son's colleague. But Leo II died a few months later and the Isaurian was left as ruler of the Eastern provinces. As an Isaurian he was unpopular: Verina plotted against him and hoped to make her paramour Patricius emperor. But when the revolution came and Zeno had fled to Asia it was Basiliscus, the commander in the expedition against the Vandals, and not Patricius, who was chosen in Zeno's room. Basiliscus favoured the Monophysites and of the orthodox opposition in the capital, headed by Daniel the Stylite, we possess in the Life a vivid account. After Zeno had returned to power Daniel gave him advice which may be regarded as a veiled criticism of his rule, but of Zeno as emperor Daniel's biographer has on the whole a high opinion: after his restoration to his throne the most holy churches enjoyed great happiness, the State was rendered glorious and the Roman Empire was strengthened. It is a remarkable tribute to an Isaurian emperor.

Zeno's successor was chosen by his daughter-in-law, the Augusta Ariadne; her choice fell upon a civil servant, Anastasius, who had recently been proposed as bishop for the see of Antioch. Anastasius (A.D. 491-518) finally banished the threat of Isaurian domination: they had performed their task, the German element in the imperial army was no longer dangerous, and thus the mountaineers could be sent back to their homes. Against the invasions of the Bulgarians, Anastasius constructed to the west of Constantinople a Long Wall, a line of fortifications stretching from the Propontis to the Black Sea at a distance of some forty miles from the capital (cf. J. B. Bury, *History of the Later Roman Empire*, 1923, pp. 435-6). It is apparently this fortification which the author of the Life of Daniel has in mind in ch. 65. For Anastasius Daniel's biographer has an enthusiastic admiration; in ch. 91 he gives an almost lyrical description of the Emperor's character, of his piety, of the complete absence of that love of money which in a sovereign is in very truth for his subjects the root of all ills. Anastasius, both in peace and war, provides for the world the fullest prosperity.

Such is the historical background of this Life of Daniel, the Pillar Saint. It was Simeon the Stylite who in the fifth century set the model for this strange form of penitential asceticism, and it was his renown which led others to follow his example. Syrian asceticism was represented rather by the solitary than by the monk who shared in the common life of a monastery; when compared with the Palestinian rule of St. Sabas it adopted extremer forms in its struggle to subdue the passion of man's intractable flesh. One form which was widely practised was that of the 'station' (stasis): the ascetic took his 'stand' and thenceforth remained immobile. Some would stand all the night in prayer, some stood continuously for years while others divided the day between sitting and standing in one and the same spot.

Simeon was born *c.* A.D. 389 on the borders of Syria and Cilicia; he became a shepherd-boy and was completely illiterate. It was the hearing of the beatitudes as they were read in church which led him to asceticism and caused him to join a monastery. Here the rigours of his mortification of the body proved incompatible with the common life of the brotherhood, so, leaving the monastery, he began his discipline as a solitary by shutting himself up in a cell not far from Antioch. Three years later he retired to a neighbouring height, and there marked out for himself a circular enclosure; to prevent himself from passing beyond this enclosure he attached himself to a large stone by a chain. After some time he ceased to use the chain, and for four years he stood within the enclosure without lying or sitting down, 'snowed upon, rained upon, and scorched'. His fame spread far and wide; pilgrims came in large numbers; the sick sought healing; all wished to touch him or to carry off some relic from the Saint. To escape the devotion of the crowds he thought of the expedient of standing upon a column and the original column was twice increased in height by the addition of a new drum. On the column in its final form — forty cubits in height — he stood for thirty years without shelter either from the frosts of winter or the scorching heat of summer. At times the glare of the sun made him completely blind. The night and the greater part of the day he spent in prayer, but twice a day he addressed the folk who thronged about the column, giving them moral counsel, settling their disputes, healing their diseases. Arabs, Persians and Armenians came on pilgrimage to the Saint; Christians came from Italy and Spain, from Gaul and from Britain. St. Geneviève of Paris wrote to him. In Rome little images of Simeon, even during his lifetime, were to be found in workshops to secure the safety of the workers (cf. Karl Holl, *Gesammelte Aufsätze zur Kirchengeschichte* II, Tübingen, 1928, pp. 388-98).

Many ascetics had their own peculiar forms of devotion: Simeon would bow so deeply in his worship that his forehead all but touched his feet. On one occasion an admirer set himself to count the number of these bowings; he had counted up to twelve hundred and forty-four and then desisted from sheer weariness: the Saint continued bowing. The crowds of his admirers had no doubts of Simeon's sanctity, but the ecclesiastical authorities frowned upon this novel form of penitential piety. It is clear that the Saint's champions developed an apologia to meet such criticism: they pointed to the strange conduct of the Jewish prophets. God, they urged, can use extraordinary means to bring home to man His messages. The apologia was successful: when Simeon died seven bishops accompanied in solemn procession the translation of the Saint's remains to Antioch.

In this Byzantine world everything was fair where sacred relics were concerned: to secure a relic guile and even open theft were justified. The dead saint would even help those who sought to steal his body. When it was thought that a certain holy man was near to death there was a free fight amongst parties from rival villages. The victors in the affray carried off the body to Antioch when the Saint, recovering, asked to be taken back to the mountain from which he had been violently transported. Immediately it was known that Simeon was dead Saracens rushed up on their camels in order to gain possession of his body by force of arms, but the sacred relic was guarded by the imperial troops under the command of the master of the soldiery. In Antioch the body rested; it remained the city's pride and protection.

It is not easy for us to picture to ourselves the life led by the stylite saints on the pillar-top. There was, of course, a balustrade or iron trellis-work around the platform: we never hear of a saint inadvertently falling from his pillar. The saint controlled all access to himself since any visitor was of necessity compelled to wait until the order was given for the ladder to be placed against the pillar (see the Life, ch. 42). To reach Daniel's first column the ladder according to one manuscript had fourteen rungs but when a column might be sixteen or eighteen metres in height the moving of the ladder can have been no light task. The Stylite's column consisted of three parts: the steps up to the platform at the base of the column, the column itself and then the enclosure at the column's top. The column of the elder Simeon had three drums, in honour of the Trinity, says the Syriac biographer. The elder Simeon, as we have seen, had no shelter at all as he stood upon his column and St. Daniel desired to follow his master's example, until he was ultimately persuaded to permit the construction of a covering. Exceptionally in Daniel's case twin columns were erected, clamped together by iron bars and a piece of masonry 'of which it is difficult to fix the position' (Delehaye). Of the extent of the space occupied by the pillar-saint on the top of the column we have no accurate knowledge; often it is not easy to decide whether visitors stood on the topmost rungs of the ladder (cf. the Life of Daniel, ch. 95) or whether they mounted on to the platform.

The Stylite soon became a magnet and drew disciples desiring to settle near the Saint; thus, as it was with St. Daniel, a monastery was formed or, it might be, as with St. Alypius, a nunnery as well.

It is terrifying to contemplate the sufferings endured through whole decades by these athletes in the school of salvation: amongst those of strict observance it was not permitted to sit or to lie down: they had taken their 'stand' and might not desert it. They sought to overcome the need for sleep and, if sleep they must, they did so, still standing, leaning against the balustrade. To increase the strain upon the rebel body St. Simeon the younger forced himself for a whole year to squat upon his heels. Only in the interest of threatened Orthodoxy might they abandon, as did Daniel, their 'stance' and descend from their column. When they had established themselves in lonely places they might be forgotten and might all but perish of hunger and thirst. We may sympathize with Delehaye's comment: 'Nous comprenons difficilement que ces hommes pieux aient pu agir de la sorte sans tenter la Providence. Leur simplicité est leur grande excuse.'

And, despite everything, they were so astonishingly long-lived. Newman's judgment is familiar: 'if these men so tormented their bodies as Theodoret describes, which it is difficult to doubt, and if, nevertheless, instead of killing themselves thereby, they lived to the great age which he also testifies, this fact was in itself of a miraculous character'. . . .

> And I had hoped that ere this period closed
> Thou wouldst have caught me up into thy rest,
> Denying not these weather-beaten limbs
> The meed of saints, the white robe and the palm.
> O take the meaning, Lord: I do not breathe,
> Not whisper, any murmur of complaint.
> Pain heap'd ten-hundred-fold to this, were still
> Less burthen, by ten-hundred-fold, to bear
> Than were those lead-like tons of sin, that crush'd
> My spirit flat before thee.

To make up what was lacking in the sufferings of Christ was no light task.

The Life of Daniel can be left to speak for itself. The author, a younger man than the Saint, writes as a disciple and eye-witness. He has consulted those who were with Daniel from the time that he came to the shores of the Bosphorus. For the 'we' accounts in the Vita see ch. 91, 95, 96 and note ch. 1 and ch. 12. There is no reason to think that he used written sources.

It will suffice to add a brief note on the chronology of Daniel's life as established by Père Delehaye: the Saint was born in A.D. 409; until he was twelve years old he lived with his parents; the next twenty-five years were spent in a monastery; then during five years he visited the most famous ascetes of his time; at the age of forty-two he arrived in Constantinople; after nine years spent in what had been a pagan temple he mounted his pillar on which he passed thirty-three years and three months. He died at the age of eighty-four years and three months in A.D. 493.

THE LIFE AND WORKS OF OUR HOLY FATHER, ST. DANIEL THE STYLITE

I

BEFORE all things it is right that we should give glory to Jesus Christ our God, Who for us was made man and for our salvation endured all things according to the Dispensation; for His sake, too, prophets were killed, and just men crucified themselves because of this faith in Him and by His grace, after having kept patience under their sufferings unswervingly unto the end, they received a crown of glory. These men our Master and Saviour Christ gave us as an example that we might know that it is possible for a man by the patient endurance of his sufferings to please God and be called His faithful servant.

For this reason I thought good to take in hand a recital of the labours of St. Daniel, yet I do so with fear; for this man's way of life was great and brilliant and marvellous, whereas I am but a witless and humble person. I fear lest I should hear those words applied to me which our Saviour spoke through the prophet David: 'But unto the sinner God saith, "Why dost thou declare my statutes and takest my covenant in thy mouth?" '[1]

Yet I do not venture to dismiss in silence those narratives about the Saint which I received from my fathers for fear lest the Lord should justly torture me in His great and terrible day for not having given into the bank the talent through His will entrusted to me for the edification and profit of the many. Being thus fortified by your prayers I will put down truthfully everything I heard from the men who were the Saint's disciples before me and I will also relate truly all the things I saw with my own eyes. For it is certain that the Lord 'will surely destroy them that speak lies'.[2] I therefore beseech you lovers of learning to cast aside all thoughts of this present life and grant me your favourable hearing.

[1] Ps. l. 16.   [2] Ps. v. 6.

2

This father among saints was the son of a father named
Elias and a mother Martha; he came from a small village
called Meratha (which is, being interpreted, 'the Caves') in the
territory of Samosata in Mesopotamia. As his mother was
barren and was reproached for this by her husband and kinsfolk, she went out one day secretly at midnight unbeknown to
her husband and stretching forth her hands to heaven, prayed
saying, 'Oh Lord Jesus Christ, Who art long-suffering towards the sins of men, Thou Who didst in the beginning
create woman to increase the race of men, do Thou Thyself
take my reproach from me and grant me fruit of my womb
that I may dedicate him to Thee, the Lord of All'. After
weeping bitterly and afflicting her soul with many lamentations, she came in to her husband and whilst sleeping beside
him saw in a vision of the night two great circular lights
coming down from heaven and resting near her.* Next morning she related the vision to her husband and kinsfolk and each
one interpreted differently the things she had told them. But
she sighed and said to herself, 'My God to Whom I prayed
will do what is best for my unhappy soul'. And not many days
later she conceived the holy man of whom we spoke.

3

So he was born; and when in course of time he had reached
the age of five years his parents took him with offerings of
fruit to a monastery near the village and the abbot asked them,
'By what name is the child called?' And when the parents
mentioned some other name, the old man said, 'He shall not
be called that, but whatever the Lord shall reveal to us, that
shall his name be'. And the archimandrite said to the child in the
Syrian dialect, 'Go, child, and fetch me a book from the table'.
For it is a custom in monasteries that many different books
should be laid in front of the sanctuary, and whichever book a
brother wants he takes and reads. So the child went and fetched
the book of the prophet Daniel, and from this he got that name.
But when the parents besought the abbot to receive him
into the monastery and let him stay with the brothers he could
not be persuaded, because the child was still so very young;
so they took him home again and he abode with his parents.

4

Now when he was twelve years old* he heard his mother say, 'My child, I have dedicated you to God'. Thereupon one day without saying anything to anybody he went out of the village for a distance of about ten miles where there was a monastery containing fifty brethren. And entering the monastery he fell at the abbot's feet and begged to be received by him. But the abbot said to him, 'Child, you are still very young in years and are not able to endure so hard a discipline; you know nothing of the monks' life; go home, stay with your parents and after some time when you are able both to fast and to sing and to endure discipline, then come back to us'. But the child answered, 'Father, I should prefer to die in these hardships than to quit the shelter of your flock!' And when, in spite of all he could do, the archimandrite was unable to persuade the child, he said to the brethren, 'In truth, my children, let us receive this boy for he seems to me to be very much in earnest'. And they all yielded to the abbot's counsel, and thus Daniel remained in the brotherhood.

5

And shortly afterwards his parents, who had sought him, found him in this monastery and rejoiced with great joy, and then besought the abbot to give him the tonsure. And he, having noticed his advancement in godliness and good disposition, sent for him and said, 'Child, do you wish me to give you the tonsure?' Daniel immediately threw himself at his feet and said, 'I beseech your Holiness, father, do it to-day!' But the abbot again said, 'You are unable to endure the discipline'. To this the boy replied, 'I know well that I am young and weak, but I trust in God and your holy prayers, because the Lord Who accepts our purpose gives us strength, for He is a God of purposes'. Then after blessing him and praying fervently over him, the archimandrite with the wisdom that had been given him by God instructed him in the things necessary for salvation. And afterwards according to custom he bade all the brethren gather together, and while they sang a hymn he bestowed upon him the holy robe of the monk. And dismissing the parents with blessings he bade them not to visit their son frequently.

6

While Daniel made progress in asceticism and in the splendour of his way of life he could not bear the scrutiny and the praise of the abbot and, still less, that of the whole brotherhood; so he planned to go to the Holy City, Jerusalem, and at the same time to visit the holy and thrice-blessed Simeon, the man on the pillar, in whose footsteps he felt constrained to follow.

Therefore he began to pray the abbot of the monastery to set him free to attain his desire, but he could not persuade him.

Soon after this, since our Master God in truth so willed it and the need of the church demanded it, the Archbishop of that time commanded all the archimandrites of the East to assemble in the capital city of Antioch. And so it happened that this abbot together with some others went, too, and amongst them he allowed the holy man also to travel with him as his disciple.

7

As God granted that the matter for which they had suffered many vexations should be brought to a satisfactory settlement, they departed to their own monasteries; and on their way they lodged in a village called Telanissae* where there was a very large monastery and monks pursuing a very noble and virtuous way of life; here, too, the afore-mentioned holy Simeon had received his training. And when the monks there began talking about the achievements of the holy Simeon, the monks from Mesopotamia withstood them, contending that it was but a vainglorious proceeding. 'For', said they, 'it is true that a man even if he were living in your midst might practise a mode of life hitherto unknown and please God, yet never has such a thing happened anywhere that a man should go up and live on a pillar'.

So the monks of that monastery persuaded them to go and see what hardships Simeon was enduring for the sake of the Lord.* And they were persuaded and went and the holy Daniel with them. When they arrived at the place and saw the wildness of the spot and the height of the pillar and the fiery heat of the scorching sun and the Saint's endurance and his welcome to strangers and further, too, the love he shewed towards them, they were amazed.

8

For Simeon gave direction that the ladder be placed in position and invited the old men to come up and kiss him. But they were afraid and declined the ascent of the ladder — one said he was too feeble from old age, another pleaded weakness after an illness, and another gout in his feet. For they said to each other, 'How can we kiss with our mouth the man that we have just been slandering with our lips? Woe unto us for having mocked at such hardships as these and such endurance'. Whilst they were conversing in this manner, Daniel entreated the archimandrite and the other abbots and Saint Simeon as well, begging to be allowed to go up to him. On receiving permission he went up and the blessed man gave him his benediction and said to him, 'What is your name?' and he answered, 'Daniel'. Then the holy Simeon said to him, 'Play the man, Daniel, be strong and endure; for you have many hardships to endure for God. But I trust that the God Whom I serve will Himself strengthen you and be your fellow-traveller'. And placing his hand upon Daniel's head he prayed and blessed him and bade him go down the ladder. Then after the holy and blessed Simeon had prayed for the archimandrites he dismissed them all in peace.

9

After they had all by the will of God been restored to their own monasteries and some little time had passed, the holy man, Daniel, was deemed worthy to be raised to the post of abbot.

Thereupon he said to himself, 'At last you are free, Daniel,* start boldly and accomplish your purpose'. When he had made trial of him who held the second place and found that he was able to undertake the duties of an archimandrite, he left everything and quitted the monastery; and when he had reached the enclosure of the holy Simeon he stayed there two weeks.

The blessed Simeon rejoiced exceedingly when he saw him and tried to persuade him to remain still longer, for he found great joy in his company. But Daniel would not consent thereto but pressed towards his goal, saying, 'Father, I am ever with you in spirit'. So Simeon blessed him and dismissed him with the words, 'The Lord of glory will accompany you'. Then Daniel went forth wishing to travel to the holy places and to worship in the church of the Holy Resurrection and afterwards to retire to the inner desert.

10

He heard, however, that the road to Palestine was dangerous, so he inquired the cause of this and was told that the Samaritans* had revolted against the Christians. But he said to himself, 'Start, Daniel, do not swerve from your purpose, and if perchance you may even have to die for your faith with the Christians, a great thing is in store for you'. Whilst he was thus deliberating with himself and walking along one fine noon-day, a monk overtook him, a very hairy man; he appeared to be a venerable man resembling Saint Simeon.

After greeting him he said in the Syrian dialect, 'Whither are you going, beloved?' And our Master, Daniel answered, 'I am going to the holy places, if it is the will of God'. And the old man replying said, 'You say rightly, "If it be the will of God", for have you not heard of the unrest in Palestine?' Daniel, the servant of God, answered, 'Yes, I have heard, but the Lord is my helper and I hope to pass through unhurt, and even if we must endure suffering, yet if we live we are the Lord's, and if we die we pass into His hands'. The old man said to him, 'Do you not know that it is written, "Do not let your foot be moved, for He that keepeth thee will not slumber"?'[1] To this holy Daniel replied, 'I told your reverence before that even death for the sake of God is good'. Then the old man waxed angry and turned away saying, 'I cannot put up with your arguing, for such is not our custom'. So Daniel, the servant of God, said to him, 'What do you bid me do? to return?' The old man replied, 'I do not advise you to return for "he that putteth his hand to the plough and turneth back is not fit for the kingdom of Heaven".[2] But if you will listen to me, there is one thing I advise.'

[1] Ps. cxxi. 3.   [2] Luke ix. 62.

Our Master, Daniel answered, 'Indeed, sir, if you advise anything that is possible and that I can do, that I certainly will do, for I see that you are both a father and a teacher'. And the old man said, 'Verily, verily, verily, behold three times I adjure you by the Lord, do not go to those places, but go to Byzantium and you will see a second Jerusalem, namely Constantinople; there you can enjoy the martyrs' shrines and the great houses of prayer, and if you wish to be an anchorite in some desert spot, either in Thrace or in Pontus, the Lord will not desert you'.

11

Whilst they were speaking of these matters, they reached a monastery, and evening had already fallen. Then holy Daniel said to the elder, 'Do you bid us lodge here?' and the old man said, 'Go in first and I will follow'. Our Master, Daniel, imagining that a bodily need constrained him, went in first and waited, but never saw him again;* and all this happened, beloved, because divine power so willed it. For had not Palestine been in a troublous state at that time, the West would never have encountered this wonderful man.

12

Of these things which I have here written down, beloved, I heard some, as I told you before, from those who were the Saint's disciples before me;* others from trustworthy men who followed the footsteps of the Saint from the beginning; and yet others I heard myself when our good shepherd related them with his own mouth — not indeed in order that we should commit them to writing, for he did not wish to receive glory from men but looked to his reward from God — but when he confirmed and comforted us and continually counselled us to abide patiently under our sufferings. And that you, beloved, may know that what I say is true, there are still living some of the devout men who frequently visited the enclosure of the Saint who bear in memory that which I will now relate, how that a certain disciple of the Saint's thinking he would achieve a work of piety and edification, sent for a painter and[1] had the

---

[1] Another reading says: 'And had the events which occurred in the reign of Basiliscus painted....'

portrait of the Saint painted above the porch at the entry to
the chapel in the quarter of the city named after Basiliscus*,
and he himself also wished to write the life of the Saint. But
when our most saintly father heard of it he was exceedingly
angry and ordered the painting to be wiped off, and the papers
to be thrown into the fire, so determined was the servant of
God not to receive glory from men. — Let us now return to
our subject.

13

When Daniel had entered the monastery and had saluted
the abbot and the brethren there, they asked him to partake of
food. But he replied that he had an old man with him and
must wait for him. So they all waited patiently for several
hours and as he did not appear they decided he must be
lodging in another monastery, so after giving thanks they took
their supper. And after supper when the monks were sleeping,
the old man came in a vision, they say, and spoke thus to the
holy man, 'Again I say unto you, do that which I counselled
you to do'. Therefore, on awakening Daniel debated within
himself what was this aged counsellor — man or angel?

Then saying nothing to anybody about this, but bidding
them all farewell after the psalm-singing in the night and
having received their 'God speed you!' he left the monastery
and started on the road to Byzantium. When he reached a
place called Anaplus* where there was an oratory dedicated to
the archangel Michael he spent seven days there in this
oratory.

14

Once he heard some men conversing in the Syrian dialect
and saying that there was a church in that place inhabited by
demons who often sank ships and had injured, and still were
injuring, many of the passers-by, and that it was impossible
for anyone to walk along that road in the evening or even at
noonday.

As everybody was continually complaining about the
destructive power which had occupied the place, the divine
spirit came upon Daniel and he called to mind that great man,

Antony, the model of asceticism [and Paul, his disciple];* he remembered their struggles against demons and the many temptations they suffered from them and how they had overcome them by the strength of Christ and were deemed worthy of great crowns. Then he asked a man who understood the Syrian dialect about this church and begged him to show him the spot.

On reaching the porch of the church, just as a brave soldier strips himself for battle before venturing against a host of barbarians, so he, too, entered the church reciting the words spoken by the prophet, David, in the Psalms:[1] 'The Lcrd is my light and my saviour, whom shall I fear? the Lord is the defender of my life, of whom shall I be afraid?' and the rest. And holding the invincible weapon of the Cross, he went round into each corner of the church making genuflections and prayers.

15

When night fell, stones, they say, were thrown at him and there was the sound of a multitude knocking and making an uproar; but he persevered in prayer. In this way he spent the first night and the second; but on the third night sleep overpowered him, as it might overtake any man bearing the weakness of the flesh. And straightway many phantoms appeared as of giant shapes some of whom said, 'Who induced you to take possession of this place, poor wretch? do you wish to perish miserably? Come, let us drag him out and throw him into the water!' Again, others carrying, as it seemed, large stones stood at his head, apparently intending to crush it to pieces. On waking, the athlete of Christ again went round the corners of the church praying and singing and saying to the spirits, 'Depart from hence! if you do not, then by the strength of the Cross you shall be devoured by flames and thus be forced to flee'. But they made a still greater uproar and howled the louder. But he despised them and taking not the slightest notice of their uproar, he bolted the door of the church and left a small window* through which he would converse with the people that came up to see him.

[1] Ps. xxvii. 1.

16

In the meantime his fame had spread abroad in those
regions, and you could see men and women with their children
streaming up to see the holy man and marvelling that the place
formerly so wild and impassable lay in such perfect calm, and
that where demons danced lately, there by the patience of the
just man Christ was now glorified day and night.

17

Now the priests of the Church of the Archangel Michael
lived nearby and they were simple folk. So when the envious
demon who hates the good saw such victories gained through
the power of Christ, he was mad with rage and suggested to
the minds of the priests an argument that ran like this: 'It is no
good thing that you are doing in letting the man dwell there;
for just look how all the world goes to him and you in consequence remain with nothing to do.* You had better go to the
city and say to your bishop, "Some man, come from we know
not where, has shut himself in near us and he is attracting
people to him, although he is a heretic. But he is a Syrian by
birth and so we are unable to hold converse with him."'" Having
reasoned thus among themselves the priests went in and reported the matter to the man who was then the bishop, namely
the blessed Anatolius, the Patriarch of Constantinople.* But the
Archbishop said to them, 'If you do not understand his language, how do you know that he is a heretic? Leave him alone,
for if he has been sent by God he will be established; but, if it
is otherwise, he will go away of his own accord before you chase
him out. Do not bring a scandal upon us and yourselves'.
With these words he dismissed them. And they went home
and kept quiet for a time.

18

But when the demons saw that they were accomplishing
nothing, they again rose in rebellion against the servant of
God and brought phantoms before him, carrying, it is said,
naked swords, and crying, 'Whence have you come, man?
give place to us for we have been living here for a long time.
Do you wish your limbs to be cut in pieces?' And then, it is
said, they came towards him with their swords and spoke again

saying to one another, 'Do not let us slay him, but let us drag him along and cast him into the water where we sank the ship!' And they made as though they would drag him away. But the servant of God arose, and after uttering a prayer he said to them, 'Jesus Christ my Saviour, in Whom I have trusted and do trust, He will Himself drown you all in the deepest abyss.' A great howling arose and they flew round his face like a swarm of bats and with a whir of wings went out of the window, and so he drove them all forth by the power of God through prayer.

19

The Devil, seeing that once more his ministers had been routed, again stirred up the priests to go to the Archbishop; and they said to him: 'Master, you have authority over us; we cannot bear that man, bid him come away from that church, for he is an impostor.' Then the blessed Anatolius sent the officer of the most Holy Church with the deacons and in the night they burst open with crowbars the door which the Saint had closed and brought him to the City. When the Saint was brought before the holy and blessed Anatolius in his palace, the Archbishop asked him, 'Who are you? and whence have you come to these parts and what is your belief? — tell us.' And the servant of God declared his blameless faith by means of an interpreter and the blessed Anatolius stood up and embraced him and besought him to remain in the palace, but the men who had brought him he dismissed, saying, 'Go, hold your peace, for I find great edification in this man'. So they left him there in the bishop's palace and went their ways.

20

In the meantime the Bishop fell into a very severe illness, so he sent for the holy man and begged him to offer prayers on his behalf that he might be freed from the illness. And, since it so pleased the Divine Power, after the Saint had made his prayer, the Bishop was cured of his illness by God's good pleasure. Thus the words of the psalm were fulfilled towards the Saint: 'He will perform the desire of them that fear Him, He also will hear their cry and will save them.'[1] After the

[1] Ps. cxlv. 19.

Bishop's recovery the servant of God asked to be allowed to depart; but the Archbishop would not agree thereto and said 'I wish you to live with me'. Then he again begged to be allowed to go, and asked him to grant pardon to the men who had slandered him to the Bishop, for the latter was threatening to excommunicate them. And the Bishop said, 'I must ask pardon of you, servant of God, for your arrest, but God has made your presence here a great blessing to me, for if your holiness had not settled there, I should certainly have departed this life'. He also implored him to let him build a cell for him saying, 'Since I am unable to persuade you to live here with me, if you will let me I will build you a small monastery,* for our most Holy Church has many a suitable spot in the suburbs of the city. Go out and look at them and whatever pleases you, I will give you'. But the holy man replied, 'If you really wish to do me a service, I beseech your Holiness to send me to the place to which God led me'. Finally the Bishop bade him be taken back with great respect and settled in the afore-mentioned church. Then the people could be seen flocking to the holy man again with joy and delight and many were granted healing so that all marvelled at the merciful grace of our Master Christ which He poured out upon His servant. And even those who had formerly wished to persecute him did not cease serving him and in all ways caring for the holy man. And he did as he had done formerly — he bolted the door and left only a small window open* through which he spoke, instructing and blessing the people, as I said before.

2 1

After a space of nine years had elapsed, the servant of God fell into an ecstasy, as it were, and saw a huge pillar of cloud standing opposite him and the holy and blessed Simeon standing above the head of the column and two men of goodly appearance, clad in white, standing near him in the heights. And he heard the voice of the holy and blessed Simeon saying to him, 'Come here to me, Daniel'. And he said, 'Father, father, and how can I get up to that height?' Then the Saint said to the young men standing near him, 'Go down and bring him up to me'. So the men came down and brought Daniel up to him and he stood there. Then Simeon took him in his arms

and kissed him with a holy kiss, and then others called him
away, and escorted by them he was borne up to heaven leaving
Daniel on the column with the two men. When holy Daniel
saw him being carried up to heaven he hard the voice of Saint
Simeon, 'Stand firm and play the man'. But he was confused
by fear and by that fearful voice, for it was like thunder in his
ears. When he came to himself again he declared the vision
to those around him. Then they, too, said to the holy man,
'You must mount on to a pillar and take up Saint Simeon's
mode of life and be supported by the angels'. The blessed one
said, 'Let the will of God, our Master, be done upon His
servant'. And taking the holy Gospel into his hands and opening it with prayer he found the place in which was written,[1]
'And thou, child, shalt be called the prophet of the Highest,
for thou shalt go before the face of the Lord to prepare His
ways'. And he gave thanks and closed the book.

22

Not many days later a monk came from the East by name
Sergius, a disciple of Saint Simeon, announcing the good end
of the Saint's life and carrying in his hands Saint Simeon's
leather tunic* in order to give it to the blessed Emperor Leo
by way of benediction. But as the Emperor was busy with
public affairs, the aforesaid Sergius could not get a hearing,
or rather it was God who so arranged it in order that the new
Elisha might receive the mantle of Elijah. When Sergius grew
weary of waiting in the City because he could not obtain a
hearing, he decided to go as far as the monastery of the
Akoimetoi,[2] now it was not possible for anyone to reach that
monastery except by passing the church and the channel by it,
as there was generally a north wind blowing. When he had
entered into the boat with many others, men and women, they
set sail. On reaching the spot where the demons used formerly
to hurl stones at the passengers and continually sank their
boats, those in the boat gave thanks to God and made mention
of the holy man.

Sergius inquired who he was, for said he, 'I should like to
be blessed by him'. They answered 'Whilst the sailors tow the

[1] Luke i. 76.
[2] 'The Sleepless ones': see the note on p. 75.

boat past, we can all land and go up to him.' And this they did.
And Sergius came and embraced the Saint. And whilst they
were talking and Daniel, the servant of God, was hearing about
the end of the holy Simeon he related his vision to Sergius,
who on hearing it said, 'It is to thee rather than to the Emperor that God has sent me; for here am I, the disciple of thy
father; here, too, is his benediction'. And taking out the tunic
he handed it in through the window. The Saint took it and
kissing it with tears said, 'Blessed be Thou, O God, Who dost
all things after Thy will and hast deemed my humbleness
worthy of the benediction which Thy servant has brought'.
Then some men from the ship upbraided Sergius for delaying
and preventing them from sailing; to them Sergius answered,
'Go on your ways and fare weil; God has led me from one
father to another'.

23

From that day he remained near the blessed Daniel, and
Sergius saw the following vision. Three young men, it seemed,
came to him and said, 'Arise, say unto father Daniel "The
appointed time of thy discipline in this church is now fulfilled,
from henceforth leave the church, come hither and begin thy
contest".' When he awoke he related what he had seen. The
blessed Daniel said to him, 'Brother, the Lord has revealed
quite clearly to us what should be done, for this dream which
your Piety saw fits in with the vision which I saw; be ready
therefore to endure hardships for the Lord and come up on
the hill and we will search out the more desolate and higher-
lying spots in these parts and judge where we ought to set up
a column. For it was not without a purpose that God guided
you to bring to my unworthiness the father's garment'. Whilst
the blessed Daniel was saying this to Sergius, lo! a certain
imperial guardsman,* by name Mark, who had been a friend
of the holy man from the beginning joined them; and now,
knowing his intention from the conversation he had overheard,
besought Daniel to allow him to provide the column. The
blessed Daniel said to him, 'Behold God has sent you according
to your faith, my son Mark, so that you may be the pioneer in
this good work; pray therefore that the good Lord may also
grant us endurance.'

24

After the guardsman had embraced the holy man and sailed away, Sergius went up to view the spot where the column was to be set; and a short distance away he saw a white dove fluttering* and then settling again. Thinking it was caught in a snare he ran towards it, and then it flew up and away out of his sight. Seeing that the place was solitary and considering the incident of the dove that it had not been shown to him casually or by chance, he gave thanks to the Lord and returned to the holy man in the church bringing him the glad tidings that the Lord had prepared for them a suitable place. Then he, too, gave thanks to the Lord Who brings all things to pass according to His will.

25

And indeed after two days men came back from the city carrying the pillar; there were with them two workmen sent by the guardsman to fix the column in whatever place it was desired. So Sergius went up with them by night and they fixed the pillar and came back reporting that the pillar was erected. Daniel gave them his blessing and sent his blessing to the guardsman, and then dismissed them. And the blessed Daniel said to Sergius, 'We do not know the measure of the circumference of the pillar'. But Sergius was unwilling to go up again and take the measurement of the column. However, the blessed man had another disciple dwelling near him by name Daniel, him he bade go up and take the measurement of the column. So he went up and as he was measuring the column, he was seen by the men who were guarding the vineyards in the neighbouring field which belonged to Gelanius, who at that time was steward of the sacred table* to the most pious Emperor Leo. They ran up and held him and asked, 'Whence are you and by whose authority are you taking the measurements of the column?' He answered them, 'I am not a stranger, I belong to the father Daniel who lives in the church and I have come upon his business. And when I saw the column I was delighted'. And when they heard his answer they let him go. And the brother went back to the City to a place called 'The Three Crosses', and ordered a balustrade,

and took it with him. Afterwards he related to Daniel everything that had happened to him and the answer he had given
to the men. The blessed man replied, 'The will of the Lord be
done!'

26

And it came to pass after three days when night had fallen
they opened the church in which Daniel was shut up, and taking the brother he went up to the spot — for Sergius had
departed to another place Thrace-wards — and they found a
long plank lying there which the inhabitants of the suburb had
prepared for knocking down the column. This they bound
with a rope and stood it up against the column, and then went
up and put the balustrade on the column, for that column was
not really high, only about the height of two men. When they
had fitted the balustrade and bound it firmly with a rope they
knelt and prayed to God. And the blessed Daniel went up and
stood on the column inside the balustrade and said, 'Oh Lord
Jesus Christ, in Thy holy name, I am entering upon this contest; do Thou approve my purpose and help me to accomplish
my course'. And he said to the brother, 'Take away the plank
and the rest of the rope and get away quickly so that if anybody
comes he may not find you'. And the brother did as he was
told.

27

The next morning the husbandmen came and when they
saw Daniel they were amazed; for the sight was a strange one,
and they came near him, and when they looked on him they
recognized him as the man who had formerly been in the
church. After having received the Saint's blessing they left
him and went to the City and reported to Gelanius, the owner
of the property. On hearing their news he was very angry
with them for not having guarded that part of his land; and he
was also annoyed with the blessed Daniel for having done this
without his consent. And he went and reported the matter to
the blessed Emperor Leo and the Archbishop Gennadius, for
the blessed Anatolius had already gone to his rest.* The
Emperor for his part said nothing. But the Archbishop said
to him, 'As master of the property, fetch him down; for where

he was he had no right to be, but he was not there on my authority'.

Then Gelanius took several men with him and went up to the servant of God, and, although it was a calm day and the air was still, yet it came to pass that suddenly the clouds gathered and a storm arose accompanied with hail so that all the fruit of the vineyards was destroyed and the leaves were stripped from the vines, for it was the time of the vintage. And it was only with difficulty that the men who were with Gelanius got away and they muttered amongst themselves, for they were astonished at the strangeness of the sight.

Gelanius then approached the blessed man and said, 'Who gave you permission to take up your stand on land belonging to me? Was it not better for you in the church? — but since you have shown contempt of me, the owner of the property, and have taken no account of the Emperor and the Archbishop, let me tell you that I have been empowered by them to fetch you down.'

28

But when he persisted and repeated his demands it seemed an unjust and illegal proceeding to his companions and they opposed its being done, 'Because', said they, 'the Emperor himself is a pious man and this man is orthodox and this spot lies at a distance from your field'. When Gelanius perceived that there would be a disturbance he said to the Saint in the Syrian language — for by birth he was a Syro-Persian* from Mesopotamia — 'Please pretend to come down for the sake of those who ordered you to descend, and then I will not allow you really to touch the ground.' So then a ladder was brought and Daniel came down about six rungs from the column. There were still several rungs before he actually reached the ground, when Gelanius ran forward and prevented his coming down the last rungs,* saying, 'Return to your dwelling and your place and pray for me'. For as Daniel was coming down he had noticed that sores and swellings had begun to appear on his feet, and he was distressed. And the blessed man went up the rungs of the ladder down which he had come, and stood inside the balustrade on the column; and after offering prayer. all received his blessing and went down from the hill in peace.

So Gelanius, when he had reached the capital, reported everything to the Emperor telling him of the patience and endurance of the man so that he won the Emperor's pity for him.

29

Not many days later Gelanius went up to the Saint asking him to allow him to change the column and have a very large one placed for him. And lo! while they were conversing a certain Sergius arrived from the parts about Thrace, a lawyer by profession, bringing with him a very young boy, his only son, by name John, who was grievously tormented by a demon. This man came and threw himself to the ground in front of the column, weeping and lamenting and crying out, saying, 'Have pity upon my son, oh servant of God; it is now thirty days since the unclean spirit first called upon the name of your Holiness; and after inquiring for you through eight long days, we have come to claim your blessing'. When Gelanius heard this and saw the old man afflicting himself thus out of pity,[1] he, too, was affected and burst into tears. And the holy Daniel said to the old man, 'He that asketh in faith receives all from God; if therefore you believe that through me a sinner, God will heal your son, according to your faith it shall be given unto you'. And he bade the young man approach; and he drew near and stood before the column. And the Saint bade them give him a drink of the oil of the saints. And it came to pass when they gave him to drink that the demon threw him to the ground and there he rolled in their midst. Then the evil spirit rose up and shouted swearing that he would go out on that very day a week hence.[2]

30

Gelanius was amazed when he saw this and besought the holy man to agree to a new column being brought; and when the Saint yielded to his entreaties Gelanius went home after receiving a blessing. And on the following day he sent stones for the steps, and the base together with the column itself and

---

[1] or by altering the punctuation '... afflicting himself, he, too, was moved with sympathy for him'.

[2] See p. 26, ch. 33.

the workmen and all the things necessary for fixing it, and for a week they were at work preparing the foundation and erecting the column. While this work was in progress Sergius returned from Thrace and the blessed Daniel said to him, 'Oh faint-hearted, why did you desert me?' Sergius fell down and received forgiveness and remained with him again. And the other brother, seeing that the Lord made all things prosper for the Saint, fashioned for himself a booth of branches and dwelt there near the Saint opposite the column. And by the grace of God the number of disciples increased and Sergius was made their superior as he was qualified by his age and had been the disciple of Saint Simeon.

31

In the meantime there came to the Saint one Cyrus,* an ex-consul and ex-pretorian prefect. He was a very trustworthy and wise man who had passed through all the grades of office owing to his extreme sagacity. But late in life he suffered from a plot hatched by Chrysaphius,* the Spatharius, and was sent as bishop to a small town, namely to Cotyaeum in Phrygia, and realizing the treachery of Chrysaphius he yielded so as not to bring his life to a miserable end. After the death of the Emperor Theodosius he divested himself of his priestly dignity and resumed his secular rank and so continued to the end of his life, for he lived till the reign of Leo of most pious memory. He used to distribute all his belongings to the poor. This man Cyrus, had a daughter called Alexandria who was afflicted by an evil spirit, and he had brought her to the holy man Daniel when the latter was still at the foot of the hill in the church, and thanks to the intercessions of the archangels and the tears and prayers of the holy man the Lord freed her from the demon within seven days. Consequently from that time forth the two men had a passionate affection for each other.

32

So when Cyrus came and found that the column had been erected, he inquired who had placed it and hearing that it was Gelanius, the steward at the imperial court,* to whom the lands also belonged, at first he was indignant that Daniel should have allowed this to be done by one who had shown him such insolence. 'Should not I far rather have been allowed to do this, if anything else was wanted?' Then the Saint began to beg and beseech him saying, 'All people everywhere proclaim your good will towards me; I accepted this column from Gelanius in order that I might not offend him. The God Whom I serve will recompense you with good things according to your faith'. And after giving him his blessing he dismissed him.

33

And it came to pass that on the following day, Saturday, Gelanius came with a large company to remove the Saint to the larger column; and as they were about to transfer the servant of God from pillar to pillar, the demon in Sergius' son[1] became agitated, for he was being forced to go out of him, and he cried with a loud voice saying, 'Oh, the violence of this false magician! When he was still in the church he drove me out of Cyrus' daughter; so I went away to Thrace and found a dwelling in this young man; and behold, he has brought me here from Thrace and now he persecutes me. What have you to do with me, Daniel? — oh violence! I must come out from this one, too!' and after reviling the Saint furiously and afflicting the young man he came out of him by the power of the Lord. As the demon came out, he created such a stench that all the crowds present could not endure the stench and had to cover their noses; and the young man lay on the ground with his mouth open so that all said he was dead and his father beat his breast as if over a corpse. Then the holy Daniel said to Sergius, 'Make him sit up and give him to drink of the oil of the saints'. And as the boy drank, vomiting came upon him and he brought up black clotted blood. Then the servant of God cried from above with a loud voice saying, 'John, what ails you? stand up!' And immediately, as if awakened from sleep, the boy said, 'What is your will, master?' and He ran forward and embraced the column, giving thanks to God and the Saint. And fear seized upon them all and for a long space of time they stretched out their hands to heaven and with tears kept shouting the 'Kyrie, eleison' (Lord, have mercy!).

[1] See p. 24, ch. 29.

34

Then with great ceremony and with an escort to guard him Daniel moved on to the taller column. And Gelanius, having seen the wonderful works of God, went down from the hill and related everything in detail to the Emperor and to all the great folk of the Court. The young man who had been cured fell at his father's feet and implored him to entreat the servant of God to grant him the holy robe of a monk and, as the old man could not be persuaded because he wished to keep his son near him, the son protested saying, 'If you will not do this, then I shall go away secretly to some other place where you will not even be able to see me'. In this way he persuaded his father who then petitioned the holy man who received his son and bade him live with the brethren. After a year had been fulfilled and the young man by the grace of God was making progress towards the good way of life the holy man sent for his father and gave the son the holy robe. Then the father was content and returned to his home rejoicing and glorifying God. After three years the young man passed away and went to the Lord after having lived a good life.

35

And when these things had thus been auspiciously accomplished Eudoxia* of pious memory came from Africa and heard all about this holy man from her own son-in-law Olybrius* of glorious memory; she rejoiced greatly and visited the Saint's enclosure.

And after prayers had been offered and she had been blessed by him she said, 'Everything I heard from my son Olybrius I have found more abundantly in your angelic presence* and the prophecies which you announced to him about my coming here when you were still in the church are also known to me. On that account am I come both to enjoy seeing you face to face and to receive a perfect blessing. Now I have many convenient lands here, therefore, if it is to your liking, I beg you to move on to land that belongs to me, for by so doing you would cause me great content of spirit'. But the Saint replied to her, 'May the God, Who has shown us sinners the face of your Piety in the flesh, grant you together with an earthly kingdom a heavenly and eternal one according to your faith. But as regards my removal you will remember that our Lord told us[1] not to move from place to place, but where each man is called — provided only that the place be pleasing to God — there, too, let him practise to remain until he leave this tabernacle; therefore as the Lord has once planted me here, it is not permissible for me to move from here. For as your Piety sees, this place is barren and I must not seek a pleasant resting-place'. When Eudoxia, the most faithful Empress, heard these words she was edified by them all and, having paid him reverence with all good-will, she came down from the hill.

36

On the following day there happened to come the elder daughter of Cyrus, the eminent man of whom we have already spoken,* and she had an evil spirit; and after staying some time in the enclosure she obtained healing through God. After his daughter had been freed from the demon and returned to her home, the most distinguished man, Cyrus, whom we have often mentioned, came giving thanks to God and to the Saint and asked to be allowed to put an inscription on the column. Though the just man did not wish this to be done, yet, being hard pressed by Cyrus and not wishing to grieve him, he allowed him to do it. So he had carved on the column the following lines:

> Standing twixt earth and heaven a man you see
> Who fears no gales that all about him fret;
> Daniel his name. Great Simeon's rival he;
> Upon a double column firm his feet are set;
> Ambrosial hunger, bloodless thirst support his frame
> And thus the Virgin Mother's Son he doth proclaim.*

These verses are still inscribed on the column and thus preserve the memory of the man in whose honour they were written.

37

Things were in this state when a certain elder born in Pontus came to the Saint's enclosure bringing with him his son, a young man of about twenty years old, who was afflicted by

[1] 1 Cor. vii. 24.

an evil spirit. And this evil spirit was deaf and dumb. Then
the father fell down before Daniel begging him to heal his son.
Now while the father and his son were still on their way the
Saint saw the young man being held fast by his own servants.
And knowing in his spirit why the man was coming, he besought God for him and asked that He would give him a
speedy healing. In consequence the demon was greatly agitated and having wrenched the young man from the grasp of
the servants who were holding him he dashed away from them.
It was Sunday and thus by the providence of God the ladder
was necessarily standing against the column. And the young
man rushed headlong to the ladder and climbed up it, but
before he had gone half way up he was cleansed and descended
in perfect health and stood in front of the column with his
father glorifying God; and other signs, too, God did at
Daniel's hands.

38

Now the blessed Emperor Leo* of pious memory had heard
from many of these things and desired for a long time to see
the man. Therefore he sent for the pious Sergius, who carried
the Saint's messages, and through him he asked that the Saint
would pray and beseech God to grant him a son. And Daniel
prayed, and through God's good pleasure the Emperor's wife,
the Empress Verina,* thereafter conceived and begot a son —
whereupon the Emperor immediately sent and had the
foundations laid of a third column.

39

Now the demon of envy could not control his envy so he
found an instrument worthy of his evil designs. A certain
harlot,* Basiane, who had lately come to Constantinople from
the East, entrapped many of those who hunted after women of
her sort. The sons of some heretics summoned her and made
the following suggestion to her: 'If you can in any way bring
a scandal upon the man who stands on the pillar in Anaplus*
or upon any of those who are with him, we will pay you a
hundred gold pieces.' The shameless woman agreed and went
up to the holy man with much parade and took with her a crowd

of young men and prostitutes and simulated illness and remained in the suburb opposite the Saint's enclosure. And
though she stayed there no little time she spent her time in
vain. As she was anxious to get possession of the money she
went down to the city and plotted after this fashion. To her
lovers she said, 'I managed to seduce the man, for he became
enamoured of my beauty and ordered his disciples to bring me
up to him by means of the ladder; but as I would not consent,
the men there planned to lie in wait and kill me; and it is with
difficulty that I have escaped from their hands'. When her
lovers heard this they thought they had gained their object
and imparted the news to all their fellow conspirators. And
thereupon as the report spread you could have seen a war
between the believers and unbelievers. While matters were
in this state, God Who rejoices in the truth and ever defends
His servants, brought it about that the abandoned woman,
Basiane, should be tormented by an evil demon in the middle
of the City and then and there should proclaim her plot and
the wrong which the licentious men had suggested to her
against the righteous Daniel, promising her money if she were
successful. And not only did she make public their names,
shouting them for all to hear, but their rank also. Then could
be seen a change in the ordering of affairs, for the faithful now
rejoiced, whilst the faithless who had threatened to throw
stones against the just man were put to shame.

40

While she was being chastised terribly for many days, the
Christ-loving inhabitants of the City took pity upon her and
led her away to the Saint and importuned him to pray to God
on her behalf that she might obtain healing. But the servant
of God said to them, 'Believe me, beloved, the former calumnies
have now become as it were blessings to me; for neither does
a man who is praised falsely benefit thereby nor does he sustain
any injury who is slandered unjustly. For he who has entrusted his soul to God rejoices rather in false calumnies — for
they procure a reward for him — than in true praises which
swell and puff up the mind'. After these words as they all
besought him to bear no malice against her, because they saw
the wretched woman being so afflicted before the column, he

bade them all stand for prayer. And stretching out his hands
to heaven in the sight of them all, he besought God with tears
for many hours that she might be healed. And it came to pass,
as he prayed, that the demon cast her to the ground and came
out of her in that same hour; and he bade them give her to
drink from the oil of the saints. And when she came to herself
she stood up and embraced the pillar weeping and praising
God. And all those who were present gave thanks to God Who
had granted such grace to the holy man: and they took her
and went away with rejoicing.

41

About that time it was revealed to the holy man by the power
of God that very great wrath from heaven was about to descend
upon the city, and he made this known to the blessed Archbishop Gennadius,* and also to the Emperor, begging them to
order rites of intercession concerning this. But as the feast of
the saving Passion of Christ was at hand, they did not wish to
disturb the people and cause sorrow to reign through the whole
city during the feast. And when the holy feast was past, the
matter was not remembered any more.*

42

Thereafter the blessed Emperor Leo of pious memory
reflected that he had often put Daniel to the test and had obtained many benefits through his holy prayers; so, through a
guardsman,* he sent a message to the Archbishop, of whom I
have already spoken, saying, 'Go up to the holy man and
honour him with the rank of priest'. — But the Archbishop was
unwilling and sent various excuses to the most pious Emperor
through the messenger. The Emperor waxed indignant at the
delay and sent again to the blessed Gennadius saying, 'If you
intend to go up, do so, for I myself am going and the will of
God is coming to pass'. Then the Bishop was afraid, so he
took some of the clerics with him, and came to the holy man's
enclosure. The reason of his coming had been made known
to the holy man beforehand. The Archbishop said, 'Father,
bless your children'. The holy man replied, 'Your Holiness
must bless both me and them'. The blessed Gennadius said
'For a long time I have wished to come up and enjoy your

prayers; I pray you order the ladder to be placed so that I may come up and receive a full blessing, for God will convince your Holiness that it is through my being busied with the manifold needs of the Church that I have not been able to do this long ago'. But the servant of God having heard these words, though the Archbishop continued to implore him to allow the ladder to be set against the column, yet refused to make any further answer.

43

Whilst all those present continued to importune Daniel and the just man still refused to consent, the day was slipping by; and as the crowd was tormented with thirst owing to the heat and the Archbishop saw that he was not achieving anything, he bade the Archdeacon offer a prayer; he himself stood and uttered a further prayer and through the prayer ordained the holy man to be a priest and said, 'Bless us, sir priest; from henceforth you are a priest by the grace of Christ; for when I had prayed God laid His hand upon you from above'.* And for a long time the crowd shouted, 'Worthy is he'. Afterwards all, together with the Archbishop, besought the holy man saying, 'Order the ladder to be put in position, seeing that you have now become what you wished to avoid'. On the just man's giving permission for this to be done, the Archbishop mounted the ladder holding in his hand the chalice of the Holy Body and the Precious Blood of our good Mediator Jesus Christ our God. After saluting each other with a holy kiss, they received the communion at each other's hands. Then the Archbishop descended from the hill and entering the palace reported all that had happened to the Emperor.

44

And the blessed Leo of pious memory rejoiced in these doings; and not long afterwards he visited the place in which the holy man dwelt and asked for the ladder to be set so that he might go up and be blessed. When the ladder was placed, the Emperor went up to the servant of God and begged to touch his feet; but on approaching them and seeing their mortified and swollen state he was amazed and marvelled at the just man's endurance. He glorified God and begged the

holy man that he might set up a double column and that
Daniel would take his stand upon it. [And when this double
column had been set up] the Bishop and almost the whole city
came up and people, too, from the opposite shore. As the
Emperor Leo importuned him incessantly to cross over on to
it there and then, the servant of God bade planks to be laid to
form a bridge from one ladder to another. This being done,
the holy man walked across to the double column. And on that
day so many received healing that all were astonished.

45

And it came to pass shortly afterwards that there was a
great fire in the capital.* So all the inhabitants were in great
distress and the majority had to flee from the city. They made
their way to the holy man and each of them implored him to
placate God's anger so that the fire should cease. At the same
time they would relate to him the personal misfortunes they
had suffered; one would say, 'I have been stripped bare of
great possessions'; another, 'As the fire was far off I felt no un-
easiness but slept with my wife and children; but suddenly the
catastrophe overtook me and now I am a widower and childless, and have barely escaped being burnt alive'. Or again
another, 'I ran away from that terrible danger only to suffer
shipwreck of my scanty belongings'. The holy man wept with
them and said, 'The merciful God wished to spare you in His
goodness and made these things known beforehand and He
did not keep silence concerning it;* you should therefore have
importuned God and escaped His terrible wrath. For once
upon a time when the Ninevites were warned by the prophet
that destruction threatened them, they escaped it by repenting.
I was not vexed by the thought that God's mercy might prove
me to be a false prophet; for I had as an example the prophet
who was angry because of the gourd; and now I beg you bear
with gratitude that which God has sent. For a master is most
truly served when he sees his servant bearing chastisement
gratefully; and then he deems him worthy not only of his
former honour but even of greater by reason of his goodwill towards him'. And many other words of counsel he spoke unto
them and turned their hopelessness into hopefulness and then
dismissed them saying, 'The city will be afflicted for seven days'.

46

When the fire had ceased, fear seized upon all the citizens. And then the most blessed Emperor Leo of pious memory took his wife and went up and did reverence to the servant of God and said, 'This wrath was caused by our carelessness; I therefore beg you pray to God to be merciful to us in the future'. — Now consider, dear reader, how the saying of the holy man's mother was fulfilled. For now he received the adoration of the two lights which his mother had seen over her bed in a vision of the night.* — After all had with one accord received a blessing, the Emperor lodged in the palace of St. Michael, which was about one mile distant near the sea.

47

One day a terrific storm arose and as for some reason the column had not been properly secured, it was torn from its supports on either side by the violence of the winds and was only kept together by the iron bar which held the two columns in the middle. Thus you could see the double column swaying to and fro with the just man; for when the south wind blew it leant over to the left side, but when the north wind blew it inclined to the right, and streams of water poured down like rivers, and the base was getting shattered, for the violent winds were accompanied by thunderstorms. His disciples sought to underpin it with iron bars, but one swing of the column smashed them, too, and very nearly killed the men who tried to withstand it. Their shouts were mingled with their tears, for they were likely to suffer the loss of their father, and in their distracted state one ordered one thing and another another. By this time they had all become pretty well desperate; there they stood trembling and aghast, turning their head from side to side as the column swayed now this way and now that, following with their eyes to see in what direction the corpse of the just man would be hurled with the column. But the servant of God answered not a word to anyone but persevered in prayer and invocations to God for aid; and through His compassion the merciful God caused the danger to cease by sending a calm.

48

On the following day the Emperor sent his chamberlain,* Andreas by name, to inquire whether the holy man had suffered any harm from the violence of the winds. When the messenger came up and saw the extremity of the danger through which the just man had passed he went back and reported it to the Emperor. When he heard it he was furious against the architect who had laid the foundation of the column so badly and the Emperor purposed to put him to death. He went up at once in all haste and when he saw with his own eyes how the column had been shaken and what the holy man had endured, he was amazed and all present glorified God. And the Emperor said to the holy man, 'For all that man could do, you were helpless and in sore peril, but as you had God to support you, you have triumphed over the plot of the devisers of evil'. Hearing of the Emperor's threat against the architect, the servant of God begged the Emperor not to do him any harm. And so a pardon was granted him, and instructions were given that the column should be fixed securely; and this was done.

49

As the Emperor was on the point of leaving, the Devil, who is ever envious of the good, devised against him a dangerous snare because of the so great affection which he cherished for the holy man; for the horse he was riding shied and reared, and then fell to the ground on its back together with its rider. The curved edge of the saddle caught the Emperor's face and grazed it a little and the crown which he was wearing was shot from his head, and some of the pearls which hung over the back of his neck were dashed from their setting. The Emperor by the will of God was preserved unhurt, and after he had gone down to the City a special act of grace was shown by God. For the Emperor was angry with the general, Jordanes*, who was his count of the stable, and the latter, seized with fear on hearing his threats, took refuge in the holy man's enclosure and obediently listening to the just man's counsel, he renounced the doctrine of the Arians and joined the community of the Orthodox faith. At the same time the Emperor was reconciled to him; for when he of pious memory heard that the holy man was anxious about the accident which he had sustained on riding home he immediately sent Calapodius, his head chamberlain, to reassure the servant of God and say, 'Your angelic presence* must not have any anxiety about me, for through your holy prayers I was preserved unhurt, and I know now why I had that accident, for when visiting your Holiness I ought not to have mounted my horse so long as you could see me; but, I beg you, pray earnestly to God to forgive me for my ignorance'.

50

Remark now, dear readers, the Wicked One's disgrace! — for just as he thought he would have some success, he was still further disgraced, for the aforementioned most pious Emperor built a palace close to the church of St. Michael and spent the greater part of his days there and became the holy man's inseparable companion. And in future as soon as he perceived the just man from a distance he alighted from his horse; similarly, too, when he went down from the hill, he did not mount until he was hidden from his sight.

51

It happened about the same time that Gubazius,* the king of the Lazi arrived at the court of the Emperor Leo, who took him up to visit the holy man. When he saw this strange sight Gubazius threw himself on his face and said, 'I thank Thee, heavenly King, that by means of an earthly king Thou hast deemed me worthy to behold great mysteries; for never before in this world have I seen anything of this kind'. And these kings had a point in dispute touching the Roman policy; and they laid the whole matter open to the servant of God and through the mediation of the holy man they agreed upon a treaty which satisfied the claims of each. After this the Emperor returned to the city and dismissed Gubazius to his native land, and when the latter reached his own country he related to all his folk what he had seen. Consequently the men who later on came up from Lazica to the City invariably went up to Daniel. Gubazius himself, too, wrote to the holy man and besought his prayers and never ceased doing so to the end of his life.

52

In the following year a storm of unbearable violence took place and caused the Saint's leather tunic* to become like a bit of tow under the searing blast of the winds, and then the wind tore off even that wretched rag from the holy man and hurled it some distance away into a gully and the holy man was exposed to the snow all night long. And as the bitterest winds dashed against his face, he came to look like a pillar of salt. When morning broke the ladder could not be dragged along to him because of the tempest's violence, so he remained as he was and very nearly became a lifeless corpse.

53

But by God's mercy a calm followed, and they brought up the ladder. His disciples saw the hair of his head and beard glued to the skin by icicles, and his face was hidden by ice as though it were covered by glass and could not be seen and he was quite unable either to speak or to move. Then they made haste and brought cans of warm water and large sponges and gradually thawed him and with difficulty restored his power of speech. When they said, 'You have been in great danger, father', he answered them as though he were just awaking from sleep and said at once, 'Believe me, children, until you woke me, I was completely at rest. When the terrible storm broke and my garment was torn off me by the force of the winds, I was in great distress for about an hour, and then after a violent fainting fit I called upon the merciful God for help. And I was wafted, as it were, into sleep and I seemed to be resting on a magnificent couch and kept warm by rich coverings and I saw an old man sitting on a seat by my head, and I thought he was the man who met me on the road when I was coming away from the blessed Saint Simeon's enclosure.* And he appeared to be talking with great love and sincerity and he pointed out to me a huge hawk coming from the East and entering this great city and finding an eagle's nest on the column in the Forum of the most pious Emperor Leo. And he came and settled down in the nest with the eagle's young and then no longer appeared to be a hawk but an eagle. And I inquired of the old man what that might mean. And he answered. "There is no need for you to learn that now, but you shall know hereafter". And whilst he held me in his arms and warmed me, the same old man said very pleasantly, "I love you dearly; I wanted to be near you; many fruit-bearing branches are to blossom from your root". And as we found pleasure in each other you did not do well in waking me; for I was delighted at meeting him'. Then the disciples said to the holy man, 'We pray your forgiveness, but truly we were in great despair; for we thought your Holiness had died. What do you think that vision means, father?' He said to them, 'I do not understand it clearly, but God will do what is pleasing to Him and expedient for us'. But his disciples tried to interpret the vision and said, 'It behoves you with the help of the Emperor to bring the corpse of the holy and most blessed Simeon to this city. For it appears from the vision that this is the pleasure of the blessed Saint Simeon'.

The servant of God said to them, 'Fetch another leather tunic and wrap me in it'.

54

And the Emperor considering the peril through which Daniel had passed, said, 'It is not right for him to stand naked and unprotected and incur such dangers'. And he went up to him and begged him to let him make him a shelter of iron in the shape of a little enclosure. But the holy man did not wish it saying: 'Our sainted father Simeon did not have anything of the kind although he was far older than myself; therefore it is right that I who am young should practise endurance and not seek ease which relaxes the body'. But the Emperor replied, 'You have spoken well, father, and I approve your resolve; for I rejoice in your endurance, when I see, too, the help of God which constantly sustains you. For this reason a crown is being woven for you; yet be willing to serve us for many years still, and therefore do not kill yourself outright, for God has given you to be fruitful on our behalf'. With these arguments he with difficulty persuaded the holy man to accept his offer; and then the shelter was made. And from that time on the holy man remained untouched by storms. All the visitors who came from different nations, were they kings or emperors or ambassadors, the Emperor in person would either take them to see the Saint or send them up, and he never ceased boasting of the Saint and showing him to all and proclaiming his feats of endurance.

55

About that time a certain Zeno,* an Isaurian by birth, came to the Emperor and brought with him letters written by Ardaburius, who was then General of the East; in these he incited the Persians to attack the Roman State and agreed to co-operate with them. The Emperor received the man and recognizing the importance of the letters he ordered a Council to be held; when the Senate had met the Emperor produced the letters and commanded that they should be read aloud in the hearing of all the senators by Patricius,* who was Master of the Offices at that time. After they had been read the Emperor said, 'What think you?' As they all held their peace the Emperor said to the father of Ardaburius, 'These are fine things that your son is practising against his Emperor and the Roman State'. The father replied, 'You are the master and have full authority; after hearing this letter I realize that I can no longer control my son; for I often sent to him counselling and warning him not to ruin his life; and now I see he is acting contrary to my advice. Therefore do whatsoever occurs to your Piety; dismiss him from his command and order him to come here and he shall make his defence'.

The Emperor took this advice; he appointed a successor to Ardaburius and dismissed him from the army; then ordered him to present himself forthwith in Byzantium. In his place he gave the girdle of office to Jordanes* and sent him to the East; he also appointed Zeno, Count of the Domestics.

And the Emperor went in solemn procession and led him up to the holy man and related to him all about Ardaburius' plot and Zeno's loyalty; others told him, too, how Jordanes had been appointed General of the East in place of Ardaburius. The holy man rejoiced about Jordanes and gave him much advice in the presence of the Emperor and of all those who were with him; then he dismissed them with his blessing.

56

Some time later it befell that a report was spread that Genseric, King of the Vandals, intended to attack the city of

Alexandria;* this caused great searchings of heart to the
Emperor and to the Senate and to the whole city. So the
Emperor sent his spatharius* Hylasius, who was a eunuch, to
inform the holy man about Genseric and of the Emperor's
intention to dispatch an army to Egypt. Hylasius went up
and delivered the Emperor's message to the holy man; and
the holy man said to him, 'Go and say to the Emperor, "Do
not be troubled about this, for God sends word to you through
me, a sinner, that neither Genseric nor any of his will ever see
the city of Alexandria; but if you wish to send an army that is
a matter for you to decide; the God, Whom I adore, will both
preserve your Piety unhurt and will strengthen those who are
sent against the enemies of the Empire".' Hylasius departed
and reported these words to the Emperor, and by the grace of
God his words came true.*

57

Thereupon the Emperor returned thanks to God and the
holy man, and went up to the ladder and asked his permission
to build a lodging for the brethren and for strangers. But the
blessed Saint opposed the idea saying, 'Saint Simeon never had
any building at all in his enclosure during his lifetime; but I
beseech your Piety to grant me the request I make of you'.
The Emperor said, 'I for my part beseech you to do so, command me if you have any wish', to which the holy man replied,
'I beg you to send men to Antioch, and to bring back the corpse
of Saint Simeon'. The Emperor rejoiced at this request and
answered, 'Do you then give orders for a house to be built
where strangers can rest, and a dwelling for the brethren: for
I see that with God's help the number of brethren and disciples
will increase, and there will be a large crowd of strangers who
will be sore put to it if they come up and find no place wherein
to lodge. For the blessed Simeon, as you said, did not live in
such a storm-beaten place, nor did people go up to him for so
many different needs but only to pray and to be blessed;
whereas you suffer annoyance in many ways from those who
are perplexed over matters of State. Through them I receive
many letters from you and rejoice to do so, for they bring me
much profit. And so let that come to pass which I wanted
when I made my request'. Then the blessed Daniel said to

the Emperor, 'Since it was for the glory of God and for the protection of brothers and strangers that your Piety proposed to do what you suggest, give orders for it to be done'. Then the Emperor planned that the martyr-chapel of Saint Simeon should be placed to the north of the column and be built with piers and vaults but no columns;* and the monastery for brothers and strangers should be behind the column. And after prayers had been offered, he returned to the city.

58

While the work was progressing well by the grace of God, the remains of Saint Simeon arrived from the city of Antioch.* Being informed of this the Emperor ordered the Archbishop to announce that the deposition of the holy remains would take place and that there would also be an all-night service in the church of St. Michael at Anaplus because the Emperor himself was in his palace there. Thus on the following day an imperial carriage was prepared in which the Archbishop took his seat and taking the remains with him went up the hill in this fashion, and all the people in untold numbers, some going ahead, and others following, made their way to the appointed place singing psalms and hymns. And many healings took place on that day of the deposition of the holy remains. After the service which followed the whole populace streamed out into the enclosure to the holy man in order to be blessed. And the Archbishop with all the clergy went there likewise; and a throne was placed in front of the column; and when the Archbishop had taken his seat he said to the holy man, 'Behold, the Lord has fulfilled all your desires; and now bless your children with your counsel'. After the deacon had said the 'Let us attend', the holy man from his pillar said to the people: 'Peace be upon you!' and then opening his mouth taught them, saying nothing rhetorical or philosophical, but speaking about the love of God and the care of the poor and almsgiving and brotherly love and of the everlasting life which awaits the holy, and the everlasting condemnation which is the lot of sinners. And by the grace of God the hearts of the faithful people were so touched to the quick that they watered the ground with their tears. After this the Archbishop offered a prayer, and then the holy man dismissed them all, and each man returned to his house in peace.

59

One day a disbelieving heretic came up to the holy man, ostensibly for prayer, with his wife and children and some girls; but instead of prayers he began uttering calumnies against the holy man and poking witticisms at him. And the crowds who were united in their belief in God said to him, 'What are you doing, man, talking thus foolishly and, instead of praying, hindering us? Why have you come up here?' He said to them, 'I, too, heard from many about this man and came up to be edified, and I found the opposite; for when I approached the column to do obeisance I found this fish lying on the step'. And from the inside of his garment he pulled out a very large fried fish, which he had prepared in the market as lunch for himself and his companions; this he showed them, casting blame upon the holy man for being a voluptuary and not temperate. They who saw it first were astonished at his scheme and then, after censuring him severely, they left him alone saying, 'You will find out what lies you are uttering against the servant of God'. And as he was returning to the city, in order that the merciful God might make manifest how He protects His servants, it came to pass that the man himself, as well as his wife and children, began to shiver with ague; then after they had reached the market of the Archangel Michael and he wanted to partake of the fish, the wretched fellow was suddenly seized by an unclean spirit, and as he was driven by the demon all round the market he confessed all the deception he had practised against the holy man. And so, being driven on by the demon, he reached the enclosure with all his friends following him. There they persisted in their repentance and made full confession. Within three days the Lord healed them after they had been given oil of the saints to drink. As thankoffering he dedicated a silver icon, ten pounds in weight, on which was represented the holy man and themselves writing these words below, 'Oh father, beseech God to pardon us our sins against thee'. This memorial is preserved to the present day near the altar.

60

At that time the blessed Emperor Leo heard from many about a certain Titus, a man of vigour who dwelt in Gaul and had in his service a number of men well trained for battle; so he sent for him and honoured him with the rank of Count that he might have him to fight on his behalf if he were forced to go to war. This Titus he sent to the holy man for his blessing; on his arrival the Saint watered him with many and divers counsels from the Holy writings and proved him to be an ever-blooming fruit-bearing tree; and Titus, beholding the holy man, marvelled at the strangeness of his appearance and his endurance* and just as good earth when it has received the rain brings forth much fruit, so this admirable man Titus was illuminated in mind by the teaching of the holy and just man and no longer wished to leave the enclosure, for he said, 'The whole labour of man is spent on growing rich and acquiring possessions in this world and pleasing men; yet the single hour of his death robs him of all his belongings, therefore it is better for us to serve God rather than men'. With these words he threw himself down before the holy man begging him to receive him and let him be enrolled in the brotherhood. And Daniel, the servant of the Lord, willingly accepted his good resolve. Thereupon that noble man Titus sent for all his men and said to his soldiers,* 'From now on I am the soldier of the heavenly King; aforetime my rank among men made me your captain and yet I was unable to benefit either you or myself, for I only urged you on to slaughter and bloodshed. From to-day, however, and henceforth I bid farewell to all such things; therefore those of you who wish it, remain here with me, but I do not compel any one of you, for what is done under compulsion is not acceptable. See, here is money, take some, each of you, and go to your homes'. Then he brought much gold and he took and placed it in front of the column and gave to each according to his rank. Two of them, however, did not choose to take any, but remained with him. All the rest embraced Titus and went their ways.

61

When the Emperor heard this he was very angry and sent a messenger up to the holy man to say to Titus, 'I brought you up from your country because I wanted to have you quite near me and I sent you to the holy man to pray and receive a blessing, but not that you should separate yourself from me'. Titus replied to the messenger, 'From now on, since I have listened to the teaching of this holy man, I am dead to the world and to all the things of the world. Whatever the just man says about me do you tell to the Emperor, for Titus, your servant, is dead'. Then the messengers went outside into the enclosure to the holy man and told him everything. And the holy man sent a letter of counsel by them to the Emperor, beseeching him and saying, 'You yourself need no human aid; for owing to your perfect faith in God you have God as your everlasting defender; do not therefore covet a man who to-day is and tomorrow is not; for the Lord doeth all things according to His will. Therefore dedicate thy servant to God Who is able to send your Piety in his stead another still braver and more useful; without your approval I never wished to do anything'.

And the Emperor was satisfied and sent and thanked the holy man and said, 'To crown all your good deeds there yet remained this good thing for you to do.* Let the man, then, remain under your authority, and may God accept his good purpose'. Not long afterwards they were deemed worthy of the holy robe, and both made progress in the good way of life; but more especially was this true of Titus, the former Count.

62

Next the Devil, the hinderer of good men, imbued Titus with a spirit of inquisitiveness and suggested that he should watch the holy man in order to see if he ate and what he took to eat. So one day he waited till about the time of lamp-lighting and then unnoticed by all the brethren he remained outside in the enclosure hidden behind the column. When the nightly psalmody took place in the oratory the brothers imagined he had stayed behind because he was sick. The following day he spent with all the others. Although he did the same thing for seven nights, he found out nothing. Finally he openly conjured the holy man to explain his manner of life to him. And the holy man granted him his wish saying, 'Believe me, brother, I both eat and drink sufficiently for my needs; for I am not a spirit nor disembodied, but I too am a man and am clothed with flesh. And the business of evacuation I perform like a sheep exceedingly dryly, and if ever I am tempted to partake of more than I require, I punish myself, for I am unable either to walk about or to relieve myself to aid my digestion; therefore in proportion as I struggle to be temperate, to that degree I benefit and the pain in my feet becomes less intense'. Titus answered, 'If you, your Holiness, who are in such a state of body and standing in such a wind-swept spot, struggle in that manner to be temperate for your own good, what ought I to do who am young in years and vigorous in body?' The Saint replied, 'Do whatever your flesh can endure; neither force it beyond measure nor on the other hand abandon it to slackness; for if you load a ship beyond its usual burden, it will readily be sunk by its weight, but if on the contrary you leave it too light, it is easily overturned by the winds. By the grace of God, brother, I understand my natural capacity and know how to regulate my food'. After hearing this Titus went away to the oratory, took his place in one corner and hung himself up by ropes under his armpits so that his feet did not rest upon the ground, and from one evening to another he would eat either three dates or three dried figs and drink the ration of wine. He also fixed a board against his chest on which he would sometimes lay his head and sleep and at others place a book and read.

63

And he did this for some long time and benefited all those who visited him; amongst these was the most faithful Emperor, Leo, for whenever he went up to the holy man, after taking leave of him, he would go in to the blessed Titus; and beholding his inspired manner of life he marvelled at this endurance and besought him to pray for him. And it pleased the Lord to call him while he was at prayer, with his eyes and his face turned upwards and heavenwards, and thus it was that he breathed his last. The brethren looking at him thought he was praying as usual. When evening had fallen, the two brethren came who had formerly been his servants and now ministered unto him and brought him all he required, and they discovered that he was dead. And when they began to lament all recognized that he had gone to his rest. His head lay back on his neck, his hands were crossed and supported by the plank and since the weight of the body was borne by the shoulder ropes his legs hung down straight and were not bent up. And as one looked on the corpse of this saintly champion it showed the departed soul's longing for God. The brethren went and told the elders who came out to the holy man's enclosure and announced to him the death of the glorious saint. When he heard of it he thanked the Lord and bade them carry out the corpse to him after the time of lamp-lighting and put it in front of the column and hold an all-night service there in his memory. The next day Titus was buried in the tomb of the elders by command of the holy man.

64

After Titus had died this holy death, one of the barbarians who had come with him and had been named Anatolius by the holy man aspired to the same kind of life in the same place, and conducting himself blamelessly therein for a long time he greatly benefited all those who visited him. Thus his fame spread on every side. As he wished to flee from glory among men he went out at night into the enclosure to the holy man and fell down before him imploring him to grant him his permission. The holy man inquired the reason and, on hearing it, prayed over him and dismissed him. After receiving his dismissal Anatolius travelled to the chapel of St. Zacharias in Catabolus (the Harbour) and took up his dwelling there in a suburb on the opposite shore; at that time Idoubingos* was general. Shutting himself up in a small cell, he lived in it for a long time; later he established a small monastery* of about twelve men, which by the grace of God and the prayers of the holy father is still in existence to-day; thus in blessedness he passed away to the Lord.

65

About that time the pious Emperor Leo married his daughter Ariadne to Zeno* (of whom we have spoken before) and also created him consul. And shortly afterwards when the barbarians created a disturbance in Thrace, he further appointed him commander-in-chief in Thrace.* And in solemn procession he went up to Anaplus to the holy man and besought him as follows: 'I am sending Zeno as general to Thrace because of the war which threatens; and now I beg you to pray on his behalf that he may be kept safe'. The holy man said to the Emperor, 'As he has the holy Trinity and the invincible weapon of the Holy Cross on his side he will return unharmed. However, a plot will be formed against him and he will be sorely troubled for a short time, but he shall come back without injury'. The Emperor said, 'Is it possible, I beg you, for any one to survive a war without some labour and trouble?' When they had received a blessing and taken their leave they returned to the city. Then the aforesaid Zeno set out for the war and soon afterwards a plot was formed against him as the holy man had foretold, but by God's assistance he escaped and reached the Long Wall and crossed from there and came to Pylae;* and later still he reached the city of the Chalcedonians.

66

Now while the patrician Zeno was still absent at the war a male child was born to him by the Emperor's daughter and received the name of Leo.* When Aspar and his sons stirred up a rebellion against the most pious Emperor Leo, He 'that maketh wars to cease unto the ends of the earth'[1] fought on the side of the pious Emperor and destroyed them both. After that Leo crowned his own grandson and namesake, emperor. And thus it came to pass that Zeno took courage and crossed from Chalcedon to the city and entered the palace and came to the Emperor Leo.

67

As time went on it befell that the pious Emperor Leo the Great fell sick and died;* he made a good end and left as successor to the throne his own grandson Leo, son of the patrician Zeno. Then the Senate convoked a meeting because the Emperor was an infant and unable to sign documents, and they determined that his father Zeno should hold the sceptre of the Empire. And thus he was crowned and became Emperor. After three years had passed the Lord took the infant, the pious Emperor Leo, into His eternal kingdom; and he went to the land of his fathers,* and left the Empire to his* father.

[1] Ps. xlvi. 9.

§ 68

The Roman government was being well administered by the will of God, and the State was enjoying a time of quiet and order, and the holy churches were living in peace and unity, when the ever envious and malignant Devil sowed seeds of unjust hatred in the hearts of some who claimed to be the Emperor Zeno's kinsmen, I mean Basiliscus, Armatus and Marcianus and some other senators. When Zeno became aware of the treachery that was being planned against him, he went up to the holy man and confided to him the matter of the plot. The holy man said to him, 'Do not let yourself be troubled about this; for all things that have been fore-ordained must be accomplished upon you. They will chase you out of the kingdom, and in the place where you find a refuge, you will be in such distress that in your need you will partake of the grass of the earth. But do not lose heart; for it is necessary that you should become a second Nebuchadnezzar, and those who are now expelling you, having felt the lack of you, will recall you in the fullness of time. You will return to your Empire, and more honour and glory shall be added unto you and you shall die in it. Therefore bear all with gratitude; for thus must these things be'. The Emperor thanked him for these words (for he had already put him to the test in the case of other prophecies of his) and after being blessed by the holy man he took his leave and went down to the City.

69

Now the malicious men whom I mentioned above had free access to the blessed Empress Verina, Basiliscus because he was her brother and chief of the Senate, and Armatus as being her nephew and Zuzus as being the husband of her sister, and Marcianus the husband of her daughter and son of an emperor. They were constantly at her side and by their guile persuaded her to conspire with them to drive Zeno from the throne. As he knew of their wickedness and that he was in danger of assassination, he took his own wife, the Empress Ariadne, and some eunuchs, and unbeknown to all he left the palace one night during a very heavy storm. They crossed the straits and landed* at Chalcedon because of their pursuers, and they escaped and reached the province of Isauria. The Empress

Verina so controlled the revolution that she secured the crown for her brother Basiliscus; who shortly afterwards attempted to do away with his own sister. However, she fled to the oratory of the Ever-Virgin Mary in Blachernae and remained there as long as Basiliscus lived.

70

Next Basiliscus — name of ill omen* — made an attack upon the churches of God, for he wished to bring them to deny the incarnate dispensation of God. For this reason he came into conflict with the blessed Archbishop Acacius* and sought to malign him so as to bring about his ruin. Directly news of this attempt reached the monasteries all the monks with one accord assembled in the most holy Great Church in order to guard the Archbishop. After some consideration the Archbishop ordered all the churches to be draped as a sign of mourning, and going up into the pulpit he addressed the crowds and explained the blasphemous attempt which was being made. 'Brethren and children', he said, 'the time of martyrdom is at hand; let us therefore fight for our faith and for the Holy Church, our mother, and let us not betray our priesthood.' A great shout arose and all were overcome by tears, and since the Emperor remained hostile and refused to give them any answer, the Archbishop and the archimandrites determined to send to the holy man, Daniel, and give him an account of these things, and this they did.

71

And it happened by God's providence that on the following day Basiliscus sailed to Anaplus, and sent a chamberlain* named Daniel, to the holy man to say, 'Do those things which the Archbishop Acacius is practising against me seem just to your angelic nature?* for he has roused the city against me and ˈˈˈˈˈˈˈˈˈˈ ˈˈˈˈ ˈˈˈˈˈˈ ˈˈˈ ˈˈˈˈˈ ˈˈˈˈˈˈˈ ˈˈ ˈˈˈˈ ˈ ˈˈˈ ˈˈˈ ˈˈˈ for us that he may not prevail against us'. After listening to him the holy man said to Daniel, 'Go and tell him who sent you, "You are not worthy of a blessing for you have adopted Jewish ideas and are setting at nought the incarnation of our Lord Jesus Christ and upsetting the Holy Church and despising His priests. For it is written 'Give not that which is holy unto the dogs, neither cast your pearls before the swine'[1] Know therefore and see, for the God Who rendeth swiftly will surely rend your tyrannous royalty out of your hands". When the chamberlain heard this answer he said he dared not himself say these things to the Emperor and besought Daniel to send the message in writing, if he would, and to seal it with his seal. The holy man yielded to the eunuch's entreaties, wrote a note and after sealing it, gave it to Daniel and dismissed him; and he returned and delivered the sealed note to the Emperor. He opened it and when he learnt the purport of the message he was very angry and immediately sailed back to the city. These things were not hidden from the Archbishop Acacius and his most faithful people; therefore on the following day almost the whole city was gathered together in the Great Church and they kept shouting, 'The holy man for the Church! let the new Daniel save Susanna in her peril! another Elijah shall put Jezebel and Ahab to shame! in you we have the priest of orthodoxy; he that standeth for Christ will protect His bride, the Church'. And other such exclamations they poured forth with tears.

72

On the morrow the Archbishop Acacius sent to Daniel some of the archimandrites who were best beloved of God; these were the blessed Abraamius of the monastery of St. Kyriakus, Eusebius who dwelt near the Exakionium* Athenodorus of the monastery of Studius* and Andreas, the vicar of the exarch,* and some others. Having chosen these he sent them saying, 'For my sake and the faith's go to the holy man Daniel, throw yourselves before his column and importune him with entreaties saying, "Do you imitate your teacher Christ Who 'bowed the heavens and came down'[2] and was incarnate of a holy virgin and consorted with sinners and shed His own blood to purchase His bride, the Church.[3] Now that she is insulted by the impious, and her people are scattered by fierce wolves and the shepherd tempest-tost, do not ignore my grey hairs but incline your ear and come and purchase your mother, the Church'. And they went and did as they were bid and threw themselves down before the column; and the holy man

[1] Matt. vii. 6. [2] Ps. xviii. 9. [3] Cf. Acts xx. 28.

seeing them lying on the ground was disturbed and began to
call to them from above, 'What are you doing, holy fathers,
mocking my unworthiness? What is it that you bid me do?'
Then they stood up and said, 'That you with God's help
should save the faith which is being persecuted, save a storm-
tossed church and a scattered flock, and save our priest who,
despite his grey hairs, is threatened with death'. And Daniel
said to them, 'He is truthful that said, "The gates of hell shall
not prevail against the holy Church"[1]; wait patiently therefore
where you are and the will of God shall be done; pray then
that God may reveal to us what we should do'. And it came
to pass that as Daniel was praying in the middle of the night,
and as the day dawned — it was a Wednesday — he heard a
voice saying distinctly to him, 'Go down with the fathers and
do not hesitate; and afterwards fulfil your course in peace!'
Obedient therefore to the counsel of the Lord he woke his
servants. And they placed the ladder and went up and took
away the iron bars round him. And Daniel came down with
difficulty owing to the pain he suffered in his feet, and in that
same hour of the night he took the pious archimandrites with
him and they sailed to the City and entered the church before
the day had begun.

73

And thus it was that when the people came to God's house
while, according to custom, the fiftieth psalm was being sung,
they saw the holy man in the sanctuary with the Bishop and
marvelled; and the report ran through the City that he had
come. All the City, and even secluded maidens, left what they
had in hand and ran to the Holy Church to see the man of God.
And the crowds started shouting in honour of the Saint saying,
'To you we look to banish the grief of the Church; in you we
have a high priest; accomplish that for which you came; the
crown of your labours is already yours'. But the holy man
beckoned with his hand to the people to be silent and addressed
them through the deacon, Theoctistus, 'The stretching forth
of the hands of Moses, God's servant, utterly destroyed all
those who rose up against the Lord's people, both kings and
nations; some He drowned in the depths of the sea, others He

[1] Matt. xvi. 18.

slew on dry land with the sword and exalted His people; so to-day, too, your faith which is perfect towards God has not feared the uprising of your enemies, it does not know defeat nor does it need human help; for it is founded on the firm rock of Christ. Therefore do not grow weary of praying; for even on behalf of the chief of the apostles earnest prayer was offered to God, not as if they thought he was deserted by God but because God wishes the flock to offer intercessions for its shepherd. Do you, therefore, do likewise, and amongst us, too, the Lord will quickly perform marvellous things to His glory'. After he had said this they took down all the mourning draperies from the sanctuary and the whole church. Daniel also wrote a letter to the Emperor saying, 'Does this angering of God do you any service? is not your life in His hands? What have you to do with the Holy Church to war against its servants, and prove yourself a second Diocletian?' And many other things like these he wrote both by way of counsel and of blame. When the Emperor received the letter and found that Daniel had come down and was in the church he was stung by the prick of fear and sent back word to him, 'All your endeavour has been to enter the City and stir up the citizens against me; now see, I will hand the City, too, over to you'. And he left the palace and sailed to the Hebdomon.*

74

When the holy man heard this news, he took the cross-bearers and the faithful people and bidding the monks guard the Church and the Archbishop he went out. As they reached Ammi, close to the chapel of the prophet the holy Samuel, the just man being carried by the crowd of the Christ-loving people, behold, a leper approached and cried aloud saying, 'I beseech you, the servant of the God Who healed lepers, to pray Him that I may be healed!' On hearing him the holy man ordered his bearers to halt; and when the leper had drawn near, the holy man said to him, 'Brother, how came you to think of asking me things that are beyond my power? for I, too, am a man encompassed with weakness even as you are'. The leper replied, 'But I beg you, I know that you are a man of God; and I believe that the God Whom you serve will grant me cleansing in answer to your prayers; for the apostles too were but men and yet through their prayers the Lord healed many'. The holy man marvelling at his faith said to him, 'Do you then believe in Him Who gave healing to many through His saints?' The leper said, 'Yes, and I believe that even now if you pray I shall be healed'. Then Daniel turning to the East asked the people to stretch forth their hands to heaven and with tears to cry aloud the 'Kyrie eleeson' (Lord, have mercy!) And when he deemed that they had done this long enough, he said to the men near him, 'In the name of Jesus Christ, Who cleansed lepers, take him and wash him in the sea and wipe him clean and bring him back'. They ran off with the man, washed him in the sea and by the power of Jesus Christ the leper was healed on the spot. When the multitudes saw this astonishing miracle they shouted unceasingly the 'Kyrie eleeson'. Then the crowds took the man that was healed, all naked as he was, and returned to the City and brought him into the Holy Church and leading him up to the pulpit declared this wondrous miracle to all. The whole city ran together and beholding him who had been a leper cleansed by God through the holy man's prayers they glorified God for making the leper spotless. And so all those in the City who had sick folk ran to the servant of God. And the Lord gave healing abundantly to them all.

75

Thereafter as the holy man with the crowd approached the palace of Hebdomon, a Goth leant out of a window and seeing the holy man carried along, he dissolved with laughter and shouted, 'See here is our new consul!' And as soon as he said this he was hurled down from the height by the power of God and burst asunder. Then sentinels, or the palace guards,* prevented those who had seen the fall from entering into the palace, saying they should have an answer given them through a window. But when the people insisted with shouts that the holy man should enter the palace but received no answer, the servant of God said to them, 'Why do you trouble, children? You shall have the reward promised to peacemakers from God; and since it seems good to this braggart to send us away without achieving anything, let us do to him according to the word of the Lord. For He said to His holy disciples and apostles, "Into whatsoever city or village ye shall enter and they do not receive you, shake off the dust of your feet against them as a testimony to them";[1] let us therefore do that'. And he first of all shook out his leather tunic and incited the whole crowd to do likewise; and a noise as of thunder arose from the shaking of garments. When the guards who were on duty* saw this and heard all the marvellous things God had wrought by Daniel most of them left all and followed him.

76

When the impious Basiliscus heard what the holy man had done in condemnation of him, he sent two guardsmen of the court and a legal secretary of the Emperor* with them to over-take Daniel and implore him to return. These men overtook Daniel and implored him in the name of Basiliscus saying, 'The Emperor says "if I indeed sinned as a man, do you as servant of Christ propitiate Him on my behalf and I will seek in everything to serve God and your Holiness".' But the holy man said to them, 'Return and say to the Emperor: Your words of guile and deceit will not avail to deceive my un-worthiness, for you are doing nothing but "treasuring up for yourself wrath in the day of wrath";[2] for in you there is no fruit of good works; wherefore God will shortly confirm his wrath upon you that you may know that "the Most High ruleth over the kingdom of men"[3] and will give it to the good man in preference to you'.[4] With these words he bade the Emperor's secretary to spread out his cloak and after shaking the rest of the dust from his own clothing into the cloak he said, 'Go, carry this to the braggart as a testimony against him and against her who is his confederate* and against his wife'. Directly after the messengers had returned and given the Emperor the just man's answer, the tower of the palace fell; since even lifeless things may feel the wrath of God to the salvation of many.

77

When the just man had arrived at the Golden Gate and saw the concourse of people, he besought them to return each to

[1] Matt. x. 11.   [2] Rom. ii. 5.
[3] Dan. v. 21.   [4] Cf. 1 Sam. xv. 28.

their own home. But they as with one voice cried, 'We intend to live and die with you; for we have nothing with which to repay you worthily; receive the resolve of your suppliants and lead us as you will, for the Holy Church awaits you'. Whilst the people were uttering these cries two young men afflicted with demons were brought to him; and after he had prayed with tears to God, they were immediately cleansed and they followed him glorifying God.

78

When they came to the chapel of St. John in the monastery of Studius* the monks came out and requested the holy man to come in and offer prayer in their prophet's shrine and to rest a little from the thronging press which encompassed him. When he consented to come in and offer prayer there was such a crush of people in the narrow passages that many only narrowly escaped being trodden to death. Then after Daniel had offered prayer in the venerable shrine and passed through to the sacristy he and the men who carried him had a short rest. And the monks had the idea of taking him through the garden to the sea and bringing him by boat to the Great and very Holy Church. When the people got wind of this, a great tumult arose among them and they shouted and said, 'Bring the just man here if you love orthodoxy; do not begrudge healing to the sick'. They also said to the just man, 'Freely you have received therefore freely give![1] if you desert us we will burn down the chapel at once'. So the holy man came out of the sacristy and addressed them, reassuring them and asking them to go on ahead of him and thus relieve the pressure of the crowd.

79

When Daniel came out of the prophet's shrine and was going on his way, behold, a certain woman, as did the woman of Canaan,[2] cried to him saying, 'Oh servant of God, have pity on my daughter, for she whom you see has now been bedridden for three years in the grip of an unknown disease, and though many doctors have visited her, not one of them has been able to help her. So now I beseech you, oh holy man, do not

[1] Matt. x. 8.   [2] Matt. xv. 22.

despise my tears for I am sorely distressed about her'. Seeing her in such terrible grief, the holy man was dissolved in tears, and raising his eyes to heaven and stretching out his hands to God he prayed; and then calling the girl close to him he sealed her with the sign of the precious Cross and said to her, 'In the name of our Lord Jesus Christ Who ever worketh our salvation and does not desert us, be thou cured of this disease'. And the girl was cured of her scourge in that hour in the sight of all the people.

80

When they drew nigh to the house of the most glorious patrician Dagalaiphus,* the patrician himself leaned out from an upper window and seeing that the holy man was being unbearably crushed by the thronging crowd, he ran down with a body of helpers and took him out of the crush and caused him to be carried into his house near the Forum of the Ox* to rest there. He himself stood in the porch and excused himself to the people by saying, 'I did this in order that my house might be blessed'. And he put Daniel into a litter and secured him well by posting men round the litter to prevent his being troubled by the crowd. And in this manner he was brought in safety to the Church without any difficulty.

81

When he entered into the most holy Cathedral he was received in great sincerity and with acclamation by the Archbishop Acacius and the holy archimandrites and all the reverend clergy and the most pious monks and the most faithful people. And all glorified the merciful God for the marvellous things that they had heard and seen which God had done through him. And they led him into the vestry that he might have a short rest from the pressure of the crowd. And behold a snake came out from some hole and wound itself round his feet; those present were terrified on seeing the animal and ran forward to kill it; but the holy man prevented them saying, 'Leave it alone, it is near its end'. and shaking it off his feet he said to it, 'Go to thy place!' and it went to the wall opposite them and in the sight of all of them it burst in pieces.

82

The patrician Herais* hearing that he was in the vestry came in, threw herself on the ground and seized the holy man's feet, begging him that she might have a son. But when she saw that on the one foot the sole had dropped away from the ankle bone and there was nothing left but the shin bone she was amazed at the man's endurance. She gave him a little cord and begged him to wind it round his inflamed foot and give it to her. But he would not suffer this to be done. Then the Archbishop Acacius and all the pious men present besought the holy man to grant her what she asked. Then the holy man consented, took the cord and placed it on his inflamed foot and gave it to her saying, 'According to thy faith may the Lord grant thee thy request for a son; and his name shall be Zeno'. And it came to pass that soon afterwards this most noble woman conceived and bore a son and called him by the name of Zeno according to the word of the Saint.

83

When all these things had been thus auspiciously accomplished by the grace of the Lord, and when Basiliscus of ill-omened name* had heard from his legal secretary of the Saint's condemnation of him and of the sudden fall of the palace tower, it did not seem to him to augur any good. And immediately without a moment's delay he entered a boat and sailed from the Hebdomon to the City; and the next day he sent senators to the very holy Cathedral to beseech the Saint to take the trouble to come as far as the palace. But he would not consent to go but said, 'Let him come himself to the Holy Church and make his recantation before the precious Cross and the holy Gospel which he has insulted; for I am but a sinful man'. The senators went back and gave this message to the Emperor, whereupon in solemn procession he at once went to the Church. The Archbishop met him with the holy Gospel in the sanctuary and was received by the Emperor with dissimulation; then after the customary prayer had been offered Basiliscus went in with the Archbishop to the holy man. And they both fell at his feet before all the people, both Basiliscus and the Archbishop Acacius. And Daniel greeted them and counselled them to seek the way of peace and for the future to refrain from enmity towards each other. 'For if you are at variance', he said, 'you cause confusion in the holy churches and throughout the world you stir up no ordinary unrest'. The Emperor then made a full apology to the holy man and the people cried out saying, 'Oh Lord, protect both father and sons; it is in Thy power to grant us concord between them; let us now hear the Emperor's confession of faith! why are the canons of orthodoxy upset? why are the orthodox bishops exiled? To the Stadium with Theoctistus,* the Master of the Offices! the Emperor is orthodox! burn alive the enemies of orthodoxy! send the disturbers of the world into exile! a Christian Emperor for the world! let us hear what your faith is, Emperor!'

These and countless other exclamations the people kept shouting, and all the time the Emperor and the Archbishop lay prostrate on the ground at the holy man's feet.

84

Then the holy man summoned Strategius, the imperial secretary, and bade the Emperor make a proclamation to the people by way of justification, and this he did. And the secretary mounted the pulpit and began to read as follows: 'We believe that your Reverences — perfect in understanding as you are — cannot fail to know that from infancy up we have been orthodox and have communicated in the very Holy Church in which our children were baptized; and that we believe in the one holy and consubstantial Trinity, and we approve your warm championship of the faith. Do not, therefore, accept any childish insinuation against us from those who say that we do not think rightly concerning the holy faith. For you know yourselves that we who are soldiers brought up and trained to arms are not able to understand the depths of the holy faith; but since it is now a time for peace and no season for controversy, I can pass over many things, since we are able completely to convince you, our beloved subjects, that we shall not be found guilty of a single one of those charges which men in their fickleness plotted to bring against us. This is our justification before God and the holy man and we have stated it clearly to you.' Having in this way appeased the holy man and the people, the Emperor was reconciled to them. And having been reconciled to the Archbishop in the sight of them all the Emperor returned to his palace. Thus did our Master God bring the enemy of His Holy Church to His feet.

85

When all minds were set at rest and the people were moving off to their own homes the servant of God returned to his usual practice of asceticism, but when he had sailed back he reached his column only with difficulty owing to the press of faithful people and of those overmastered by divers illnesses. Therefore with great danger and much distress he made the ascent of his column and summoned them all, and after praying to God he dismissed them all restored to health. To the clergy and monks and the people who had remained behind he said, 'It was not with honesty of purpose that the persecutor appeared to make peace with us; be patient therefore and you will soon see the glory of God; for the Lord will not overlook the affliction of His servants and His holy churches'. And thus it was accomplished by the will of God, for after a short time Zeno, the Emperor, returned with his wife, the Empress Ariadne, the daughter of royal parents.* Thenceforth the holy churches rested in much contentment and the State grew glorious and the Roman government waxed in strength. And the aforesaid usurper met with his due reward, as the servant of God had foretold. And thereafter the Emperor often went up to the holy man returning thanks to the merciful God, and also to the Saint, reminding him of the things which he had foretold should happen.

86

Once a goldsmith came up from the City to the holy man with his wife and they brought with them their seven-year-old child who had never walked from birth but spent his life crawling along. This goldsmith came to the holy man and throwing himself and his child in front of the column, he besought the holy man saying, 'Oh servant of God, have pity on my young child who longs to stand up but cannot do so, for nature conceived him contrary to nature; grant me this joy, oh servant of God, for I have followed your holy footsteps; do not send me away, I pray you, with my petition unfulfilled'. The holy man replied, 'Do not be so impatient in your words; for your zeal towards God, if accompanied by faith and patience, will release your son from his calamity; do not be discouraged but go with the child and remain by the holy relics of Simeon,* the holy servant of God and our father; anoint the child's feet with the holy oil and bring him back here when prayer is being offered, and we trust in God that He will give him healing'. The man did as the holy man had ordered him, and on the seventh day, when prayer had been offered in the enclosure, the boy suddenly jumped on to the steps of the pillar and went up and embraced the column; all marvelled and glorified God for this wonderful happening. And his parents gave thanks to God and to the holy man and took the boy home in health. When the boy grew to be a man he frequently visited the holy man, received a blessing and returned home.

87

A certain man travelling to Constantinople from the East fell among robbers who stole from him everything that he had with him, mutilated his body, cut the sinews of his knees and leaving him half dead, went their ways; but by the providence of God they had not inflicted any mortal wound on him. Some wayfarers who came to that place picked him up and carried him to the city of Ancyra, for it was close to that city that this had befallen him. There they took him to the bishop who ordered him to be conveyed to the hospital and cared for there. But while his wounds were tended he was not able to walk. He therefore made this request of the bishop, 'I was travelling to Constantinople in fulfilment of a vow making my way to our lord Daniel, who stands on the column, when I met with this accident; and now that, thanks to you, I have been healed it behoves me to fulfil my vow. I pray you, therefore, servant of God, to send me safely to Constantinople to the holy man'. The bishop, since he thought that this was a pious request, gave him money for his expenses, also a beast and two men to conduct him to the holy man Daniel. So the men took him and brought him to the holy man's enclosure and then carried him and laid him in front of the column. The man cried aloud and told the holy man the reason for which he had come and related what had happened to him and how he had been saved by the help of God and the bishop. The holy man sent thanks to the bishop for the kindness he had shown to the man and after furnishing those who had brought him with supplies for their journey he dismissed them in peace with presents for the bishop. He handed over the man to some of the servants with orders to carry him and bring him to the enclosure daily at the hour of prayer, and to anoint him with the oil of the saints; the man's legs hung down as if they did not belong to him. After a few days, one Friday when the Saint had said the prayers as usual and all had said 'Amen', the man suddenly leapt from the litter, and stood on his feet and said with a loud voice, 'Bless me, oh servant of God'. And he quickly ran up the steps and embraced the column giving thanks the while to God.

88

Here I think it would be reasonable to make known the faith which lay hidden in Hippasius, the 'second centurion'.[1] This man was so rich in the great poverty of Christ that the cures performed by Christ's disciples he accepted as though wrought by the Lord Himself; for if any one of his house, be it son or daughter or man-servant or maid servant, fell ill or suffered from anything, he judged himself unworthy to seek the intercession of the Saint, but would send letters asking for the Saint's prayers. On receiving the holy man's written reply he would lay the letter, as if it were the miracle-working hand of Jesus, on the sufferer and immediately he received the fruits of his faith.

89

A certain woman had a son of twelve years, Damianus by name, dumb from birth; him she brought to the holy man's enclosure and signing to him not to go away, she left him and departed. Then when the brethren saw the boy staying there and saying nothing to anybody, they brought him to the holy man. He, beholding him, ordered that he should remain in the monastery, saying, 'The boy shall be God's minister'. The

[1] Matt. viii. 5-13; Luke vii. 2-10.

brethren said, 'He is dumb, master!' He said to them, 'Moisten his tongue with the oil of the saints'. But the brethren suspected that from stress of poverty the mother had suggested to him to feign dumbness; so very often when the boy was asleep they woke him suddenly by making a noise; and at other times they would prick him in the body with needles or pens to try whether he would speak. But he said nothing, as he was held by the power of dumbness. One Sunday, after some considerable time had passed, when the holy Gospel was going to be read aloud, and the deacon had announced the lesson from the holy Gospel of St. Matthew, the boy shouted out ahead of the others, 'Glory be to thee, oh Lord!' And after uttering this first cry he in future surpassed all the brethren in his singing of the psalms. A certain chamberlain, Calopodius by name, had built an oratory to the holy Archangel Michael and came to the holy man asking him to give him some brethren for this oratory in Parthenopolis.* And together with the brethren the holy man gave him this boy to sing the psalms and he became God's minister, as the servant of God had foretold about him. So great are the achievements of grace, so great the gifts of our Master to His sincere servants; he came not speaking and became a good speaker, he came voiceless and gained a beautiful voice, he was deserted by his mother as dumb and he proved to be the wonderful herald of the church.

90

Many other marvellous works, too, were performed by God through His servant Daniel which neither words can describe nor tongue relate; these we must of necessity omit so as not to prolong our story unduly; for those we have told are sufficient to confirm the faithful and to lead the faithless to turn to the faith. But let us attempt to describe how resolute and inflexible was the faith of the holy man.

Through the Devil's working a tumult once arose in the most holy churches, for tares had sprung up from vain disputations and questionings, so that some of the monks, who were renowned for good living, through their simple-mindedness and through their failure to consider the matter with precision, left the most Holy Church and separated themselves from the holy fellowship and liturgy. These mischief-makers came to the holy man and tried to confound him with similar arguments, but he who kept the foundation of the holy faith unmovable and unshakable answered them saying, 'If the question which you raise is concerning God, your inquiry is no simple or ordinary matter, for the Divinity is incomprehensible; and it will be sufficient for you to study the traditions of the holy apostles about Him and the teaching of the divine Fathers who followed in their steps and not trouble yourselves any further. But if the matter in dispute is about human affairs, as, for instance, if one priest has removed another, or has accepted one to whom the others object, all such things must be submitted to the judgment of God and to the rulers themselves to judge according to the divine canons; for we are the sheep and they are the shepherds, and they will give account to God for the flocks entrusted to them; let us abstain from vain and dangerous questionings and let us each consider that which concerns ourselves knowing that it is not without danger that we separate ourselves from our holy mother, the Church. For her bridegroom is the true Shepherd Who is able to recall to His fold the sheep that have strayed and to lead those who have not strayed to better pasture. Therefore it suffices us to believe unquestioningly in the Father, Son and Holy Ghost, and to receive the incarnate dispensation of our Lord Jesus Christ and his birth from the Virgin in the same way as He Himself was pleased to do in His own lovingkindness, for it is written: 'Seek not out the things that are too high for thee, neither search the things that are too deep for thee'.[1] With this and similar counsel and warning he led their hearts away from soul-destroying questionings and kept them unshaken in the faith.

91

He also foresaw the death of the Emperor Zeno and this he made known to him through one of those who often came to visit him, first by ambiguous messages, and then later he warned him clearly that he would receive the recompense for his good and evil deeds. He told Zeno that owing to his faith in God and his good deeds he might have full confidence when

---

[1] Ecclesiasticus iii. 21.

he came into the presence of God; but he must be mindful to abstain from all covetousness, and he must excel in the good ordering of his life and banish all informers and treat with generosity all those who had sinned against him; for by nothing is God better pleased than by forgiveness and gentleness. These things he said before Zeno's death; and to us he foretold that after her husband's death the Christ-loving Ariadne would reign over the Empire because of her perfect faith in the God of her fathers. And that with her would reign a man who loved Christ and had devoted his whole life to hymns to God and to vigils, who was a model of sobriety to all men and who in gentleness and justice would surpass all those who had reigned at any time; 'he will turn aside, too', he said, 'from that love of money which according to the apostle is "the root of all evil".[1] He will govern the State impartially and honestly, and throughout his reign he will grant peace and confidence to the most holy churches and to the order of monks. In his time the rich shall not be favoured, neither shall the poor be wronged, for this above all, both in peace and in war, will be the surest guarantee of prosperity to the world.' All these predictions were confirmed shortly afterwards, for when Anastasius* had been elected Emperor, his acts in themselves were sufficient proof to the world that the Saint's prophecies had been fulfilled, and those who dwelt in the holy man's enclosure realized this more especially since they received all manner of benefits.

92

During the holy man's first illness, from which he was expected to die, the pious sovereigns of whom I have spoken moved by divine zeal, displayed great eagerness to honour his memory, for they brought from the capital a very large tomb of precious stone and splendid metal-work which can be seen to this day in the consecrated enclosure, a very wonderful sight for visitors and of surpassing lavishness, and whatever was needed for the funeral they supplied with the greatest generosity. And it is superfluous to mention the munificence of the liberality of the pious sovereigns and their unfailing protection. This devotion to the Saint which was so fruitful

[1] 1 Tim. vi. 10.

and a fountain of kindly deeds the servant of God heard of after his recovery and said, 'All these acts are truly great and worthy of their faith in God and sufficient to call down the goodwill from above upon them, but a resting-place of stone and one so distinguished does not befit me; for I desire the earth only according to God's command: "Dust thou art and unto dust shalt thou return".[1] The rulers will receive a far greater recompense from God; but I myself wish to be buried deep down in the earth and have the remains of holy martyrs laid above me, so that, if anyone should wish to visit my resting-place to strengthen his faith, he may pay his reverence to the Saints and from them receive the reward of his good deeds and free himself from condemnation'. This wish we carried out according to his orders after his second illness and actual translation. For above his revered grave lie the relics of the three holy children, Ananias, Azarias and Misael. These were brought from Babylon by the Emperor Leo of pious memory during the lifetime of the holy man, and were deposited by Euphemius,* the most holy Archbishop of the imperial city, who out-rivalled all others in his zeal for showing honour to the holy man; so we did not experience any feeling of separation from our blessed and glorious father. And at the moment of Daniel's blessed death the sovereigns increased their gifts, for they bought tens of thousands of candles and illuminated both the oratories; and beginning at the very top of the column they filled with candles all the spiral scaffolding built for the descent of the holy corpse.

93

So great a grace of prophecy was granted to this holy man that three months before his falling asleep he foretold to us that within a few days he would quit the dwelling of his body and go to dwell with the Lord. And from that time on he did not converse with those that resorted to him about present day matters only, but by foreknowledge he also announced future events to them, strengthening them with words of good counsel, and he gave injunctions to his usual attendants and to us how his precious body was to be brought down from the column.

[1] Gen. iii. 19.

And in every instance in which we obeyed him things turned out propitiously for us; but if perchance we did anything contrary to his command, or as we thought fit, being satisfied with our human planning, it was sure to turn out contrariwise for us; for he had been deemed worthy by God of the prophetic gift.

94

And as he had been granted this wonderful grace the glorious man also told us beforehand of Herais,* the servant of God, and said that moved by spiritual zeal she would not allow his holy body to be brought down except by the means she herself would provide, and he warned us that nobody should oppose her in this intention, and this, too, came to pass. For this most noble servant of God, Herais, generous as ever, made lavish provision for the funeral of our thrice-blessed father Daniel supplying an abundance of candles and oil beyond measure and gold for distribution to the poor and a great quantity of wood. And she ordered a number of men who were experienced in such works to erect a structure spiralwise round the column and about the entrance to the oratory where the much-enduring body of the noble champion of the ascetic life was to lie, so that it might not be injured by the onrush of the crowd trying to snatch a relic. And according to the command of the holy man nobody hindered her in this pious purpose.

95

Seven days before his falling asleep he summoned the whole brotherhood, from chiefest to least, and some he bade stand quite near him on the top of the ladder and listen to his words. When he knew they were assembled, he said, 'My brothers and children, behold, I am going to our Master and Lord, Jesus Christ. God Who created all things by His word and wisdom, both the heaven and the earth and the sea and all that in them is, Who brought the race of men into being from that which was not, He Who is terrible to the angels but good to men, Who "bowed the heavens and came down"[1] upon the earth "like rain upon the mown grass",[2] upon the holy virgin

---

[1] Ps. xviii. 9.   [2] Ps. lxxii. 6.

Mary, the mother of God, and was pleased to be incarnate of her, as He alone understands, and to be seen by men upon earth, Who "took away the sins of the world"[1] and suffered for us, and "with His stripes"[2] upon the Cross healed our spiritual wounds, and "nailed the bond that was against us to the wood of the Cross",[3] He will strengthen you and will guard you safe from evil and will keep your faith in Him firm and immovable if you continue in unity with each other and perfect love until you draw your last breath. May He give you grace to serve him blamelessly and to be one body and one spirit continuing in humility and obedience. Do not neglect hospitality; never separate yourselves from your holy mother, the Church, turn away from all causes of offence and the tares of heretics, who are the enemies of Christ, in order that ye may become perfect even as also your heavenly Father is perfect. And now, I bid you Farewell, my beloved children, and I embrace you all with the love of a father; the Lord will be with you.' These words he ordered to be read aloud to the brethren by those who had stood nearest to him and caught the words, for he was lying down. When this had been done, and the brethren had heard the holy father's prayer and farewell they burst into such weeping and wailing that the noise of their lamentation sounded like unto a clap of thunder. Once again the holy man prayed over us and then dismissed us telling us not to be faint-hearted but bear up bravely, 'and make mention of me in your prayers!'

96

From that hour on, as if moved by some divine providence, the body of faithful people came up of their own accord. And they would not move from the holy man's enclosure until Euphemius, the most holy Archbishop of this imperial city, arrived. He mounted the column and looked, and then standing high up on the ladder, announced to all the people, 'The holy man is still alive and with us; do not be troubled; for it is impossible for his holy body to be consigned to the grave before news of his death has been published to everyone and all the holy churches everywhere have been informed'. And this was done.

[1] John i. 29.   [2] Is. liii. 5.   [3] Col. ii. 14.

But I must not forget to mention the greatest thing of all which was indeed worthy of wonder. Three days before his falling asleep in the middle of the night he was allowed to see at one time all those who had been well-pleasing to God. They came down and when they had greeted him they bade him celebrate the divine and august sacrament of the Euchar- ist, and two brethren standing by were allowed to be hearers of the words and to make the due responses. And directly he had completed the liturgy of God he woke up from his trance and coming to himself he asked for the holy communion to be administered to him; this was done and he partook first, and we all at that hour of midnight also partook of the Holy Mysteries just as if he had been administering to us the holy sacrament. Then, bidding farewell to the crowds who sur- rounded him, he bade the brethren present throw incense into the censer without ceasing.

97

Just about the time of his holy departure from this life a man vexed with an unclean spirit suddenly cried aloud in the midst of the people, announcing the presence of the saints with the holy man, naming each one of them; and he said, 'There is great joy in heaven at this hour, for the holy angels have come to take the holy man with them, besides there are come, too, the honourable and glorious companies of prophets and apostles and martyrs and saints; they are tormenting me now, and to-morrow at the third hour they will drive me out of this tabernacle; when the holy man is going to his home in the heavens and his saintly corpse is being brought down, I shall come out.' And this did indeed happen. Our glorious father Daniel died at the third hour on the following day, a Saturday, December 11th in the second indiction (A.D. 493), and at the time of his death he worked a miracle in that the man with an unclean spirit was healed.

98

When they took down the railing they found his knees drawn up to his chest, and his heels and legs to his thighs. And whilst his body was being forcibly straightened, his bones creaked so loudly that we thought his body would be shattered;

yet when he was laid out, he was quite entire except that his feet had been worn away by inflammation and the gnawing of worms. The weight of the hair of his head was divided into twelve plaits, each of which was four cubits long; likewise his beard was divided into two and each plait was three cubits long. Most of the Christ-loving men saw this.

They clad him, as was his wont, in a leather tunic, and a plank was brought up and laid on the column and he was placed on it.

99

At early dawn the Archbishop Euphemius, dearly beloved of God, came and went up the column by the spiral way and kissed the precious corpse, and thus, too, did all the faithful high dignitaries and officials, for they went up* to the head of the column, gave their benediction and kissed his blessed body and came down.

But the people demanded that the holy man should be shown to them before his burial, and in consequence an extraordinary tumult arose. For by the Archbishop's orders the plank was stood upright — the body had been fixed to it so that it could not fall — and thus, like an icon, the holy man was displayed to all on every side; and for many hours the people all looked at him and also with cries and tears besought him to be an advocate with God on behalf of them all. When this had been done, behold, all the people suddenly saw clearly with the naked eye three crosses in the sky above the corpse and white doves flying round it.

100

Next there was great anxiety about the manner of bringing it down for the funeral; for the Archbishop Euphemius was afraid that the corpus might be torn asunder by the crowd, so he ordered it to be put into a case of lead, and this coffin the aforementioned 'illustris', the most pious Herais, also provided. This coffin was raised on the shoulders of the most holy Archbishop Euphemius and he bore it together with the noblest officials and pious men, and they brought down the corpse by way of the spiral stairway without its being hurt.

But in order to receive a blessing the people rushed forward in front of the entry to the chapel and as the planks could not bear such a sudden rush they parted from each other and all the men who were carrying the coffin were thrown to the ground with the holy corpse. By the grace of the Lord the carriers did not suffer any injury nor did they give way, but they most marvellously withstood the onrush of the crowd so that among those countless thousands of men, women and children not a single one sustained any harm.

And Daniel was brought into the oratory and laid to rest underneath the holy martyrs as he had wished.

101

These few short reminiscences out of many, beloved, we have recorded in this our work as best we might. We rejected a multitude of words in order to avoid satiety, and although numberless incidents have been omitted, we are assured that these will suffice the faithful for remembrance and give them all that they desire.

Now let us in a short summary review his whole life down to the end of his time on earth.

Our all-praiseworthy father Daniel bade adieu to his parents when he was twelve years old, then for twenty-five years he lived in a monastery; after that during five years he visited the fathers and from each learned what might serve his purpose, making his anthology from their teaching. At the time when the crown of his endurance began to be woven the Saint had completed his forty-second year, and at that age he came by divine guidance, as we have explained above, to this our imperial city. He dwelt in the church for nine years, standing on the capital of a column, thus training himself beforehand in the practice of that discipline which he was destined to bring to perfection. For he had learned from many divine revelations that his duty was to enter upon the way of life practised by the blessed and sainted Simeon.

For three and thirty years and three months he stood for varying periods on the three columns, as he changed from one to another, so that the whole span of his life was a little more than eighty-four years.

During these he was deemed worthy to receive 'the prize of his high calling';[1] he blessed all men, he prayed on behalf of all, he counselled all not to be covetous, he instructed all in the things necessary to salvation, he showed hospitality to all, yet he possessed nothing on earth beyond the confines of the spot on which the enclosure and religious houses had been built. And though many, amongst whom were sovereigns and very distinguished officials occupying the highest posts, wished to present him with splendid possessions he never consented, but he listened to each one's offer and then prayed that he might be recompensed by God for his pious intention.

102

While we bear in mind our holy father's spiritual counsels, let us do our utmost to follow in his steps and to preserve the garment of our body unspotted and to keep the lamp of faith unquenched, carrying the oil of sympathy in our vessels that we may find mercy and grace in the day of judgment from the Father, the Son and the Holy Ghost now and henceforth and to all eternity, Amen.

[1] Philipp. iii. 14.

NOTES

Introd., p. 1   For the whole subject of the asceticism of the Stylite Saints see the masterly study of Hippolyte Delehaye, *Les Saints stylites* (=Subsidia Hagiographica, vol. 14), Brussels, Société des Bollandistes, 1923; the text of the Life of Daniel, pp. 1-94. There is a previous publication of the Life in *Analecta Bollandiana* 32 (1913), pp. 121-229; this has an index of proper names which is lacking in the later edition. For a study of the new historical material contained in the Vita cf. *English Historical Review* 40 (1925), pp. 397-402.

The reader of the Life of Daniel will naturally be interested in the life of Daniel's master Simeon: for that life the sources are (i) Theodoret, *Historia Religiosa*, ch. 26, the account of an eye-witness; (ii) a Syriac Life of which there is a German translation by Hilgenfeld in H. Lietzmann, *Das Leben des heiligen Symeon Stylites* (=Texte und Untersuchungen zur Geschichte der altchristlichen Literatur, edd. A. Harnack and C. Schmidt, vol. 32, Heft 4), Hinrichs, Leipzig, 1908; (iii) a Greek Life — the text in Lietzmann, ibid.; (iv) Evagrius, *Historia Ecclesiastica*, Book I, ch. 13; of this there is an English translation in Bohn's Ecclesiastical Library, *History of the Church by Theodoret and Evagrius*, London, 1854, pp. 272-6. Of these sources there is an admirable study by P. Peeters recently published in *Analecta Bollandiana* 61 (1943), pp. 29-71, *S. Syméon Stylite et ses premiers Biographes* which shows that our most reliable source is the Syriac Life.

Antioch might share with Constantinople the possession of the saint's relics, but the pillar remained and about the pillar the devotion of Simeon's Syrian admirers raised a majestic church. The remains of that church have been closely studied of recent years and a note of the principal publications may be of interest:

H. W. Beyer, *Der Syrische Kirchenbau* (=Studien zur spätantiken Kunstgeschichte, edd. Richard Delbrück and Hans Lietzmann, vol. 1), De Gruyter, Berlin, 1925, pp. 69-72: the building of the church dated between A.D. 460 and 490.

H. C. Butler, *Early Churches in Syria: Fourth to Seventh Centuries*, ed. E. Baldwin Smith. Princeton Monographs in Art and Archaeology, Princeton University, 1929, pp. 97-109. For Simeon's column see p. 100: height 40 ft.: it is suggested that the summit was 6 ft. square.

Daniel Krencker and Rudolf Naumann, *Die Wallfahrtskirche des Simeon Stylites*, etc. Abhandlungen der Preussischen Akademie der Wissenschaften Jahrgang 1938 Philosophisch-historische Klasse Nr. 4, De Gruyter, Berlin, 1939 — a sumptuous publication: account of excavations in the spring of 1938 with plans and photographs, but see the review by A. M. Schneider in *Göttinger Gelehrte Anzeigen* for 1939, pp. 335-42; G. de Jerphanion, in *Voix des Monuments* N.S., Pontificio Istituto Orientale, Roma, 1938, pp. 111-33 and in *Orientalia Christiana Periodica* 9 (1943), pp. 203-11.

Readers may be glad to have a reference to the French translation of the life of another stylite saint: François Vanderstuyf, *Vie de Saint Luc le Stylite* (879-979), Patrologia Orientalis, edd. R. Graffin and F. Nau, Tome 11, Fasc. 2 (1914).

For the history of the period covered by Daniel's life cf. J. B. Bury, *History of the Later Roman Empire*, Macmillan, London, 1923, vol. 1; Otto Seeck, *Geschichte des Untergangs der antiken Welt*, vol. 6, Metzler, Stuttgart, 1920, with an *Anhang* of notes, 1921; Ernst Stein, *Geschichte des spätrömischen Reiches*, vol. 1, Seidel, Vienna, 1928. For details of the struggle between the Germans and the Isaurians cf. E. W. Brooks in *English Historical Review* 8 (1893), pp. 209-38.

ch. 2, p. 8   'two great lights': for the explanation of the vision see ch. 46.

4, p. 9   'When he was twelve years old ' For the admission of children into monasteries at this time cf. the case of Heliodorus who was received into the monastery of Eusebonas when he was only three years old: for sixty-two years he never left the monastery and he told Theodoret that he had no idea what a pig or a cock might look like. Theodoret, *Historia religiosa*, Migne, Patrologia Graeca, vol. 82, coll. 1468.

ch. 7, p. 10   Telanissae: the Greek text of Theodoret has the form Telanissos or Telanessos: the Syriac form is Telneschin or Telneschil: cf. H. Lietzmann, *Das Leben des heiligen Symeon Stylites* (see above), p. 205.

7, p. 10   For the apologetic for St. Simeon's strange form of asceticism see Theodoret, *Historia Religiosa*, ch. 26, Migne, Patrologia Graeca, vol. 82, col. 1473, and in Hilgenfeld's translation of the Syriac Life in Lietzmann, op. cit., ch. 117, pp. 163-5.

9, p. 11   'at last you are free': a surprising consequence of his appointment as abbot.

10, p. 12   The revolt of the Samaritans. Hatred of the Christians led to many revolts of the Samaritans: in 484 Zeno took Gerizim from the Samaritans and built there a church dedicated to the Virgin. After the violence of the Samaritan revolution of 529 many of their synagogues were destroyed: some of the Samaritans became Christians, while others escaped into Persia.

11, p. 13   For the reappearance of the old man see ch. 53.

12, p. 13   On the writer's sources of knowledge see the Introduction, p. 6.

12, p. 14   'in the quarter of the city named after Basiliscus': ἐπάνω τοῦ προπύλου τῆς εἰσόδου τοῦ μαρτυρίου τὰ κατὰ Βασιλίσκον. τὰ κ.Β. is curious and we are not sure how the words should be translated.

13, p. 14   a place called Anaplus: cf. J. Pargoire, *Anaple et Sosthène*, Izvyestiya russkago arkheologicheskago Instituta v Konstantinopolye 3 (1898), pp. 60-97. Pargoire has shown that the word Ἀνάπλους has many meanings: (i) the navigation of the Bosphorus up against the current from Constantinople to the Black Sea or the whole of the Bosphorus itself; (ii) the S.W. coastline of the Bosphorus from the suburb of Sycae (Galata) to the narrows halfway between Constantinople and the Black Sea; (iii) a specific place (or perhaps to two specific places), as in this Vita, where Anaplus=the modern Roumeli-Hissar.

14, p. 15   'Paul his disciple' — a mistake which was corrected by the author of the shorter Life who omits the name of Paul. Antony is, of course, St. Antony, 'the first monk', whose Life was written by Athanasius.

15, p. 15   'a small window': σεμνὴν θυρίδα cf. ch. 20 s.f. θυρίδα μικράν; see ch. 20 μοναστήριον σεμνόν, ch. 64 s.f. καὶ συστησάμενος σεμνὸν μοναστήριον ὡσεὶ ἀνδρῶν δώδεκα. It is not easy to see how σεμνός comes to mean 'small'.

ch. 17, p. 16   'with nothing to do': ὑμεῖς ἀδιοίκητοι μένετε. We are not sure of the translation of ἀδ.

17, p. 16   'the blessed Anatolius': Anatolius was Patriarch of Constantinople from 449 to July 3rd, 458. For the date of his death cf. Franz Diekamp, *Analecta Patristica* (=Orientalia Christiana Analecta, No. 117), Pontificium Institutum Orientalium Studiorum, Roma, 1938, p. 55 note.

20, p. 18   'a small monastery': see note on ch. 15.

20, p. 18   'a small window': see note on ch. 15.

22, p. 19   St. Simeon's leather tunic: δερμοκούκουλλον. There is a difficulty here, since Simeon's instruction before his death was that the skins which were his only garments should be his sole covering after death. The writer of the Syriac Life says 'and this was done'. Hilgenfeld in Lietzmann, *Das Leben*, etc., ch. 123, p. 168. — The leather covering may of course have been abstracted after Simeon's death to be presented to the Emperor, as later the Saint's relics were carried to Constantinople. Peeters writes: 'S'il y a contradiction entre les deux textes, on ne la résoudra pas en accordant a priori la préférence au narrateur grec', *Analecta Bollandiana* 61 (1943), p. 59. Perhaps δερμοκούκουλλον should be translated 'leather tunic with its cowl', cf. ch. 52 *infra*.

22, p. 19   'the sleepless ones': the monks who sought to maintain prayer both night and day within the monastery: to 'pray without ceasing'. Cf. the article by E. Marin s.v. 'Acémètes' in the *Dictionnaire de Théologie catholique*, edd. A. Vacant and E. Mangenot, vol. 1, Paris, 1903, coll. 304-8. The founder of the body of 'sleepless monks' was Alexander, who formed a monastery in Constantinople c. 420. The monks had attacked Nestorius who was at that time supported by the Court. In consequence they were driven from the capital and took refuge in the monastery of Rufinianae of which Hypatius was abbot. Later they moved fifteen miles farther up the Asiatic shore of the Bosphorus to Irenaion=the modern village of Tchiboukly opposite Stenia — for the identification of Stenia with Sosthenion of the Byzantines see Pargoire, op. cit. (note on ch. 13), pp. 61-5. At Irenaion the

ch. 22, p. 19
(*cont.*)

'sleepless monks' built a large monastery housing some 300 monks: they were divided into separate choirs and thus praise to God was sung continuously without pause night or day. A vivid account of the sufferings of the Akoimetoi before they settled at Irenaion is given in the Life of St. Hypatius by Callinicus of which there is a useful edition, Leipzig [1895], and that story is re-told by J. Pargoire, *Les Débuts du Monachisme à Constantinople*, Revue des Questions historiques, N.S. 21 (1899), pp. 133-43.

23, p. 20

'guardsman': Silentiarius. The silentiarii formed the body of 'ushers who kept guard at the doors during meetings of the Imperial Council and Imperial audiences'. J. B. Bury, *History of the Later Roman Empire*, Macmillan, London, 1923, vol. 1, p. 33 note. Cf. ch. 42 *infra*, and see A. Vogt, *Constantin VII Porphyrogénète, Le Livre des Cérémonies, Commentaire*, Les Belles Lettres, Paris, 1935, pp. 46-7.

24, p. 21

'fluttering': θωπεύουσαν. θωπεύειν means to 'flatter'. There is apparently no parallel to its meaning in this passage which can be only to 'flutter'. It has been suggested that in English 'flatter' and 'flutter' are forms of the same word and that it has undergone a change in meaning similar to that in the case of the Greek θωπεύειν, though this differentiation has been marked in English by a vowel change. See Maurice Leroy, *Nugulae byzantinae*, Annuaire de l'Institut de philologie et d'histoire orientales et slaves 6 (1938), pp. 95-9.

25, p. 21

'steward of the sacred table': καστρήσιος τῆς θείας τραπέζης. For the imperial table and its controller ὁ ἐπὶ τῆς τραπέζης, cf. Constantine Porphyrogenitus, *De Ceremoniis* (Bonn edition), p. 463 (cf. pp. 70, 484); J. B. Bury, *The Imperial Administrative System of the Ninth Century* (=British Academy Supplementary Papers I), Oxford University Press, 1911, pp. 125-6. The Castresios (Castrensis) would appear to have been his subordinate; he is mentioned by Constantine VII, ibid., pp. 742, 744.

27, p. 22

Anatolius, cf. ch. 17. For a biography of Gennadius see Franz Diekamp, op. cit. (note on ch. 17), pp. 54-70, and see ch. 41-3 *infra*.

28, p. 23

'a Syro-persian from Mesopotamia': 'Syro-persian'= a Persian subject speaking Syriac. Leroy argues that in the case of such compound words the first part describes the country of origin and the second part the habitat. He compares Mark vii. 26. Maurice Leroy, loc. cit. (note on ch. 24), pp. 102-4.

'the last rungs': In the Vienna MS. of the Vita the word 'four' is added here: if this reading were adopted the ladder used for Daniel's first column would have had ten rungs.

ch. 31, p. 25   Cyrus. For the famous Praefect of Constantinople and Praetorian Praefect of the East cf. J. B. Bury, *History of the Later Roman Empire* (see note on ch. 23), vol. 1, pp. 227-9. His buildings in the capital caused the crowd in the Hippodrome to shout 'Constantine built the city, but Cyrus renewed it'. See further the article by Otto Seeck in Pauly-Wissowa-Kroll, *Realencyclopädie der classischen Altertumswissenschaft*, vol. 12, Stuttgart, 1924, coll. 188-90. Cf. ch. 36 *infra*.

31, p. 25   Chrysaphius: the all-powerful eunuch under Theodosius II. See J. B. Bury, op. cit., vol. 1, pp. 229, 235-6; Otto Seeck, *Realencyclopädie*, vol. 3 (1899), coll. 2485-6 — 'the Spatharius' — see note on ch. 56.

32, p. 25   On Gelanius see note on ch. 25.

35, p. 27   Eudoxia, the daughter of Theodosius II and Eudocia, married Valentinian III in 437 and in Ravenna was declared Augusta in 439. In 455 her husband died, and in the same year Gaiseric, the Vandal, invaded Italy, sacked Rome and carried off as prisoners Eudoxia and her two daughters, Placidia and Eudocia. In 462, under the terms of a treaty of peace concluded with Gaiseric, Eudoxia and Placidia were restored from captivity and returned to Constantinople. Of her later history we know nothing. See the article by Otto Seeck, *Realencyclopädie* (see note on ch. 31), vol. 6 (1907), coll. 925-6.

35, p. 27   Olybrius, a member of the aristocracy of Rome, escaped from the western capital when it was sacked by Gaiseric and as the present Vita shows reached Constantinople; he had probably been betrothed to Placidia, the daughter of Eudoxia, while in Italy: this would explain his inquiries which Daniel had answered concerning the return from Africa of Eudoxia and her daughter. Gaiseric (whose son Huneric had married Placidia's sister Eudocia) desired Olybrius to be de-

ch. 35, p. 27   clared Emperor in the West. Olybrius was sent to
    (cont.)   Italy by Leo, and after the death of Anthemius ruled
                  there as emperor for seven months. He died — sur-
                  prisingly — a natural death. It is doubtful whether
                  he was recognized as Emperor by the East Roman
                  Court; on the circumstantial story given by Malalas
                  of Leo's attempt to procure the assassination of
                  Olybrius see J. B. Bury, *English Historical Review*,
                  vol. 1 (1886), pp. 507-9. The story is unsupported
                  by any other authority; how did Malalas learn the
                  details which he gives (Malalas, p. 374, Bonn ed.)?
                  See Ernst Stein, *Geschichte des spätrömischen Reiches*,
                  vol. 1 (see p. 73), pp. 582-3, and T. Hodgkin, *Italy
                  and her Invaders*, vol. 2, ed. 2, Oxford, 1892, index.
                  s.v. 'Olybrius', and probable genealogy, p. 474.

35, p. 27   'your angelic presence': παρὰ τῷ σῷ ἀγγέλῳ i.e. 'with
                  your angel'='with your angelic self'. For this curious
                  use of the word 'angel' see H. Grégoire, *'Ton Ange' et
                  les Anges de Théra*, Byzantinische Zeitschrift 30
                  (1929-30), pp. 641-4. Professor Grégoire thinks that
                  this form went out of use after the seventh century: it
                  was too 'osé de saluer un ange dans un chrétien vivant,
                  fût-il un saint'. 'On se contente d'expressions plus
                  prudentes comme ἰσάγγελος ['equal to the angels'],
                  ἀγγελικός ['angelic']; on parla d'âmes concitoyennes
                  des anges'. Cf. *infra*, ch. 49, 71.

36, p. 28   Cyrus. See note p. 77, ch. 31.
36, p. 28   On this epigram cf. Père Delehaye's article *Revue des
                  Études grecques* 9 (1896), pp. 216-24. Delehaye sug-
                  gested that the inscription was the work of Cyrus him-
                  self: he has contributed several epigrams to the Greek
                  Anthology: cf. vii. 557; ix. 136, 623, 808, 809; xv. 9.

38, p. 29   The Emperor Leo I. For the reign cf. J. B. Bury,
                  op. cit. (see note on ch. 23), vol. 1, pp. 314-23;
                  Ensslin in *Realencyclopädie* (see note on ch. 31), vol. 12
                  (1925), coll. 1947-61.

38, p. 29   The Empress Verina, cf. the note on ch. 55.
39, p. 29   'a certain harlot': the Greek text has an otherwise
                  unknown word τυφάς: Maurice Leroy proposes to read
                  τρυφάς: cf. his study of the Greek words for prostitute,
                  op. cit. (see note on ch. 24), pp. 106-9.

39, p. 29   Anaplus: see note on ch. 13.
41, p. 31   Gennadius: see note on ch. 27.
41, p. 31   'the matter was not remembered': see ch. 45.

ch. 42, p. 31	'guardsman': Silentiarius; see note on ch. 23.
43, p. 32	On this remarkable ordination to the priesthood see H. Delehaye, *Les Saints stylites*, Brussels, 1923, p. lvi.
45, p. 33	The great fire (cf. ch. 41) — September 2nd, 465 (for references cf. Ensslin, *Realencyclopädie* — see note on ch. 31 — vol. 12, coll. 1959). A great part of the capital was destroyed by the conflagration which is probably to be identified with that reported in *Chron. Pasch.* (Bonn cd.), vol. 1, p. 598, which was the greatest ever known: the fire spread from sea to sea. The Emperor fled from Constantinople and crossed to the Asiatic shore where he remained for six months.
45, p. 33	'did not keep silence', etc.: or, as in the abbreviated version of the Vita: 'God in His mercy and wishing to spare the people disclosed these things to me and I did not keep silence, but more than once I declared them and besought men that they should repent and my words were counted as idle babbling. You should have obeyed my words and have escaped from such anger. For formerly the Ninevites...'
46, p. 34	'the two lights': see ch. 2 *supra*.
48, p. 35	'his chamberlain': see note on ch. 71.
49, p. 35	Jordanes, son of John, the Vandal Master of the Soldiers, who was murdered in Thrace in 441. Jordanes was consul in 470. For his appointment as general on the Eastern front see ch. 55 *infra*.
49, p. 36	'your angelic presence': see note on ch. 35.
51, p. 36	Gubazius, King of the Lazi: In 456 Marcian had attacked Colchis and had called upon the King of the Lazi to abdicate or to depose his son, as it was against tradition to have two joint rulers. Gubazius abdicated and agreed to come to Constantinople to discuss the relations of his kingdom towards the Empire. In 466 Gabazius pays his visit. Lazica lay at the eastern extremity of the Black Sea. See the sketch-map in V. Chapot, *La Frontière de l'Euphrate*, Fontemoing, Paris, 1907. On Lazica see ibid., pp. 13 14, and the chapter on *L'Extrémité du Pont-Euxin et les Régions caucasiques*, ibid., pp. 363-73.
52, p. 37	'the Saint's leather tunic': see note on ch. 22.
53, p. 37	'the man who met me on the road': cf. ch. 10.
55, p. 39	This is an important section; it tells us for the first time how Zeno was brought to the notice of the Emperor. For Ardaburius and his father Aspar see

ch. 55, p. 39 (cont.)	Otto Seeck in *Realencyclopädie* (see note on ch. 31), vol. 2 (1895), coll. 607-10.
55, p. 39	Patricius: not to be identified with Aspar's son of that name (J. B. Bury, op. cit. (see note on ch. 23) vol. 1, p. 317 note). Later Patricius became the paramour of Verina: she plotted against Zeno in order to raise Patricius to the throne. In this she failed, as her brother Basiliscus was made Emperor and he put Patricius to death (cf. Bury, ibid., pp. 390-1). For Jordanes see note on ch. 49.
56, p. 40	So far as we know this is the only place where a threatened Vandal attack upon Egypt is mentioned.
56, p. 40	spatharius: spatha=a long sword. Spatharii appear as private soldiers maintained, as were the bucellarii, by generals and other potentiores. Here Hylasius is clearly a member of the troop of imperial guards, cf. R. Grosse, *Römische Militärgeschichte*, Weidmann, Berlin, 1920, pp. 137-8, 285-6.
56, p. 40	The biographer here is very discreet: it is true that Gaiseric did not attack Egypt, but the combined naval expedition of the forces of the East and of the West of the Emperor directed against the Vandal kingdom ended in a complete catastrophe. The expedition was under the command of Basiliscus and it was ruined by his incompetence. It was said that he had been instigated by Aspar to betray the fleet under the promise of empire: Priscus, a contemporary, states that he was bribed by Gaiseric [for sources: E. W. Brooks, *English Historical Review* 8 (1893), p. 213]. It is not necessary to accept either of these attempts to explain the disastrous failure. For Gaiseric or Genseric see: Thomas Hodgkin, *Italy and her Invaders*, vol. 2, 2nd ed., Clarendon Press, Oxford, 1892, pp. 227 sqq.; F. Martroye, *Genséric, La Conquête vandale en Afrique et la Destruction de l'Empire d'Occident*, Hachette, Paris, 1907; E. A. Gautier, *Genséric, Roi des Vandales*, Payot, Paris, 1932. For the range of Gaiseric's hostile action see the account of his attack on Greece, Gautier, p. 254. For the disastrous attack on Africa by the Empire, Gautier, pp. 255 sqq.; Hodgkin, p. 446; Bury, op. cit. (see note on ch. 23), pp. 335-7.
57, p. 41	'but no columns': ἐκτὸς κιόνων. We do not know how this should be translated: it seems as if ἐκτὸς must mean 'free from'.

ch. 58, p. 41   The relics of St. Simeon. Since Antioch continued to regard the body of St. Simeon as its great protection we must conclude that a part only of the Saint's remains was brought to Constantinople. 'Il n'est pas nécessaire d'admettre, dans un pays où la division des corps saints n'était pas regardée comme un sacrilège, que l'on n'a pu enrichir la capitale sans dépouiller complètement Antioche.' Delehaye, *Les Saints stylites*, p. lvi.

60, p. 43   'at his endurance': Here we have adopted a change in punctuation.

60, p. 43   'to his soldiers': his bucellarii — i.e. soldiers serving under a military commander as his own private troop. The word is said to be derived from bucella = fine white bread as distinguished from the ordinary rations of the common soldier. See Grosse, op. cit. (note on ch. 56), p. 287.

61, p. 44   We owe this translation to Professor Dawkins; cf. ch. 49 (short version). περὶ δὲ 'Ιορδάνου καὶ τοῦτο τὸ ἀγαθὸν τῇ σῇ ἔμενεν ὁσιότητι.

64, p. 46   We know nothing about Idoubingos.

64, p. 46   'a small monastery': see note on ch. 15.

65, p. 46   Zeno marries Leo's daughter Ariadne. Since Zeno was consul in 469 the marriage presumably was celebrated in the winter of 467-8. Brooks placed it in 466, *English Historical Review* 8 (1893), p. 212. Leo had previously promised that Patricius, Aspar's son, should marry Ariadne. 'Henceforth there were two factions at the Court of Constantinople, the Isaurian and the barbarian . . . For the next twenty years the history of the Empire turns upon the struggle between these factions.' Brooks.

65, p. 46   Apparently in 470 Anagast revolted in Thrace; this would explain Zeno's mission to Thrace. Anagast later claimed that his revolt had been instigated by Ardadurius and produced letters from Ardaburius in support of his assertion (John of Antioch, frag. 206). This revolt may in its turn have led to the murder in the palace in 471 of both Aspar and Ardaburius (ch. 66 *infra*).

65, p. 47   'came to Pylae': see note p. 191.

66, p. 47   Birth of Leo II. Leo was in his seventh year when he died in November 474. He must therefore have been born in 468. Malalas xiv (Bonn ed.), p. 376; Seeck, *Regesten der Kaiser und Päpste*, Metzler, Stuttgart, 1919, p. 425.

ch. 67, p. 47   Death of Leo I: January 18th, 474.

67, p. 47   'went to the land of his fathers': this reads oddly here — ἐπορεύθη ἐν τῇ γῇ τῶν πατέρων. Presumably such texts as 1 Kings viii. 34, 48; 2 Chron. vi. 25, 38 are interpreted as signifying Heaven.

67, p. 47   'his father': οἰκεῖος has merely the force of the possessive pronoun.

68-9, p. 48   For the plot organized by Verina in concert with her brother Basiliscus with the object of dethroning Zeno, the husband of her daughter Ariadne, see Bury, op. cit. (note on ch. 23), vol. 1, pp. 390-7.
Armatus, nephew of Verina, was the lover of Zenonis, the wife of Basiliscus: he was created a Master of the Soldiers by his uncle and was his colleague in the consulship in 476.
Marcianus, the son of Anthemius, the Roman Emperor in the West, had married Leontia, the second daughter of Leo I. His participation in the revolt of Basiliscus (475) is to be distinguished from his later attempt to overthrow Zeno, on which see Bury, op. cit., vol. 1, p. 395. Cf. the article by Ensslin, *Realencyclopädie* (see note on ch. 31), vol. 14 (1930), coll. 1529-30. We do not know of any other mention of Zuzus. It is to be noted how carefully the writer shields Verina and puts on others the responsibility for the attack on Zeno.

69, p. 48   'and landed': ἐποίησαν ἔκοταβλα. We do not know how these words should be translated: is it 'they landed' or does it mean literally 'they took horse'?

70, p. 49   'Basiliscus—name of ill omen': Basiliscus—a diminutive of Basileus='a little emperor'. For the Monophysitism favoured by Basiliscus see J. B. Bury, op. cit. (note on ch. 23), vol. 1, p. 403; Ernst Stein, op. cit. (see p. 73), p. 538; for the Encyclical of Basiliscus anathematizing the Creed of Chalcedon cf. Zechariah of Mitylene, Book V, ch. 2 — in the translation of E. W. Brooks (Methuen, 1899), pp. 105-7; in the German translation of K. Ahrens and G. Krüger (Teubner, Leipzig, 1899), pp. 60-2.

70, p. 49   Acacius: Patriarch of Constantinople, A.D. 471-89.

71, p. 49   chamberlain: a cubicularius. On these trusted servants of the Emperor see the article by Rostowzew, *Realencyclopädie* (see note on ch. 31), vol. 4, coll. 1734-7.

ch. 71, p. 49   'your angelic nature': literally 'to your angel'; see note on ch. 35.

72, p. 50   The Exakionium, more usually Exokionion or corrupted into Hexakionion=the district outside (ἔξω) the wall of Constantine to the south of the City. Cf. Van Millingen, *Byzantine Constantinople* (Murray, 1899), pp. 18 sqq. and map opposite p. 19.

The Monastery of Studius. Studius, a patrician from Rome, founded in 463 the famous monastery dedicated to Saint John the Baptist. It lay south of the Exokionion (see note *supra*). Delehaye has shown that the monastery was always known as 'of Studius' and never as 'Studium'. *Analecta Bollandiana* 52 (1934), pp. 64-5. Exarch. Probably here=the superintendent of the monasteries of the capital.

73, p. 52   The Hebdomon=seven miles from the central milestone in the capital. Its site at Makrikeui on the shore of the Sea of Marmora, three miles to the west of the Golden Gate, was determined by Van Millingen: *Byzantine Constantinople*, pp. 316-41 and map opposite p. 316. See further Heinrich Glück, *Das Hebdomon und seine Reste in Makriköi* (=Beiträge zur vergleichenden Kunstforschung Heft 1), Vienna, 1920 (illustrated), and for the most recent excavations cf. *Échos d'Orient* (Bucharest) 38 (1939), 146 sq.

75, p. 53   'sentinels or the palace guards': φρουροί εἴτουν φύλακες τοῦ παλατίου. Of the precise meaning of these terms we are not sure; are they synonymous? Cf. φρουροφυλακή in the Lexikon of Sophocles.

75, p. 54   'the guards who were on duty': οἱ σχολάριοι οἱ τὰ ἐκσκούβητα ποιοῦντες. Cf. J. B. Bury, op. cit. (note on ch. 23), vol. 1, p. 37: 'The Scholarians were picked men and till the middle of the fifth century chiefly Germans, mounted, better equipped and better paid than the ordinary cavalry of the army. There were seven schools at Constantinople each 500 strong.' They were under the control of the Master of the Offices. 'The decline of the Scholarian Guards is attributed by Agathias (v. 15) to Zeno, who bestowed appointments on Isaurian relatives of no valour.' Bury, ibid., p. 401. Cf. R. Grosse, op. cit. (see note on ch. 56), pp. 93-6.

76, p. 54   'two guardsmen': here silentiarii — for these Court ushers see note on ch. 23.

ch. 76, p. 54   'a legal secretary of the Emperor': ραιφερενδάριον. On the Referendarii see J. B. Bury, *Magistri Scriniorum*, ΑΝΤΙΓΡΑΦΗΣ *and* ΡΕΦΕΡΕΝΔΑΡΙΟΙ, Harvard Studies in Classical Philology 21 (1910) (Harvard University), pp. 23-9. 'The *referendarii*, who might be described as legal secretaries of the Emperor . . . acted as bearers of the unwritten answers of the Emperor, in judicial matters, to the persons concerned, and they might be employed on various special missions. From the nature of the case they might possess much influence on the imperial decisions', p. 29.

76, p. 54   'against her who is his confederate': presumably Verina

78, p. 55   'monastery of Studius': see note on ch. 72.

80, p. 56   Dagalaiphus: son of Areobindus (consul in 434) and married to the daughter of Ardabur. He was consul in 461.

80, p. 56   Forum of the Ox (βοῦς): at Ak Serai, not far from the harbour of Eleutherius (see map in Van Millingen, *Byzantine Constantinople*, at p. 19).

82, p. 57   We do not know of any reference to Herais in other sources; cf. ch. 94.

83, p. 57   'Basiliscus of ill-omened name': see note on ch. 70.

83, p. 58   Theoctistus had been appointed Master of the Offices by Basiliscus; he was a doctor from Alexandria. See Zechariah of Mitylene, translation of Hamilton and Brooks (Methuen, 1899), p. 104. For his part in the religious controversy of the reign, ibid., pp. 104, 110. In the translation of Ahrens and Krüger (Leipzig, 1899), pp. 59, 65.

85, p. 59   Zeno's return to Constantinople: Armatus, the nephew of Basiliscus, went over to the side of Zeno, cf. E. W. Brooks, *English Historical Review* 8 (1893), pp. 217-18. Zeno had fled from the capital on January 9th, 475, and the fall of Basiliscus must be placed at the end of August 476; see Seeck, *Regesten* (note on ch. 66), p. 426.

86, p. 60   'The holy relics of Simeon': see ch. 58.

89, p. 62   Parthenopolis: where is this place?

91, p. 64   Anastasius: Emperor 491-518.

92, p. 65   Euphemius: Patriarch of Constantinople, 490-6.

94, p. 66   Herais. Cf. ch. 82.

99, p. 69   ἀνιέντες: we have translated as though the text read ἀνιόντες.

ST. THEODORE OF SYKEON

INTRODUCTION

WE have chosen this biography for translation since it gives the best picture known to us of life in Asia Minor in the Byzantine period before the Arab invasions of the Empire. St. Theodore was a contemporary of St. John the Almsgiver, and it may suffice to refer for the historical background to the references given on p. 263.

The references in this Life to the general history of the Empire are few and slight, but for the Persian invasion of East Roman territory see ch. 49, 54, 120.

The Emperor Heraclius later transported St. Theodore's body to Constantinople in order that its presence there might protect the capital from the Persian attack: [cf. C. Kirch, *Nicephori sceuophylacis encomium in S. Theodorum Siceotam,* Analecta Bollandiana 20 (1901), pp. 249-72].

THE LIFE OF ST. THEODORE OF SYKEON

3

In the country of Galatia there is a village called Sykeon under the jurisdiction of the town of Anastasioupolis which belongs to the province of Galatia Prima, namely that of Ancyra, Sykeon lies twelve miles distant from Anastasioupolis.*

The public highway of the imperial post* ran through this village, and on the road stood an inn kept by a very beautiful girl, Mary, and her mother, Elpidia, and a sister Despoinia. And these women lived in the inn and followed the profession of courtesans.

At that time when Justinian of pious memory was Emperor[1] certain imperial decrees were being dispatched from the capital, and thus it chanced that a certain well-known man, Cosmas by name, who had become popular in the Hippodrome in the corps of those who performed acrobatic feats on camels, was appointed to carry out the Emperor's orders.

On this man's journey to the East he stayed for some time in the inn, and seeing Mary and how fair she was, he desired her and took her to his bed. From this union she conceived and saw in a dream a very large and brilliant star* descending from heaven into her womb. She awoke all trembling with fear and related the vision she had seen in the night to Cosmas, the imperial messenger, and he said to her, 'Take good care of yourself, dear, for perchance God will watch over you and give you a son who will be deemed worthy to become a bishop'. With these words he left her in the morning and went on his way rejoicing.

4

Next the woman visited a holy father who could foresee the future who lived six miles off near the village of Balgatia,* and related to him what she had seen in her dream. The old man said to her, 'I tell you of a truth that the son who shall be

[1] reigned A.D. 527-65.

88

born of you will become a great man, not as men hold great-ness, but he will be well-pleasing to God. For a brilliant star is held to signify the glory of a king by those who are expert in interpreting visions; but with you it must not be read thus. For it is the brilliant adornment of virtues and graces which God has sent down upon the babe in your womb that you saw in the likeness of a brilliant star; for thus He is wont to conse-crate His worthy servants in the womb before they are born'. When Theodosius who had been appointed bishop of the town of Anastasioupolis heard of her vision, he, too, by God's inspiration gave to her the same interpretation.

5

When her full time was accomplished, Mary bore the servant of God; and after some days had passed, she carried him, as is the custom among Christians, to the Holy Church of the Orthodox and showed him to the priests who baptized him in the name of the Holy Trinity and named him 'Theodore', thus showing by this name that he would be the 'gift of God'. When the child was about six years old, his mother wanted him to enter the Emperor's service in the capital, so she made ready for him a gold belt and expensive clothes and everything else necessary, and then she prepared herself for the journey. On the night when she intended to start, God's holy martyr, St. George,* appeared to her and said, 'What is this plan, lady, which you have made for the boy? do not labour in vain, for the King in heaven has need of him'. And in the morning she arose and related her vision and wept saying, 'Assuredly death has drawn near to my boy'. After this she abandoned her journey. She wore herself away with increasing care of her son, and when he was eight years old she gave him to a teacher to be taught his letters. By the grace of God he was quicker at learning than all the other boys and made great progress.

He was beloved by all and in his daily life became known to all for his virtues; for when he played with the others he always beat them, but no oath or blasphemy nor any unfitting word ever escaped his lips, nor did he allow the others to use one. And whenever any dispute arose in their games, he at once withdrew and through his actions put an end to it.

6

Now there lived in the house a God-fearing man called Stephen who used to make skilfully prepared dishes. The women by this time had become quite respectable, for they had abandoned their profession as prostitutes and followed the path of sobriety and godliness. They now relied upon the goodness of the fare when they entertained the many governors and officers who came to the inn, and they congratulated Stephen who had made the food so tasty. Whenever he received any money, either from the women or their guests, he spent it on the churches where he prayed regularly morning and evening. During Lent, although he prepared all the food for the women, he fasted till the evening partaking of nothing except perhaps a little boiled wheat* and water.

The women loved him and looked upon him as a father because he was such a true lover of Christ. The boy noticing this abstinence was moved by divine love and desired to copy Stephen's mode of life, according to the words of the apostle who said, 'Remember them that have the rule over you who spake unto you the word of God; and consider the issue of their life and imitate their faith . . . For it is good that the heart be stablished by grace; not by meats wherein they that occupied themselves were not profited'.[1] 'For meat commendeth us not to God.'[2]

His mother and the other women, unconscious of his heart's desire, compelled him to eat with them when he returned home from school at the dinner-hour; so when school was over he no longer came home for dinner but spent the whole day in the school fasting and in the evening he would come back and go off with the pious man, Stephen, to the holy churches and there pray and partake of the body and blood of Christ. Returning home he would share with Stephen his boiled wheat and water. However much the women and even Stephen himself urged him, he could not be persuaded to do as they wished. Then his mother asked the schoolmaster to send him home at the dinner-hour as she wished to persuade him to eat at least a little vegetable food, because he was getting run down from want of food and from eating only so late in the day. The schoolmaster accordingly sent him away with the other boys, but

[1] Heb. xiii. 7, 9.   [2] 1 Cor. viii. 8.

Theodore did according to the song of David which says: 'In the Lord I have trusted; how shall ye say to my soul, Flee as a bird to your mountain?'[1]

7

When he came out of school he went up the rocky hill which lay near the village. Here there was a shrine dedicated to the martyr St. George. The Saint would guide him to the spot appearing visibly before his eyes in the form of a young man. Entering the shrine Theodore would sit down and busy himself with the study of the Holy Scriptures; and after midday he went back to the school and returned home in the evening. When his mother inquired why he had not appeared at dinner-time, he tricked her saying either that he had not been able to say his lesson and was therefore kept in*; or that he had a pain in his stomach and therefore had no appetite. So she again sent word to the master to send him home with the others, and he replied that since he had received her message he always did send him away with the others. Then she found out that he went up to the shrine and so she sent some of her servants to fetch him, and they brought him down to her. She threatened him and told him to come straight home from school to her; but he continued to act as he had been accustomed to do. His mother was very troubled about him, but in spite of all her threats and advice she was quite unable to make him change his fixed purpose, or to break the rules of abstinence which he had prescribed for himself.

8

When he was about twelve years old an epidemic of bubonic plague fell upon the village and it attacked him along with the others so that he came near to dying. They took him to the shrine of St. John the Baptist near the village and laid him at the entrance to the sanctuary, and above him where the cross was set* there hung an icon of our Saviour Jesus Christ. As he was suffering great pain from the plague suddenly drops of dew fell upon him from the icon, and immediately by the grace

[1] Ps. xi. 1.

of God, freed from his suffering, he recovered and returned to his home.

As Theodore was sleeping at night with his mother and the women who lived with her Christ's martyr, George, came to him, and, steeping all the others in deep slumber, woke him up. The first few nights he came in the form of the Stephen whom we have already mentioned, and later, in his own person, and said to him, 'Get up, master Theodore, the dawn has risen, let us go and pray at the shrine of St. George'. Theodore got up readily and with great joy and the Saint led him away from the house up to his shrine, while it was still dark, so that the boy beheld some of the temptations caused by the demons, for the wicked demons, the enemies of truth, appeared on either side of him in the semblance of wolves and other wild beasts, and with gaping mouths they rushed upon him as though to kill him, in order that they might cause him through fear to give up his good purpose. But Christ's martyr took hold of him and, like a man wielding a sword, chased them from him, so that Theodore was no whit alarmed by the sight of the wild beasts but became even more zealous and never missed his visits to the shrine.

9

When he began to adopt this habit, his mother and the women sleeping with her would wake up in the morning, and not seeing him in his bed they suspected that he had crept out and was spending the nights in the martyr's shrine; and they wondered how it was, since he slept between them, that he got out so successfully without anybody noticing it. They were afraid he might be devoured by some beast, since a fierce wolf, which carried off children, had lately been haunting the neighbourhood; so they tried to coax him not to go up to the shrine, at least before sunrise, as it was a wild, and fearsome place. However, the boy would not be persuaded and when awakened by the martyr at the appointed hour he went off to the shrine. When the women did not find him in bed in the morning, they became very angry and sent servants who brought him back dragging him by the hair. His mother whipped him and tied him to the bed with his arms behind his back, and gave him no food.

That night God's holy martyr, George, appeared to Theodore's mother and the other women, girt with a sword, which he drew as he came towards them saying threateningly, 'Now I shall cut off your heads because you ill-treat and punish the boy and prevent his coming to me'. On their swearing solemnly that they would never do it again, he took back his threat and disappeared.

The women woke up from fright and loosed the boy and comforted him, imploring him not to be angry with them for their mistakes. They asked him how he dared go up to the shrine before dawn, to which he replied, 'First I went up with Stephen and afterwards with a very handsome and fine young man'. So they concluded that that must be the martyr they had seen in their dream, and yielding to the martyr's urgency they no longer tried to force the boy but said, 'God's will be done!'

Theodore had a tiny sister called Blatta who sympathized with him and loved him dearly. Her heart was set on doing God's will and often she went up with Theodore to the shrine in the daytime, and she tried to imitate him in every act of self-denial.

10

The boy had made very good progress in learning to read, when one day he went into the church of the holy martyr, Gemellus,* which was near his home and spent the night there. And he saw himself as though he were in the presence of a king surrounded by a strong bodyguard and a woman clad in purple at his side, and he heard the king say, 'Fight the good fight, Theodore, that you may receive full pay in the heavenly army, and on earth I will give you glory and honour in the sight of men'. When he had heard this voice, he awoke.

He was twelve years old when his heart was stirred by the message given to him by the King, Christ, in this vision, and in his zeal to follow the path leading to those better things which pertain to salvation he began to shut himself up in one of the cellars of his home from Epiphany to Palm Sunday, and during two weeks in Lent, the first and the middle one, he spoke to no one at all but offered prayers to God alone, and practised abstinence as he had done before.

11

Now when the devil, the enemy of truth, saw that Theodore
was industriously acquiring the spiritual weapons of virtue
against him, he determined to destroy him. Accordingly one
day he assumed the appearance of one of Theodore's school-
fellows, Gerontius by name, and took him and led him up to
the cliffs of a place called Tzidrama, and, setting him on a
lofty crag of the cliffs there, put the temptation to him which
was put to our Saviour, and said. 'If you are willing, master
Theodore, to display your powers of conquest, display them
here and jump down from this cliff.' But Theodore looked at
the height which was really great and said to Gerontius, 'It is
high and I am afraid'. The devil said to him, 'In the eyes of
all the boys you are considered braver than I, and you outshine
me, but in this matter I am no coward and will throw myself
down'. The boy answered him, 'Don't do it! You may lame
yourself, or even be killed'. As the other asserted he could do
the feat without any danger, Theodore finally said to him, 'If
you will, then I will too'. So the devil standing with him on the
rock jumped down, and alighting on his feet shouted up to
the boy Theodore, saying 'See, I have done it! If you dare,
come down too, that I may see your bravery: if you can, as in
all else, distinguish yourself in this test too'. Whilst the boy
stood debating within himself full of fear at this utterly useless
ordeal, and staggered at the boldness of the supposed Gerontius, who had never previously been so bold, George, the
martyr of Christ, suddenly appeared and taking Theodore by
the hand, led him away from the place, saying, 'Come, follow
me, and do not listen to the tempting of him who is seeking
your soul; for he is not Gerontius but the enemy of our race'.
And so saying the holy martyr brought him to his oratory.

12

One day when Theodore was staying in the chapel of St.
George his mother and his mother's mother came up to him
and with much coaxing tried to force him to come down home
saying that they expected the visit of some important friends.
But the boy could not be persuaded by them to go down, for
he fulfilled literally the words of holy scripture which says,
'The friendship of this world is emnity with God, and whoever

would be a friend of the world maketh himself an enemy of God.'[1] and 'No one can serve God and Mammon.'[2] He also regarded the wealth of the world as nought and wishing to get rid of it, he unbuckled his gold belt, took off his necklace and the bracelet from his wrist and threw them down in front of the women saying, 'You suspect that these things may get lost and it is because of them you trouble me. Take them then and begone! for I will not leave this place.' And the women took them and went as they could not persuade him. For all his thoughts were towards the Lord Whom he imitated and in Whose footsteps he followed; he fled from his parents and ran to God; he gave up wealth and houses in order to be rewarded a hundredfold and inherit eternal life,[3] as the Lord who has promised this says: 'He that wishes to come after me, let him deny himself and take up his cross and follow me!'[4]

For the boy nobly mortified his body, keeping it under and wearing it down, as though it were some alien thing which warred against his soul; and on his forehead he bore the Cross; and just as Peter and James and John and the rest of the apostles 'left all and followed Jesus'[5] so this boy likewise believed in the witness of the Scriptures and sought earnestly to mould his life thereon.

13

Further, he wanted to imitate David in his holy hymn-writing and accordingly began to learn the psalter. With difficulty and much labour he learnt as far as the sixteenth psalm, but he could not manage to get the seventeenth psalm by heart. He was studying it in the chapel of the holy martyr Christopher* (which was near the village) and as he could not learn it, he threw himself on his face and besought God to make him quick of learning in his study of the psalms. And the merciful God, Who said 'Ask and it shall be given you',[6] granted him his request. For as the boy got up from the ground and turned to the icon of our Saviour in prayer, he felt a sweetness more pleasant than honey poured into his mouth. He recognized the grace of God, partook of the sweetness and gave thanks to Christ, and from that hour on he memorized the psalter easily

---

[1] James iv. 4. [2] Luke xvi. 13. [3] Luke xviii. 29.
[4] Matt. xvi. 24. [5] Luke v. 11. [6] Matt. vii. 7.

and quickly, and had learnt the whole of it by heart in a few days.

And he would wander about to all the churches, 'with psalms and hymns and spiritual songs singing and praising the Lord';[1] and wherever a commemorative service in honour of a saint was being held, he attended it with joy. Similarly, on the occasion of the all-night service for the holy martyr Heuretus* held in the town of Iopolis,* fifteen miles away, he left at the hour of supper and ran fasting to this service and after praying and partaking of the divine mysteries of Christ, he returned and reached his home at midnight. For he was an exceedingly swift runner, so much so that several times for a wager he ran a race of three miles with horses and outstripped them.

14

Taking instructions from proverbs — from such texts as 'And if thou hearest of a man of understanding, get thee betimes unto him';[2] and 'With the holy thou wilt be holy and with the elect elect',[3] he acquired a great affection for the servants of God and wherever he heard of a righteous man, he would go to him and learn his manner of life gathering like a busy bee the flowers of the man's virtues* as if he were storing up food.

Now there was a certain holy father, Glycerius, by name, in a place called Trapezas about ten miles off, and Theodore went to him desiring to be blessed by him in order that like Elisha, the miracle-worker, who after being blessed by Elijah received a double portion of his spirit and grace, he himself might also in a similar manner through the blessing of our Saviour be deemed worthy of greater virtues and graces. 'For the blessing of a father establisheth the houses and the labours of children.'[4] When the man of God saw him, having by divine aid learnt of the virtuous manner of life that was flowering in him, he received him cordially and smiling at him said, 'Do you like the monkish habit, my son?' to which Theodore replied, 'Yes, certainly, father, I like it very much indeed and I long to be thought worthy of it myself.'

[1] Col. iii. 16.   [2] Ecclesiasticus vi. 36.
[3] Px. xviii. 26. (text of the Septuagint Ps. xvii. 26-7).   [4] Ecclesiasticus iii. 9.

Now there was a drought in that district, and they both went out and stood in the open air in front of the apse of an oratory of St. John the Baptist which stood there. Then the blessed man said to the lad, 'Let us bend our knees in prayer, son, so that the Lord may be merciful and send down rain on the earth, and by that we shall know whether we are among the number of the just'. Whilst they prayed, the sky became covered with clouds and after they had risen from prayer the Lord sent down much rain upon the earth. Filled with joy at His goodness the old man, with a smile on his face, said to the boy, 'From henceforth, my son, whatsoever you shall ask of the Lord, will be granted unto you. Therefore carry out your desire, and the Lord God will be with you and will give you increase both in bodily stature and in virtuous living'. When the boy had received the old man's blessing, he embraced him and returned home.

15

By now he had reached the age of fourteen and decided within himself to bid a final farewell to his home and take up his abode in the martyr's oratory. And he did indeed bid farewell to the women, and went up to the oratory and lived there giving thanks to God; but as his mother and the women who lived with her still did not realize that he had irrevocably chosen his blessed mode of life and that his resolve was no youthful fancy, they used to carry up to him fresh white loaves, and divers kinds of boiled and roast birds. Theodore took them all indeed in order to satisfy them and because his fasting was in secret; however, he never touched any of these things but after his mother and her sister had gone down* he would come out of the chapel and throw all the food out on the rocks and go in again, and the birds and beasts ate it up. Or if by chance a man passed by, he would take them from the rock. The boy's nourishment was from the gifts brought to him in the martyr's chapel and if sometimes these failed, he was content with bread alone.

16

Once he heard tell of a certain place called Arkea eight miles away that it was impossible for anyone to go near it, especially at the midday hour, because it was rumoured that Artemis, as men called her, dwelt there with many demons and did people harm even unto death. As he was astonished at such a report he used to set off at a run for that place during the days of July and August, after he had recited the psalms set for the third hour, and would spend the whole afternoon there in the places supposed to belong to Artemis. And as no evil manifestation showed itself to him owing to Christ's protection, he returned to the chapel.

In this chapel Theodore dug and made for himself a dark cave underground beneath the step of the altar. On the night of the Feast of the Epiphany[1] when some of the clergy and laity had gathered round him he went down with them from the chapel to the ford of the river, and he alone entered into the water and stood there until all the reading from the prophets, apostles and Gospels was over as well as the rest of the liturgy; so that at the end of the service he could only with difficulty pull up his feet all covered with mud and icicles frozen on to them, and thus he re-entered the oratory with psalm-singing.* And when the day had dawned, he celebrated the feast and then retired to his underground pit where he lived in silence until Palm-Sunday, so that all who saw and heard this raised their hands to heaven and said, 'We thank thee, O Father, Lord of heaven and earth, that thou didst hide these things from the wise and understanding, and didst reveal them unto this babe; Yea, Father, for so it was well-pleasing in Thy sight'.[2]

Now his grandmother, Elpidia, truly sympathized with him and loved him more than her two daughters; and she came up to the chapel and stayed with him all the time of his silence and ministered to him and gave him a little nourishment of fruit or some vegetable salad, but this only on Saturdays and Sundays, for the other days he touched nothing at all; and this abstinence he practised until Palm-Sunday.

When Theodosius, at that time bishop of the town of Anastasioupolis, heard these things about Theodore, he rejoiced about him and spoke highly of him to all men, saying

---

[1] In the Greek church the baptism of Christ in the Jordan is commemorated on the day of Epiphany, January 6th.
[2] Matt. xi. 25.

that it was through the stirring of God's spirit that he accomplished such things.

17

(*Summary*) A black unclean demon causes Theodore to fall ill from cold but is turned to flight by St. George, and Theodore is restored to health. The Saint gives Theodore a promise that the wicked demon will not trouble him in future. And the merciful God 'who gave to his holy apostles power against unclean spirits and to banish diseases'[1] gave to him also power against the demons to cast them out from men and to heal the sick.

18

After the feast of holy Easter a man appeared in the oratory one day with his only son who was troubled by an unclean spirit; and the man, emboldened by faith, besought the virtuous boy, Theodore, to heal his son. But the virtuous child of Christ did not know what he ought to do for him and indeed was greatly perplexed, for he was so young. But the father of the demoniac gave him a little whip and said to him with tears, 'Dear master, servant of Christ, take this and rebuke my child and beat him and say, "Come out, come out from this boy, you unclean demon, in the name of my Lord!"'

The righteous boy did as he was told; and the demon was disturbed and began to disparage him and to call him an impostor, and if Theodore said anything to him the devil just repeated the same words, and for two days he gave him no answer at all. Then on the third day Theodore, the child of Christ, did as he had done before with the boy and the demon, now disturbed again, began to cry out; 'I am coming out, boy, I am coming out, I will not resist you, give me one hour!' Then Theodore moved away to the altar and the demon shouted out, 'Oh, the violence of the Nazarene who excites these forces against us! for ever since He came down upon the earth He wins men against us, and now He has given authority to the son of the harlot to cast us out. Woe is me, wretch that I am, to be expelled by such a child! for I cannot withstand the grace which has been sent down upon him from heaven. Woe will come upon our kind from this harlot's action, because

[1] Matt. x. 1.

he will drive out many of us from men. But the dreadful thing
for me is that he has made a beginning with me and I dare not
return to my father the Devil, after being expelled by such a
child. For if it had been done by an old man, my shame would
not be great; accursed be the day on which you were born!'
Whilst he was speaking Theodore, the child of God, took some
oil from the lamp and touched the boy's head and with the sign
of the Cross rebuked the demon saying, 'Come out then, you
most wicked spirit, and do not talk so much nonsense!' And
the demon with a shriek cast down the boy at his feet and went
out of him. And the boy that was healed lay like a corpse, so
that Theodore was in much concern and thought that he was
dead. But the father said to him, 'Give him your hand, master,
and raise him up. And immediately the boy came to himself
and stood up, and through the grace of God Theodore restored
him to his father in complete health. And this became known
throughout all the neighbourhood so that all gave glory to God
who bestows wisdom and grace even upon children.

19

(*Summary*) Theodore determined to imitate St. John the
Baptist by living in a desert place. So he went up into the
interior of the mountain and there found a rock to shelter him.
He dug beneath the rock and made for himself a' spacious
cave. He blocked up the entry and lived there in secret. At
that time some soldiers were passing through the district.
When the members of his family had searched for Theodore
high and low — in the oratory and everywhere else — and
could not find a trace of him they came to the conclusion that
he had been carried off by the soldiers, and they urged the
then governor of the province to arrest the soldiers and institute
an inquiry about the boy. Since they still could not find him,
they thought that he had been eaten by wild beasts, and his
mother, his kinsfolk and their acquaintances mourned him for
a long time as though he were dead. For two years Theodore
remained hidden in the cave. A single pious deacon alone
knew his secret; he gave to Theodore his tunic — for before
that he had worn linen clothes — and brought him the scantiest
fare, water and vegetable salad. He told no one where Theodore was hidden.

20

(*Summary*) But God made his virtue known to all men.
Since Theodore's kinsfolk noticed that the deacon on many
different occasions went up to the mountain, they suspected
that he knew where the boy was; so they called him into the
house and adjured him with frightful oaths to tell them anything he knew. On account of the oaths and in fear lest Theodore should die through the violence of his mortification he
disclosed to them the place. With joy they went to the mountain and brought Theodore out looking like a corpse. They
carried him to the oratory of St. George. When he came into
the air he fainted and did not speak for a long time. His head
was covered with sores and pus, his hair was matted and an
indescribable number of worms were lodged in it; his bones
were all but through the flesh and the stench was such that no
one could stand near him. In a word people looked on him as
a second Job. His relations besought him when he had regained consciousness to come home with them to be looked
after, but he would not be persuaded.

21

When Theodosius, the holy Bishop of Anastasioupolis,
heard how Theodore had been carried half-dead out of his
cave, he immediately went to him in the chapel. And when he
saw him, he shuddered at the sores on his head, kissed him and
ordained him 'lector' . . . And on the following day he ordained
him sub-deacon and then priest, saying 'Behold, God deems
you worthy to be granted, one after the other, the orders in the
hierarchy of the Church, so that you can celebrate the sacred
liturgy to the edification of those coming to the oratory; and
may the Lord our God, the generous bestower of gifts in which
He has made you to share, deem you worthy hereafter to be
clothed with the office of bishop and entrusted with the care of
a flock. For as you have now received the gift of these four
talents* and are soon to receive the habit of a monk, you are
only short of one. May God give you that one, too, after you
have doubled the number of your saintly deeds. Therefore
advance in faith and in the flower of virtue and pray for me'.
And after blessing Theodore and embracing him, he returned
to his city.

Theodore, the servant of God, was only eighteen years old at that time and consequently many people found fault with the bishop saying that the ordination was invalid, since Theodore had not reached the proper age. Whereupon the holy Bishop Theodosius replied to them, 'I, too, am well aware that it appears uncanonical to some to ordain a man contrary to the rules of age and without any witnesses. For the apostle Paul says in his injunctions to Timothy: 'Not a novice lest being puffed up he fall into the condemnation and snare of the devil.'[1]

'But just as that same Paul judged Timothy, young as he was, worthy of a bishopric, so I too ordained this youth in the name of the Lord, and I shall never be brought to shame by his manner of life. For God assured me that he was worthy of the priesthood, and most certainly this boy is from God. Therefore do not regard his youthfulness, but regard rather the nobleness of his soul, just as Samuel was told concerning David.[2] For "It is not the long-lived that are wise, nor the aged that understand judgment'[2] 'and, again, as Elihu declared in the book of Job "But there is a spirit of God in man and it is the breath of the Almighty which teaches"[3] and works with the young, and renders their manner of life pious and virtuous.' After the bishop had spoken thus, all were fully satisfied with his words; and Theodore, the young athlete of Christ, made progress in wisdom and spiritual understanding, and the grace of God was upon him.

22

Now these doings of his childhood and youth have been written by me George,* his unworthy servant and disciple; some of them I learnt from his contemporaries and school-fellows, who lived and associated with him at that time and actually saw these things with their own eyes, but the majority of them I gathered from the lips of the holy and saintly man himself, when he lived alone and would narrate these things with pleasure in order to arouse in us a longing and desire for them. And I have written them after his death so that the young, through hearing of his virtuous manner of life as a

[1] 1 Tim. iii. 6.   [2] Cf. 1 Sam. xvi. 6 sqq.
[3] See Job xxxii. 8-9 (Septuagint).

child, may strive to emulate his angelic and blameless life, and be accounted worthy of the Kingdom of Heaven, through the grace of Christ our God to Whom with the Father and the Holy Spirit be glory both now and for ever, world without end.[1] Amen.

The Lord Jesus Christ, our true God, the sun of righteousness, the ineffable light, the ever-flowing fount of immortality, the life undefiled, the salvation of our souls, the giver of wisdom, inspired even me George, your sinful servant, with the passionate desire to tell, and you, my God-loving readers, with a burning longing to hear the manner of life of our great and holy father, Theodore, now among the saints, for that life until its close was supremely virtuous and crowned with miracles.

For I have been deemed worthy to narrate to you the story of his early years. And in reliance on the prayers of you all, I now venture to take up the tale afresh, and I look to God to be my guide and to bring my task to its completion.

23

So then Theodore, the most holy servant of God, was deemed worthy of the priesthood by our Saviour God at the age of eighteen, and with godly wisdom he strove to show himself like unto a prudent man in accordance with the Lord's appointment, praised be His name.* Thus he left his parental home which was built upon sand and all the earthly things therein, resolving within himself never to set foot in it again, and in full assurance of faith he devoted himself body and soul and with a sincere heart to God.

He founded his dwelling on the hallowed spot which was literally and figuratively made of rock,[2] where there stood the revered oratory of the holy and glorious martyr George, in order easily to repel the attacks of alien winds* and to ward off the uprising of the flood, that came like waters in their wake. And thus with his faith firmly based on the rock of Christ and with the help of the holy martyr commemorated in the oratory he spent his time on all the God-inspired Scriptures deeming them to be the sources of eternal life.[3] Most often did he ponder over the holy Gospel and he was continually pricked in heart, especially when he considered the descent from heaven

---

[1] Literally 'to the ages of the ages'.   [2] Matt. vii. 24-5.   [3] John v. 39.

of our Lord and Master, Jesus Christ, His incarnation and life on earth, and how He deigned to suffer and be crucified in Jerusalem, and to be buried and to rise again. Through marvelling and wondering that these things should have taken place on earth, he was seized with the desire to travel and to worship at the holy places of the Christ which His immaculate feet had trodden, and also because of the words of the prophet Zecharias, 'Every race and every tribe shall be accursed which goeth not up to worship them'.[1]

24

And further as his mother and sister, his aunt and grand-mother had come up to visit him, he bade them farewell, and finding by God's providence another willing and anxious to make the same journey, he took him as his companion and started out, forgetting all difficulties in his longing for the desired goal. When he reached Jerusalem, the ardently desired city of the holy places of Christ, he adored the Holy Cross, the place of the life-giving Resurrection, the sacred manger and the glorious place of the Ascension and all the other holy spots commemorative of the saving Passion of our great God and Saviour, Jesus Christ. He further visited all the monasteries and the various fathers confined in cells round about the city, and the hermits in the inner desert. After receiving a blessing from them he would inquire into the manner of life of each of the more earnest ones, and recorded their answers that he might imitate their example. In his wanderings he came down to the Jordan where our Saviour and God was baptized, and arrived at the neighbouring monastery of our Lady, the Mother of God, called Chouziba.* After praying and saluting the archi-mandrite there and the holy fathers who were with him he begged them to grant him the angelic habit of a monk. As the archimandrite had been fully instructed by God about him he invested him with the robe of a monk without hesitation or delay. Then they all joined in the prayer that Theodore might prove well-pleasing unto God and well-reputed among men. When their spiritual joy and feasting on his account had had free course, he embraced them and after receiving their

1 See Zech. xiv. 17.

approval he left the monastery and returned to his own country, Galatia, and entered the oratory of the holy martyr George.

There he dwelt with great joy, his face like Moses' shining with glory and grace, and he further built himself up by fasting and sleeping on the ground, by vigils, and by psalm-singing; in consequence he received from God an inflow of still greater gifts of grace to strengthen him in his fight against unclean spirits and all kinds of diseases.

§ 25

Now his mother minded not the things of the Lord but the things of the flesh,[1] and did not feel for her son that intense longing and affection for their children which like a fire consumes some mothers. She left her most holy son, took the portion of the inheritance due to her, and was joined in marriage to a notable man, David by name, a leading citizen (protiktor) in the metropolis of Ancyra.

But her sister, Despoinia, and her mother, Elpidia, and the Saint's sister, Blatta, could not bear to be separated from him, but rather through observing his virtuous life they strove as far as possible to imitate him, purifying and ennobling themselves by sobriety and chastity, by almsgiving and prayers. When Despoinia died she left him all her worldly goods and was buried by him in the church of the holy martyr, St. Gemellus. And his sister, Blatta, a virgin of twelve years old, the most holy man took to the metropolis of Ancyra and placed her in the charge of the dedicated virgins in the convent called Petris; and after she had received the habit of a nun he dedicated her to the Lord, for she was winning many victories in her spiritual life, and then he returned to his own place. His blessed sister lived three years and then passed to her rest having borne testimony by her good works; when her most holy brother, who had also been her guide into the Kingdom, heard of her death, he sent her forth as a bride to the heavenly bridal-chamber and rejoiced in Christ. His grandmother, the blessed Elpidia, loved him exceedingly and sympathized with him, and would often come up and view his ascetic contest and glorify God who had made a rose-bearing, fruitful bough of piety to grow out of the thistles of harlotry and had raised

[1] Cf. Rom. viii. 5.

up a child of Abraham out of useless stones.[1] And stretching forth her hands to heaven she prayed for him that his mind should remain undisturbed and raised above material things ever giving glory to God, and that he should keep his faith 'stedfast and unmoveable'[2] unto the end.

She also left her rooms in the inn and gathering all her belongings together wanted to remain with him always in order to enjoy still greater gladness and at the same time to minister to him. However, he would not allow this, but asked her to come to the convent of St. Christopher lying to the East and there he persuaded her to remain. And the children who came to him plagued by unclean spirits he used to send to her (especially if they were girls) to receive treatment and to be taught their duties by living with her and that those who wished to remain after they were cured might be enrolled among the nuns.

And for such services as he himself required he hired a man from the neighbouring village of Kastina.

26

(*Summary*) A man, inspired by a passionate love of God, came to Theodore from the village of Spaninae and asked to be allowed to stay with him. This was granted and he became so zealous a disciple after receiving the habit of a monk that he healed a man tormented by a demon.

On another occasion a woman came from the village of Konkatis, suffering from a serious malady of the womb. She was cured by the Saint's prayers, and then left for the village of Mossyna, also called Enistratos, where her son, Philoumenus, was teacher in the children's school. Him she brought to the Saint asking that he might live with him. (There is a lacuna in the MS. towards the end of this chapter and the close of this incident is lost.)

27

There lived in this village (presumably Mossyna) a very excellent smith — him the holy man ordered to make a very narrow iron cage that he might enter therein and standing in it pass his days of fasting. So the men of the village impelled

[1] Cf. Matt. iii. 9.   [2] 1 Cor. xv. 58.

by faith one and all brought their agricultural tools in order that his bidding might be executed, and in this way the cage was fittingly finished for his holiness.

He wanted to take it away at once and return to his own monastery, but the men of the village begged him to leave it there until they made a second one of wood on the same pattern, and to do them the favour of passing his accustomed period of seclusion in it the following winter, so that they might have it as a protection in memory of his holiness and afterwards they would give him the iron one.

He gave the promise on these conditions; then they assembled and accompanied him with a religious procession and re-established him in his sanctified place during the Great Week of our Saviour's Passion and afterwards returned to their own homes.

Then they made the wooden cage and in the following winter they returned with a religious procession and fetched him and escorted him to their village. And he entered into the wooden cage, which was standing in the church of St. John the Baptist, and in it he observed his fast from Christmas to Palm Sunday. On that day he came out and the inhabitants of the village formed a religious procession and carrying the iron cage accompanied him and restored him before the feast to his own place. After receiving his blessing they returned to their homes. He had the cage suspended above the cave on the face of the rock in mid-air, and ordered iron rings to be made for his feet, fifteen pounds in weight, and similar ones for his hands, and a cross with a collar of eighteen pounds weight and a belt for his loins of thirty-three pounds and an iron staff with a cross on it.

28

He further wished to have a very heavy corselet, and by God's foresight a man came and brought him a coat of triple mail* called a 'lorica'; weighing fifty pounds, which the saint accepted and gave thanks to God Who speedily fulfils the desire of them that ask in faith. But he feared for himself because his body continued to grow more lusty, and because he was assailed by the passions of the flesh; so he invented for himself a perpetual bond of remembrance by immediately hanging the two rings round his feet and determining never to take them off but carry them with him even to the grave. When the day of the incarnation of our Lord Jesus Christ came round on which He was born of Mary the all-Holy Virgin and Mother of God, he put on the corselet over his hair-tunic, girt on the iron belt, placed the cross round his neck, the circlets round his hands and in this guise entered into the cave practising abstinence till the 'Paralepsis';* then coming out of the cave again he went into the cage, keeping under* his body and bringing it into subjection by the confined space and by fasting, by frost and by the weight of the irons hanging round his body. By these means he humiliated and put to shame the power and the varied attacks of the enemy. He did not touch any bread at all nor even any pulse from Christmas day to Palm-Sunday, his sole food was an apple or a salad of vegetables, and this only on a Saturday and Sunday.

29

The prescribed amount of his psalm-singing was great, so that he would rest for a while and then repeat the same Psalms over again, and the fatigue from this under wintry conditions was beyond all description. For when a snowstorm came and the wind was blowing he was shot at by the violence of the wind as with an arrow while the snow fell and often the water coming in at his neck would run down under his tunic to his feet, and his hair-garments were drenched with water. When a frost came the ice caused him no little anguish and his feet would freeze to the boards on which he stood. For from cock-crow on he forced himself not to move his feet at all from the platform on which he stood and not even to lean forward, even for a minute, against the iron railings of his cage until the evening.

So that in the earlier periods for two years when the frosts were so severe that even trees and large jars were split asunder, his feet became glued to the boards and in the evening when he pulled them up his feet were, so to say, 'stripped', as the soles of his feet remained on the boards, like sandals.

He endured this for two years, but from that time on, when his feet were held fast by the frost, his attendant would take warm water and pour it on his feet and thus the frost which

held them was gradually thawed and he could move from his
narrow platform.

30

Another time when the feast of Easter fell towards the end
of the month of April, and the sun had been shining very
fiercely during Lent as in summer, it happened that owing to
his abstinence and the brilliant sunshine he fainted and fell
down inside his cage as if dead. So Philoumenus, beloved of
God, covered the cage with his cloak to make some shade for
him. But when the athlete of God came to his senses and saw
the garment shading the cage he was very indignant and upbraided Philoumenus severely and bade him tear it away and
never do so again. Now God 'who glorifieth them who
glorify Him'[1] wished to prove that it was through faith* — not
from the desire to please men, but from a single-hearted
devotion to God — that Theodore had been led to choose this
manner of life, and of this He gave manifest witness and
assurance enough to all since wild beasts in the presence of the
Saint became quite tame and mannerly, while from him there
came a stream of mighty miracles wrought amongst men.

At the beginning of his period of seclusion in the cage a
most formidable bear used to come to him for three successive
years and on receiving some food (eulogia) from his hand
would go away quietly without doing an injury to any of the
bystanders — Again, a wolf came to the entrance of his cave
when he was shut up there and stood waiting. His servant,
Marinus by name, went out and suddenly catching sight of the
beast was terrified and ran in and told the Saint about it; but
he, smiling a little, said, 'Do not be afraid, you coward, where
is your manhood? for the wolf has not appeared to do you any
harm but driven by a belly like yours it has come in search of
food. So take this, brother, and carry it out to him so that not
only in the case of men but also in that of wild beasts the commandment of God may be fulfilled which says, "Give to everyone that asketh thee".'[2] So the servant took a piece of bread and
a slice of apple from the store of food from which the Saint was
wont to give presents (eulogiae) to his visitors, and going out
threw only the slice of apple to the beast and tried to drive it

---

[1] 1 Sam. ii. 30.   [2] Matt. v. 42.

away. The wolf seized and ate it, and then stood still again and would not budge, just as if something were still owing to it; then the servant threw the piece of bread, too, and it at once galloped off, and he went in and told his master of the impudent conduct of the animal.

31

(*Summary*) Theodore while in seclusion in the cage cleanses two lepers — one by blessing some water and pouring it over him after signing him with the sign of the Cross — the other, a priest named Epiphanius, known as Kollouras, from the village of Dioskonis, by lending him his tunic to wear.

32

(*Summary*) Elpidia the blessed, Theodore's grandmother, was utterly filled with all joy and delight at his virtuous mode of life and at the shining glory of his miracles. She had carefully provided everything necessary for the support of the women under her care; some had renounced this world, others were ill, and she had already created a very fine convent. She now came to the days in which she was to die and during this time because of an intense longing for him, but still more because she somehow foreknew that it would be a farewell visit, she stayed closely by him, praying with him and singing with him . . . Later after a slight illness she passed away peacefully in her sleep and was buried by Theodore with due honour.

33

(*Summary*) A man came from the metropolis of Ancyra and brought the news of the death of the Saint's mother, Mary, so that he might send and receive her dowry, as she had died childless; Theodore did not pay even the slightest attention to this but said to the messenger, 'You are lying and not speaking the truth; for my mother has not died'. On the other's insisting on the fact that he had seen it with his own eyes he again replied to him, 'I told you that you are not speaking the truth; for my mother has not died and is not dying; Heaven forbid! but she is present with me and is alive and will remain with me for ever'. And he continued to give no more thought to the matter; but he made supplication to God on her behalf, while fasting for a week, imploring Him to grant her forgiveness for her failings.

34

One day the treasurer of the holy church of the town of Heliopolis, Theodore by name (also called Tzoutzus) came when the Saint was in seclusion shut up in his cave, and through his servant he unfolded the following story to him with many tears. 'Have pity on me, oh servant of God, for the tragedy which has befallen me! I sent my elder son to collect the church-taxes from the villages and he has taken the whole sum and made off! and though I have run about and searched for him everywhere I have not been able to find him. I therefore implore your holiness to pray to God to restore him to me, because all my substance is insufficient to pay back to the Church the large sum he has taken.'

And the holy man sent this reply to him, 'If you will agree that when he is found you will not give him a beating nor compel him to give up more money than the amount he stole, God will be entreated and will restore your son to you; but if you will not consent to this, he will not be restored to you.' Then the father agreed to these terms on oath and said, 'If you bid me, I will also give him some of my own money, if only I receive the dues belonging to the Church which he has taken, so that I or my children may not be made destitute by repaying them.'

Then the holy man prayed to the Lord to hold up the man who had committed the theft in whatsoever place he might be and to make known with all speed where he would be found. And the Saint sent a message to the father saying, 'Go and stay at home and do not worry nor be anxious about him; for I trust in God to restore him to you soon if you carry out what you have promised.'

The man believed him, since several times before he had received assurance of his miraculous powers, and went home with joy, regarding the Saint's promise as a pledge that could not fail.

Now the holy man's prayer reached the son in a place close to the city of Nicaea and did not allow him to depart thence, but he kept wandering about in a circle in that one place and never got any further, though he seemed to himself to have travelled a long way. In that same place there happened to be some men who knew him and the treasurer and had already heard talk of what had happened, so when they recognized him and saw the senseless way in which he was walking they asked him many times where he came from, and where he was going. Finding that he gave contradictory answers they laid hold on him, and sent word to the treasurer. The latter came and took the stolen gold away from him and returned to the holy man giving thanks to God.

35

A woman once came with her husband from the village of Kalpinus during the days of Lent and she was being evilly treated by a demon. When the Saint rebuked the demon, the latter cried out saying, 'Oh! violence! do not be angry with me, iron-eater,* servant of the Most High, do not send me away into the fire of punishment. For it is not I who am guilty, for I entered into this woman against my will, at the command of one Theodotus, surnamed Kourappus, of the village of Mazamia'. The servant of Christ said to him, 'Behold, I command you in the name of Jesus Christ, the Son of God, not to trouble her in her works from now on until she comes back here again'. The demon became quiet and then the Saint told the man to take his wife and go back home and gather in their crops and afterwards return to him. They did as he ordered, went home, secured their summer crops and their vintage and then went back again. As they entered into the church of the Archangel and saw the Saint's face, the demon began to torture the woman savagely; her husband declared on oath saying that she had not been troubled by the demon at all from the day that he received the Saint's command until that moment. They stayed there one week and as the demon could not bear the rebukes of him who was truly a worker of miracles, he cast the woman down at the feet of the Saint and went out of her. The woman was quite cured and departed with her husband for her home in great joy.

36

On another occasion in the village of Mazamia, which lies on the Upper Siberis in the territory of Mnezine, a large swarm of locusts appeared about June and covered the district like a cloud and ate up the summer crops and the fruit of the vineyards. When the villagers saw this terrible scourge, which had come upon them, having heard of the miracles wrought by the Saint they came to him in a religious procession, threw themselves at his feet and besought him to come and by his acceptable prayers free them from this ill which was afflicting them. He accordingly went with them and lodged in their Catholic church of St. Irenicus (for he was ever wont to lodge in a church). On the morrow he led a religious procession to the plain and ordered the villagers to stand in a certain place and pray to the Lord for mercy. He himself took three locusts in his hand and stood praying to the Lord about them. And whilst he prayed, the three locusts died in his hand; then after giving thanks to the Lord he said to the people, 'Let us return to the church, children; for the Lord will speedily show His mercy in our midst'. And so, having recited the holy liturgy, they returned to the church of St. Irenicus. On the morrow the villagers went out to the plain and found every locust dead; and they glorified God.

37

But he that is ever envious of good deeds and the doers thereof and of the servants of Christ aroused in Theodotus, a special vessel of his, envy at this miracle and the determination to kill the holy miracle-workers.

Theodotus dwelt in the same village as the Saint and was a skilled sorcerer, thoroughly versed in wickedness. The Evil One did not know that not only would he fail in his projected plan and be put to shame, but would also be punished by being deprived of his instrument of wickedness. Theodotus had seen the miracle of the locusts performed by the Saint, and he also remembered how the demon who served him had shortly before been cast out of the woman. He himself had put the demon into the woman, and the demon after his expulsion had returned to him. Thus incited by the enemy who haunted him and inflamed by the malice of his attendant demon he sent his

envoys to attack the Saint and, if possible, so to injure him that
he should die.

Those who were sent did not dare even to show themselves
to him face to face whilst he was awake but waited for his hour
of sleeping; and then stealthily, like thieves, they sought to
attack him — thieves indeed they were and powerless to harm
him openly.

But the divine power which guarded him routed them; however the bolder in wickedness among them had the effrontery
once more to draw near to him to wreak their wickedness and
again the grace of God like a fire issuing from him scorched
them and drove them away. After they had assaulted him
several times seeking to do him injury and had always suffered
in the same way, they at last returned shamefacedly to the man
who sent them. He questioned them why they had returned
without accomplishing anything and taunted them, 'Why,
your power is nothing', he said, 'since you were not strong
enough to approach and put your spell upon him even when he
was asleep, how then are you going in future to meet him face
to face?' The envoys retorted, 'We are more anxious than you
to prove ourselves able and invincible in the missions on which
you send us; but when we tried to approach him, a great flame
of fire issued from his mouth — not natural fire which we
despise — but divine fire which lives in him — and we were
scorched; that is why we came back with nothing done. We
attacked him, too, through his food and drink, but the blessing
which he always says over it made all our power to harm him
of no effect.'

38

Meanwhile Theodotus, still greatly vexed in spirit by his
defeat, became yet more infuriated. With great skill he inserted a deadly poison into a fish and charged some other
agents of his to see to it that the Saint should eat the fish.
But when the Saint through the grace of God and through the
blessing which he said over the fish did not take any harm,
then indeed Theodotus was ashamed at the failure of his
murderous designs and reflected upon the weakness of demons
and the power of God which is so great and marvellous that it
prevails even over demons and poisons and locusts. Becoming

sober after the intoxication which was the devil's work, he
came to a recognition of God and went and threw himself at
the Saint's feet, wailing and weeping and begging to obtain
mercy. But the Saint questioned him to learn the reason of his
lamentations and supplication, whereupon he then related to
him in detail the story of his plottings and the answers of the
demons and also revealed to him the diabolic craft he possessed
to the hurt of many souls, and implored the Saint both to
release him from it and also to grant him holy baptism. And
the Saint replied, 'If you wish to be received by God and
deemed worthy of pardon from Him for these doings, then
first of all make a full confession of all your deeds, and if you
still have any book of magic bring it forth. Then loose from
the spell of your magic every person whom you have bewitched
and every house or beast or anything else, whatsoever it be,
and in future never put a spell on anyone but devote yourself
to repentance; and I will implore God to grant you forgiveness
for your past sins. For God receives those who repent for "He
willeth that all men should be saved and come to the knowledge
of the truth." '[1] And the magician promised and swore that
he would fulfil all the Saint's behests; he brought all his books
of magic and burnt them in Theodore's presence and asked to
be baptized. After the Saint had given him instruction and
cleansed him by fastings and works of charity he gave him the
bath of incorruption,[2] and thus added him to the ninety and
nine sheep that had not strayed, and by this act proved himself
one who put into practice the teaching of James, the Lord's
brother, for 'he converted the sinner from the error of his way
and saved his soul from death and covered a multitude of sins'.[3]

39

After the Saint had returned to his monastery, it happened
that he fell so ill of a desperate sickness that he saw the holy
angels coming down upon him, and he began to weep and to
be sorely troubled. Now above him there stood an icon of the
wonder-working saints Cosmas and Damian. These saints
were seen by him looking just as they did in that sacred icon*
and they came close to him, as doctors usually do; they felt his
pulse and said to each other that he was in a desperate state as

[1] Tim. ii. 4.   [2] Cf. Titus iii. 5.   [3] James v. 20.

his strength had failed and the angels had come down from heaven to him. And they began to question him saying, 'Why are you weeping and are sore troubled, brother?' He answered them, 'Because I am unrepentant, sirs, and also because of this little flock which is only newly-instructed and is not yet stablished and requires much care.' They asked him, 'Would you wish us to go and plead for you that you may be allowed to live for a while?' He answered, 'If you do this, you would do me a great service, by gaining for me time for repentance and you shall win the reward of my repentance and my work from henceforth.' Then the saints turned to the angels and besought them to grant him yet a little time while they went to implore the King on his behalf. They agreed to wait. So the saints departed and entreated on his behalf the heavenly King, the Lord of life and death, Christ our God, Who granted unto Hezekiah the King an addition unto his life of fifteen years.[1] They obtained their request and came back to the Saint bringing with them a very tall young man, like in appearance to the angels that were there, though differing from them greatly in glory. He said to the holy angels, 'Depart from him, for supplication has been made for him to the Lord of all and King of glory, and He has consented that he should remain for a while in the flesh'. Straightway both they and the young man disappeared from his sight, going up* to heaven. But the Saints, Cosmas and Damian, said to the Saint, 'Rise up brother, and look to thyself and to thy flock; for our merciful Master Who readily yields to supplication has received our petition on your behalf and grants you life to labour for "the meat which perisheth not, but endureth to everlasting life"[2] and to care for many souls.' With these words they, too, vanished.

Theodore immediately regained his health and strength;* the sickness left him and glorifying God he resumed his life of abstinence and the regular recital of the psalms with still greater zeal and diligence.

40

Through the grace bestowed on him by God Theodore continued to work many miracles against every kind of illness and weakness, but especially did he make supplications to

---

[1] 2 Kings xx. 6.   [2] John vi. 27.

God for aid against unclean spirits; hence, if he merely rebuked them, or even sent them a threat through another,* they would immediately come out of people. Some persons were so profoundly impressed by these miracles that they left their homes, journeyed to him, and entering upon a life of contemplation joined the monastery; others again who had obtained healing would not leave him but stayed with him, giving him such service as he needed.

Now since the oratory of the holy martyr George was small* and could not contain those who recited the offices as well as those who stayed with the Saint and others* who came up to pray, he built on its right hand side a very fine house (dedicated to Michael, the holy commander-in-chief of the angels) which was comfortable both in winter and summer; on its left it had a small oratory dedicated to St. John the Baptist, and one on the right dedicated to the most blessed Mother of God, the ever-virgin Mary. In this house he ordained that the community of Brothers should officiate in order that both those who were waiting either to be healed of an illness, or for the expulsion of evil spirits, and those who had come up to pray, might rest awhile in the hallowed church of the Archangel, which was open day and night, and listen to the service and join in the prayers and find healing.

41

(*Summary*) Theodore sends his fellow-worker, Philoumenus, to the bishop of Anastasioupolis to be ordained priest and abbot of the monastery in order that Theodore might be freed from the cares and toils of the office.

42

As through the grace of God the size of the holy and venerable monastery was greatly increased, a need was felt for holy vessels of silver (for the existing ones were of marble); so the holy Theodore sent his archdeacon to the capital, Constantinople, to buy a chalice and a paten of silver for the service of the immaculate mysteries. The archdeacon went and bought from a silversmith a pure and well-finished vessel, so far as concerned the quality of the silver and the workmanship, and he brought it back to the monastery.

Before the celebration of Communion on the morrow, the archdeacon brought the chalice and paten into the vestry, uncovered it to show it to the Saint and to use it for the Oblation. But when the Saint looked at them he recognized through his gift of discernment the manner of their use and their defect,' and condemned them as being useless and defiled. But the archdeacon, who looked at the appearance and not at that which was hidden, pointed out the perfect and well-wrought workmanship and the quality proved by the five-fold stamp upon it and thought by these facts to convince the Saint. But the Saint said, 'I know, yes, I know, son, that so far as eyes can see it appears a beautiful specimen of craftsmanship and the worth of the silver is evident from the stamps on it, but it is another, an invisible cause, which defiles it. I fancy the defilement comes from some impure use. But if you doubt it, pronounce the verse for our prayers and be convinced.' Then whilst the archdeacon chanted the verse of Invocation, the Saint bent his head in prayer, and after he had filled the chalice, the chalice and the paten turned black as silver* does when it leaves the fire of the oven. The brothers, seeing this, glorified God who made invisible things visible at the hands of His servant. When the archdeacon took them and locked them up they appeared once more as pure silver; then he returned to Constantinople and gave them back to the dealer in silver and told him the reason. The latter made inquiries of his manager* and his silversmith who fashioned the vessels, and found out that they came from the chamber-pot of a prostitute; he told the archdeacon the blunder that had been made and begged him to pray that he might be forgiven for his mistake, at the same time marvelling at the Saint's foreknowledge. He gave him other pure and very beautiful vessels and these the archdeacon carried to the holy servant of God, and reported to him and to the brothers the cause of defilement in the earlier vessels, and they all gave thanks unto God.

43

In the village of Buzaea, which belonged to the city of Kratianae, the inhabitants wanted to build a bridge over the torrent which ran through it, as the latter often became swollen by many streams and could not be crossed. They hired

workmen and when the work had almost reached completion
and only a few stone slabs were still needed to finish it the
workmen at the Devil's instigation went to a certain hill not
far off and dug out some slabs from it on the excuse, as some
said, that they were needed for their work; but the majority
said that they had stolen away a treasure that was hidden there.
Then there issued from the place where they had dug for the
stones a host of unclean spirits; some of them entered into
sundry men and women of the village and afflicted them
savagely, others again brought illnesses upon the remaining
inhabitants, while yet others hung about the roads and the
neighbourhood and did injury to beasts and travellers; hence
great misery arose in the village and despair at the misfortunes
in their homes and in the countryside. Then they bethought
themselves of Theodore, the servant of God, and by prayers
in his name they tried to exorcize the unclean spirits when they
showed signs of activity, and they found that the spirits showed
no little fear when his name was uttered over them, and became docile and were reduced to subjection. With all speed,
therefore, they made for the monastery and by dint of many
supplications they persuaded him to come with them. When
Theodore drew nigh to the village the spirits which were
afflicting men felt his presence and met him howling out these
words: 'Oh violence! Why have you come here, you iron-
eater,* why have you quitted Galatia and come into Gordiane?
There was no need for you to cross the frontier. We know why
you have come, but we shall not obey you as did the demons of
Galatia; for we are much tougher than they and not milder.'
When he rebuked them they at once held their peace. On the
morrow all the inhabitants were gathered together, and those
possessed by evil spirits surrounded the Saint who had ordered
a procession of supplication* to be formed which went right
round the village and came to the hill from which they said the
demons had come out. Then he rebuked them by the divine
grace of Christ and by the sign of the holy Cross and by beat-
ings on his chest, and after offering up prayers for a long time
he bade them come out of the people and return to their own
abode. They uttered loud shouts and tore the garments which
covered the sufferers and threw them down at his feet and then
came out of them. But one very wicked spirit which was in a

woman resisted and would not come out. Then the Saint caught hold of the woman's hair and shook her violently and rebuked the spirit by the sign of the Cross and by prayer to God and finally said, 'I will not give way to you nor will I leave this spot until you come out of her!' Then the spirit began to shriek and say, 'Oh violence, you are burning me, iron-eater! I am coming out, I will not resist you, only give us something that you are wearing'. The Saint loosed a sandal from his foot and threw it into the hole in the hill whence they had entered into people and straightway the spirit hurled* the woman down at the feet of the Saint and came out of her.

Then the Saint halted again and prayed to the Lord that He would drive together all the spirits, which were still remaining in the neighbourhood and in the roads to the injury of travellers, and would shut them up once more in the place from which they came out. And through the grace of God they were all collected, and to some who saw them they looked like flying blue-bottles or hares or dormice, and they entered into the place where the stones had been dug out, which the Saint then sealed with prayer and the sign of the Cross, and bade the men fill up the hole and restore it as it was before. He then led the procession back to the village, and from that time on that place and the inhabitants of the village and all the neighbourhood remained safe from harm to the glory of Christ our God, the prime author of healings.

And the Saint returned and came to his monastery.

44

(*Summary*) Theodore is asked to go to Herakleia in the province of Pontus to pray in the church of the Virgin in Herakleia.* Theodore similarly frees the house of Theodore Latzeas, a distinguished landed proprietor, from demons who had come out of an excavation made in his house and had thus caused great suffering in the family and in the city as well. In Herakleia and on his return journey he performed many miracles of healing.

45

On another occasion, as great mortality was occurring among men and oxen in the metropolis of Ancyra, leading citizens (protiktores) of that metropolis came to the monastery to the servant of God and took him and led him away to their city. Some among them had daughters who were nuns in the convent of the Holy Mother of God, called Beeia and they besought the Saint to bless and strengthen their daughters in their faith; and they persuaded him to lodge there and to pray for them.

The Saint appointed a day of supplication when the whole city and neighbourhood assembled and he went in procession with them and offered prayers to God and thus released them from the plague which held them in its grip; and to stay the deaths among the oxen he blessed water for sprinkling over the cattle and thus freed them, too, from death. The inhabitants of the city thereupon gave thanks to God and accompanied the Saint to his monastery.

The river Siberis, as it ran through the village of Sykeon near the monastery, passed close by the cornfields and was undermining the arable land and little by little was carrying away much of the soil; so the Saint, trusting fully in God, came and ordered the river in the name of Christ to change its bed and no longer approach the cornfields. After planting a wooden cross and offering a prayer, by the grace of God he induced the river to quit those fields. In the same river several men had met a violent death when crossing it, so this ever-memorable man went right into the middle of the river at the spot where the accident had occurred and by offering fervent prayer to God he, by the mercies of Christ, made the river, from that time forth, always safe and easy to cross.

46

A boy, called Arsinus, who had an unclean spirit and suffered terribly was brought to him from a monastery. The Saint received him but was not anxious to cure him quickly ⟨...illegible...⟩ time. When the boy was fully grown up he begged the Saint to ask God that he, too, might be cured as all the others were who came to the Saint. The Saint replied, 'If you will agree to adopt a good and strictly disciplined mode of life your request shall be fulfilled and you shall very soon be deemed worthy of healing'. And Arsinus agreed to these conditions. As the servant of Christ wished to go and inspect the convent of the holy martyr Christopher, he took Arsinus with him. And when they reached the deep valley of the Xerorruax, thinking that in this place the proper time had come, the Saint stood and prayed to God concerning him. And as the demon was disturbed he began to suffer and was actually raised from the ground,* and while Arsinus was hanging in the air the demon wailed and said, 'I am coming out, iron-eater, only release me and I will go out at once'. And as the demon said this he suddenly saw that Christ's holy martyr, Christopher, was also present, coming to meet Christ's servant; so he howled more loudly and tore the boy grievously and dashed him down at the Saint's feet and went out of him. And when Arsinus came to himself Theodore took him with him and went to the convent of the martyr Christopher. There by his prayers and by his admonitions and strict precepts he fortified the nuns who dwelt in the convent, and he encouraged them to lead a holy life — a life befitting their vows with fear towards God and modesty toward man. For great fear of him came upon them.

47

After Theodore had returned from this convent to his own monastery Arsinus obtained a small cell from him in which he shut himself up, living in perpetual seclusion, and every third day eating some bread and a few vegetables or pulse and drinking water, while in Lent he ate the same food but only on Saturdays and Sundays. There were two others, Evagrius and Andreas, who adopted this severe mode of life, living each in his own small cell near Arsinus and striving earnestly to accomplish the salvation of their souls so that the great servant of God shared their joy and prayed over them and glorified God. After some years the idea entered their hearts to travel to the Holy City and worship at the holy places there; and as the three were of one mind about this they fell at the feet of the most holy Theodore begging him not to forbid their desire but to dismiss them with his blessing. They were dismissed and went off and offered their prayers and Evagrius decided to remain there; he entered the Laura of Mar Saba, lived a life of virtue there and showed by his deeds that he was a disciple of the inspired and holy father, Theodore.

48

But Arsinus and Andreas returned to Galatia to the most holy Saint and begged him to give them his permission with his blessing to go away and live in seclusion in different places by themselves. He offered prayers for them and gave his approval of their purpose, and then they started, each to a place which gave him satisfaction. Andreas settled eight miles from the monastery on the hill by the village Brianeia, and there lived a strict and virtuous life; he also made a wooden cage and suspended it in the air and remained shut up in it from Christmas day to Palm Sunday, and he continued the same self-discipline which he had practised in the monastery.

Arsinus, on the other hand, went up to the country lying round the upper reaches of the river Siberis and came to the village of Galenae; he found a place to his liking outside the village, which was a haunt of demons and was eager to stay there. So he stood and prayed to God saying, 'Oh Lord, the God of my father Theodore, save me, a sinner, through his prayers and help me in my endeavours and my strivings to please Thee in this place'. And straightway he confined himself in a wooden cage and passed that winter in it; afterwards he built a very lofty column and went up on to it, and continued to practise his usual abstinence and every form of virtuous self-discipline. After he had persevered therein for forty years and bound on his brows the crown of endurance as a worthy disciple of Christ's servant, Theodore, he fell peacefully asleep.

49

There were many others, too, who had been instructed by the holy miracle-worker, our father Theodore, and were adorned with every virtue; some of these died after passing their life near him, while others let their light shine in divers other places. Of these one was Reparatus, the son of high-born parents, who entered the monastic order after being prepared for it by Theodore's encouragement and counsels and by the convincing evidence of many miracles. Then he was instructed in works by him, and by him was bidden to settle in a small cell in the village of Kolonosos in Lycaonia, where he lived a very godly life in imitation of his teacher. Another was Elpidius who after some years' instruction in the monastery, having conducted himself there in seemly fashion, went away later to the East near Mount Sinai and there dwelt in seclusion practising strict self-denial until his death; because of his seclusion and his piety the fathers in those parts nicknamed Elpidius 'Hesychos' (or 'the secluded one').

Leontius who lived in retirement near the village of Permataia had also been instructed for some years by the all-holy servant of Christ; he followed so fair and virtuous a rule of life that he was occasionally deemed worthy of the grace of prophecy, and foretold the invasion of the lawless Persians which took place later. He said that he himself would be killed by them; and this actually occurred, because he refused to leave his cell and interrupt his seclusion; so he died a martyr's death.

And Theodore who practised strict virtue on the hill of Dracon was instructed by him and took the habit; later he became the abbot of the monastery of Saint Autonomus.* Stephen again, the abbot of the monastery of St. Theodore* near the river Psilis, was a pupil of his and had been judged worthy by him of taking the habit (of monk); he also lived a life of virtue. And very many others there were, though because of their number I pass them over in silence, for I do not wish by lingering over an account of their doings, to shorten, and thus leave incomplete, the eagerly desired story of their and our great shepherd. (Close of chapter omitted.)

50

A great longing seized Theodore to travel to the Holy City, Jerusalem; so he took two brethren and started on his journey. At that time there was a great drought in Jerusalem and all men were straitened because the pits and cisterns were dried up; for the city itself and the neighbouring monasteries collect the water for their needs from the rain which falls from the houses and then conduct it into pits and cisterns because there are no natural springs or fountains. Consequently the lives of all, both of men and beasts, were endangered by this lack of water, and though they made supplications they did not gain their request, as God was evidently reserving this favour to redound to the praise of his great servant.

Now it happened that some men from Galatia were there

who knew this great servant of God and the miracles worked
by him, and they spoke about him in the Holy City and in the
monasteries to those they chanced to meet and said, 'We have
a holy father in our country who by one single prayer can fill
the whole world with rain to the full, as Elijah, the prophet,
did in the time of Ahab, King of Israel'.

51

When the Saint reached Jerusalem and had adored the life-
bestowing Cross and worshipped in the Church of Christ's
Holy Resurrection and had gone round to all the sacred places
in the city and to the monasteries, the monks, who had already
proclaimed his miracle-working way of life, when they had seen
him, now talked about his presence both in the City and the
monasteries. And so priests sent by the Patriarch as well as
monks and the most illustrious citizens came to him and besought him to propitiate God on their behalf by his prayers,
that He might send them rain. However, he asked to be
excused, pleading that he was unworthy of so great an honour,
but they declared that they believed that, if only he would join
in prayer with the other fathers, they would certainly be
deemed worthy of the gift of rain. And he said to them 'Now,
as you say you believe, so shall it be for you'.

And he bade them order a procession with prayer and he
said to those taking part in the procession who had changed
into their best clothes,* 'Take off these garments, children,
that they may not get drenched through and you be vexed in
spirit thereat; for I say unto you that according to your faith
God will speedily show his mercy on your behalf'. So they
went in procession and halted for prayer at a certain spot by
the Saint's command, and there he spread out his hands to
heaven and prayed to the Lord for a long time. Whilst he
prayed a small rain-bearing cloud appeared coming up from
the West; and when he had finished his prayer and had bidden
them turn homewards, the sky grew black with clouds and the
rain began to come down in torrents so that they returned at a
run and their clothes were soaked, and thus the procession
ended with hymns of praise to God. So through the virtue of
the prayer offered to God by His servant the rains spread over
the country like a river, and all the pits and cisterns were filled.

But in order to avoid being troubled by the crowd when this miracle became noised abroad, he quickly left the City and returned to his monastery.

52

Similar wonders to this he performed during a time of great drought in other places also which were not far from the monastery.

In a village called Reake a threatening cloud would periodically appear suddenly over the country-side and pour down hail-stones upon the vineyards, when the fruit was ripe; and the men of the village were in great distress as they had not been able to enjoy the fruits of their husbandry for several years. Accordingly they came to the monastery and entreated the blessed man and brought him back with them to their village. He formed a procession of supplication and they went round the vineyard and the fields and, after offering prayer, he placed four wooden crosses at the four angles of the boundary-line and after doing this returned to the monastery and through his holy prayer that threatening cloud never overshadowed that village again. In return for this benefit the men of the village from that time to the present day yearly bring to the monastery a fixed measure of wine and grapes of various kinds.

53

Omitted as being similar to ch. 45. — Here the river Kopas is forbidden to encroach on the village of Karuas.

54

At that time Tiberius of pious memory was ruling over the empire, and after appointing Maurice, the Chartularius, as general he sent him to the East to the Persian war to fight against them. And after Maurice had defeated them he was ordered by the Emperor to return to the capital. As he was passing through the districts of Galatia he heard talk about the servant of Christ. (These were the days of the blessed man's abstinence and he was in seclusion in his cave.)

Maurice went up with his brother Peter and his attendants and fell at the Saint's feet and begged him to pray for them that their journey to the Emperor might have a happy issue.

The blessed and glorious man bade him stand up and prayed to God for him, as if by divine revelation he said to Maurice, 'My son, if you bear in mind to pray to the holy martyr George, you will shortly learn to what glorious post in the Empire you are called; only, when you reach those heights be sure to remember the needs of the poor'. When Maurice asked to know precisely what dignity he meant to which he should be called, the Saint led him apart from his companions and told him plainly that he would become emperor.

After Maurice and all the men with him had received the Saint's blessing he left with joy and reached Constantinople.

And according to the Saint's prophecy Maurice succeeded to the imperial throne on the death of Tiberius, and remembering Theodore's words he sent him a letter asking him to pray for him and for his Empire that it might be preserved in peace and untroubled by enemies and bade him make any request he liked.

The blessed man sent the most blessed Philoumenus, the abbot, to the Emperor and also wrote a letter in order to secure some small gift of food for the monastery to meet the needs of the poor who looked to them for support. On receiving the letter the Emperor made a grant to the monastery of 200 modii of corn annually, and sent it to him together with a chalice and a paten.

55

(The fame of Theodore spreads ever more widely and the monastery continuously gains new recruits.)

When the blessed man saw the vast crowds that assembled and realized that the chapel of St. George was too small, he gave the rest of the money he had inherited to build a church worthy of the holy martyr George with three apses and an oratory on the right dedicated to the holy martyr Plato.*

A trench was being dug for the foundations of the building which was to be set apart for the catechumens and dedicated to the holy martyrs Sergius and Bacchus.* This lay higher up the hill. The workmen had blasted several rocks with fire and vinegar and then rolled them down (the land being uncultivated and rocky), when they happened to come across one enormous rock which they got out and tried to roll down into the garden behind the apse: but it stuck in one place and could not be moved in any way. After a large number of workmen had tried hard for a long time and yet could not move it, the servant of God hearing about it came to the place, touched the rock and said, 'Blessed Lord, move it away from here further down, for we need this space', and at once at his words it moved and began rolling down at a violent pace. Now right in its course stood an apple tree, and as it was likely to be caught by the rock the blessed man was grieved at heart and cried out, 'Go to one side of the tree and do not do it any harm!' And immediately, like an intelligent person, the rock bent aside from its attack on the tree, and passed it by without hurting it.

56

Again, at the place called Arkea, which we have spoken of before (ch. 16), the men of the village of Euarzia, eight miles from the monastery, had burnt unslaked lime for the building of the church; then they loaded the lime on their own wagons and on many others that had come to help from the neighbouring villages, and the saintly God-inspired man was also present. They had started and were making for the holy monastery; when they were about half way, they were overhadowed by a large cloud. From it there fell a heavy shower of rain. The farmers were terrified and desperate, thinking that their wagons and oxen would be burnt by the lime because of the downpour of rain. As the Saint was walking behind them they began to shout to him at the top of their voices saying, 'Quick, master, we and our beasts are threatened with death', and they began with all haste to unharness the beasts from the wagons. But the Saint caught them up and prevented their unyoking the oxen from the wagons. Standing and stretching up his hands to God he prayed; then he mounted on the leading wagon and sat down and went on his way singing psalms. And immediately the cloud was split in two, and it rained to the left and to the right of their road, so that the water from both sides ran underneath the wagons, but above them not even a single drop of rain fell; in this wise they were saved and reached the holy monastery glorifying God Who works marvels through His servant.

57

(*Summary*) The church is completed and Theodore foretells that a bishop of that same place* will dedicate it, God intending to grant to Theodore a yet further sign of his favour by making him a bishop.

58

After the death of Timotheus, the Bishop of Anastasioupolis, the clergy and the land-owners living in that town went to the metropolis Ancyra to the most blessed Archbishop, Paul, and asked him to appoint the great servant of God, Theodore, the archimandrite of the monastery of Sykeon, as bishop of their most Holy Church. Paul was greatly pleased at their excellent choice and gave them permission to fetch the Saint. (Now it was the time when he gave himself to prayer and he was shut up in seclusion in his cave.) So when the clergy and land-owners of Anastasioupolis reached the monastery they went up to the cave and begged him to give himself to them as their shepherd; however, he absolutely refused to listen to their request and would not yield himself to their wish; so they resorted to more forcible means and fetched him out of his cave and placed him in a litter and carried him off. The monks of the monastery and all those who were staying there grieved and lamented at his being separated from them, so the Saint sent them a message by a brother saying, 'Do not be in any way cast down, children, for believe me I shall certainly never forsake you; for nothing on earth shall separate me from my life with you'. When he reached the metropolis, Ancyra, the most blessed Archbishop Paul received him with joy and ordained him bishop and gave him much encouragement, telling him how someone in Anastasioupolis at that time had seen in a vision a very large and radiant star coming from heaven and standing above their church, shining and casting its light over the town and all the surrounding countryside. On leaving the metropolis of Ancyra holy Theodore went to Anastasioupolis with the most holy bishop of the town of Kinna by whom he was enthroned.

Like the star that had been seen he continued to cast his light over the city through his divine gifts of healings, his continual fastings, his hymns of praise to God, and his generosity to those in want; in a word, through all his virtues and good deeds he exalted the renown of the city which had welcomed him, inspiring in the citizens such a virtuous activity that their city became the envy and the admiration of other towns and thus it really proved its right to its name of 'Resurrection' (Anastasis). It was fittingly entitled the city of Anastasius (Anastasioupolis); it rose to fame not from its fortifications and the embellishment of imperial gifts: not from the size of its population or from the exceeding wealth and power of its prosperous inhabitants, but rather because it was enriched by such deeds of the inspired man as we have described and on account of these deeds it was fortified not by men alone — it was its fortune to be ruled and inhabited also by angels, and to be always under the oversight and guardianship of the heavenly King Christ. It was upon these that its courage and its victories were based.

59

(*Summary*) Theodore consecrates the church which he had built to the holy martyr George amid scenes of great rejoicing. He then returned to Anastasioupolis where he worked many miracles, the sick would be brought on beds for him to touch them; and such was the grace bestowed on the Saint by our Lord Jesus Christ that if he merely rebuked evil spirits, or often even if he only sent his rebuke through a messenger* they would immediately hasten to leave their victims.

60

(*Summary*) Another time when the Saint was in seclusion in the chapel of St. Plato and had given orders that no woman should be admitted, a man came to the church with his wife who was afflicted by a demon and quite beyond control. She broke the candelabra in the church. A servant came and told the Saint about the woman. He had laid down as a rule for himself that standing or sitting he should not leave a narrow platform.* He gave to his servant some consecrated oil with which to anoint the forehead, hands and ears and bade him command the demon to depart and it did so. The woman was never after possessed by the demon.

61

Although many such miracles were daily wrought by the Saint through the grace of God abiding in him, a certain deacon of the cathedral in Anastasioupolis, called Dometianus, disbelieved in them and was not a little sceptical and was offended in him. Now one day, a Sunday, a man from the metropolis of Ancyra came to the Saint and brought his son who was dumb.

As they arrived at the time of the administration of the Holy Communion in the Catholic church of the Holy Wisdom they went up to participate; and when the boy yawned, the Saint said to him, 'Say Amen, child!' and the child immediately obeyed him and pronounced the 'Amen'. The father began with a loud voice to glorify God and to proclaim the wonder that had been wrought. Whilst all present were amazed and singing praises to God the Archdeacon Dometianus suddenly fell to the ground. Some of the clergy rushed forward and lifted him up; he was all trembling, so they asked what had happened to him. And he answered them as follows: 'When the boy pronounced the "Amen", and the father cried out that he had been freed from dumbness, I did not believe that he spoke the truth but thought he was falsely claiming for the Saint a fraudulent glory and then I saw as it were a flame of fire come out of the child's mouth.' After saying this he was supported and led to the Saint, at whose feet he fell and besought him to offer prayers for him so that the power and wrath of the Devil which had issued from the boy might not come to him. After the Saint had heard the whole tale, he said to the deacon, 'This has happened to you, my son, because you cherish some unbelief in your heart about the gift of Christ which is shown in healings; but cast it aside, "be thou faithful and not unbelieving".[1] For it is not we, but our good God, Who even now works these miracles (whatever they may be) so that we may not have any excuse for saying that He has shown no sign in our time, and that through beholding these miracles we may also believe in those which took place before us in the lifetime of the saints and thus increase in faith and serve God wholeheartedly.' After the blessed man had spoken thus, the deacon himself confessed his unbelief and when the Saint had prayed for him he was freed from his shuddering

[1] John xx. 27.

and his fear and continued in health and from henceforth he would come to the Saint in complete confidence.

62
(*Summary*) Theodore visits Jerusalem for the third time having as his companions on the journey John, the archdeacon from his own monastery, and Martinus from the village of Dougaia, out of which he had cast a legion of devils. He decides not to return to his own country but to spend his life in one of the monasteries in Jerusalem, for he thought that, since he had been absorbed in the cares and administration of his bishopric, he had fallen away from the monastic standard.

63
(*Summary*) He goes to the monastery of Mar Saba and lives in the cell of a brother named Andreas; when the time for his period of seclusion came round, Andreas made him a seat and on that he sat without rising from Christmas to Palm Sunday. After Easter his companions urge him to return to his bishopric, but he refuses to leave the monastery. St. George appears to him in a vision and bids him start at once for Galatia; Theodore seeks to resign his bishopric but St. George promises him that, if he returns, he will shortly free him from his burden as bishop, only he must not desert his palace, nor leave his flock without tendance. On waking Theodore obeys and returns to Anastasioupolis.

64
(*Summary*) On his return journey with two disciples they reach the monastery of Druinoi in Galatia and enter it to rest there. Anicetus, the guest-master, is curious about the father's identity which the disciples had been forbidden to reveal. However, by an incautious remark made by Theodore himself at dinner, 'In truth children, we have eaten like Galatians', the secret can no longer be kept. The abbot hears the news with joy and at the night service he and all his monks join in procession with lighted candles to meet him at the door of the oratory of St. Paul and fall at his feet and then welcome him warmly. They prepare a feast for him and ask him to stay with them and rest from his journey for several days. This he

consents to do on condition that he may be 'bedmaker' during his stay.

65

(*Summary*) The news of his being in the monastery soon spread and many flocked to it in order to receive his blessing; others brought their sick to be healed. A woman brought to him a dumb boy; Theodore opened the boy's mouth, breathed into it and made the sign of the Cross over it and straightway the boy spoke. Another boy was brought to him who was quite unable to walk; the Saint moved back from the boy a little way and then said, 'Come to me, child, in the name of the Lord'. Immediately the boy left his mother's side and walked across to Theodore.

66

(*Summary*) He is then invited to the neighbouring monastery of St. Stephen, known as Vetapes, and is next taken by Amiantus, the bishop of Kinna, to that town that he might bless it. He is met by a procession and a festival is celebrated in his honour. He returned to Druinoi and then started for Anastasioupolis; on the journey crowds assemble to receive his blessing.

67

(*Summary*) On the way he cured a dumb youth with the same method of healing as in ch. 65 (save that in this case Theodore breathed into the mouth three times) and the saying of the 'Amen' as in ch. 61. In this case also he had previously given the youth 'the holy body of Christ'.

68

(*Summary*) The inhabitants of Anastasioupolis welcomed his return. A paralysed woman was brought on horseback on a pack-saddle; he directs them to take her to the monastery: he followed two days later. He bids the paralytic hold on to the railings of the pulpit; he takes oil from the 'unsleeping lamp' and makes the sign of the Cross on her forehead, hands and feet and bids her go to her own house rejoicing: she then walks without support.

69

The Saint once gave orders to some carpenters to make a wooden chest for storing corn and pulse for the monastery's use. And he commanded them not to touch any meat until the work which he had ordered was finished, and that then they could go to the village and eat. (For meat was never eaten in the monastery all the year through, except on three saints' festivals when the crowd which came to the festivals were fed.) A few days after the Saint had gone away to Anastasioupolis, the foreman brought in some meat secretly and ate it, whereupon he was immediately stricken with fever and lay half-dead, and his life was despaired of. When the Saint in Anastasioupolis heard the news about him from a brother who had come from the monastery he said 'Verily the saying of the Holy Scripture is true, "Obedience is life, disobedience death!"* For the man had disobeyed my injunction and eaten meat in the monastery and that is the reason why he is ill'. He left the city and came to the monastery and going to the place where the sick man lay he said to him, 'Do not conceal from me what you really did, brother; for you ate meat, did you not?' and the other answered that that was so. The blessed man then said, 'Now see and recognize, that it is not God who sends wrath upon us, but we bring it upon ourselves. Believe me, brother, that when I did not allow you any meat I did not do so from niggardliness as you supposed but in order to preserve the purity and sanctity of this holy place. Rise now in the name of Jesus Christ, finish your task and for the future take care not to disobey'. Then be blessed him and placed his hand on him, and the man was at once relieved of the fever; he got up the same day, and began to finish the rest of the work.

70

(*Summary*) When the Saint had returned to Anastasioupolis a man came to the monastery and with the abbot's consent remained in the church of the holy martyr George, though visitors generally remained in the church of the Archangel. The Saint in Anastasioupolis is told by St. George in a vision that the visitor had secretly taken some pork into the chapel of St. George; he sends a messenger to the abbot, Philoumenus, who makes a search and discovers the pork in the possession of the visitor.

71

(*Summary*) Aemilianus, the bishop of the town of Germia*, invited Theodore to stay with him. They meet in the church of the Archangel at Germia. At that time the annual festival of the Mother of God in the village of Mousge took place which was held conjointly by the Bishops and the inhabitants of the two towns of Germia and Eudoxias, in each case the whole town turning out in procession and meeting at Mousge. Theodore accompanied Aemilianus and on arrival at the church a woman named Eirene who had been grievously afflicted by evil spirits for many years and who was bedridden caught sight of him from outside the church. Then she was moved by the spirits and throwing off her cape and her covering she forced her way with loud yells through the crowd in front of her, reviling the blessed Theodore, the demons cursing him since they were humiliated through his presence. On seeing her the whole crowd began to repeat the 'Kyrie eleison' (Lord, have mercy!). But the woman was lifted off the ground* and with her hands bound above her head she was carried through the air from the pulpit to the rails of the sanctuary, while the demons kept on crying out that the Saint was making appeals to God against them, but after the reading of the Gospel she was borne down to the ground and lay at the entrance to the sanctuary and licked the dust with her tongue. After the service Theodore turned towards her, seized her by the hair and in the name of Christ ordered the evil spirits to depart from her. This they did, wailing as they went. On the death of her husband and children she bade farewell to the world and took up her abode in a cell near the church of the Virgin where she lived as a solitary. Later Theodore returned to Anastasiou-polis.

72

There came to visit him the chief elder of the village Araunia Andreas by name and he kept him several days.

Then it happened that Andreas' child, named Cometas, fell

grievously ill and was at the point of death. So as the child was at the last gasp and not uttering any sound nor recognizing anyone the men of the village prepared his grave and his mother in Anastasioupolis sent the elder John to convey this news to her husband, so that he might hurry home to his child's funeral. At that hour the holy Bishop Theodore after reciting the liturgy was taking some food; Andreas, the father of the child, was with him. When the elder John who had been sent had arrived he told Andreas the reason for his coming. And when the blessed Theodore heard it he did not allow him to leave at once, saying, 'I, too, will come with you, for I want to go to my monastery and visit the brethren; but first let us enjoy the good things given to us by God and then we will start. For I trust in God that we shall find your child alive; for he is not dying now but he will recover and be given back to you in good health'. After saying this he bade the elder John, who had brought the message, to come in also and eat with them. After they had risen from table the blessed man went to the village and all the inhabitants came out to meet him with torches and censers. As it was evening he went into the church and having blessed the crowd he read the evening office and then went away to the house of the chief elder Andreas. Seeing the child failing fast he stood in prayer and besought Him who has power over life and death, Christ our God, to restore the child's life and give him back alive to his parents. After his prayer the Saint nodded and spoke to the child, who opened his eyes and looked hard at him but was unable to give him any answer (for he had also lost his power of speech). Again bending his head the servant of God prayed to the Lord to fulfil his prayer and to raise up the child in health. And having finished his prayer he spoke to the child saying, 'Cometas, look up and tell us how you are and give an answer to your father that he may not grieve about you'. Again the boy opened his eyes and looked at him intently and gave him an answer to his questions. Then having made the sign of the Cross on his forehead, on his hands and on his feet the Saint took the boy's right hand and made him sit up saying, 'In the name of our Lord Jesus Christ Who raised up the dying child of the centurion do you rise up and be well, for it is He also who now gives you life'. And he commanded that something should be given him to eat.[1] So they brought him food and he ate. Being invited to supper by the parents the Saint allowed the elder John to carry the child and bring him in to supper. So the elder John holding the child at supper gave him from the dishes placed before him so that the child took more food than the others and all who saw it joined in great joy with the parents glorifying God Who gives life even to the dead at the request of His servants. On the following day the child, now restored to health, began to walk. And the blessed man left the village and went to the monastery.

73

During those days he welcomed a saint of the desert gifted with foresight, Antiochus, as I believe he was styled, who was returning from Constantinople to the East. For he had gone up to the Emperor Maurice to ask his help on behalf of a town which had been pillaged by barbarians. He had eyebrows that met each other and was an African by race, about one hundred years old, and the hair of his head was as white as wool, and hung down to his loins, and so too did his beard, and his nails were very long. It was now sixty years since he had touched wine or oil or other drinks; and he had not tasted bread for thirty years. His food was uncooked vegetables with salt and vinegar and his drink, water. The facts about each other had been revealed to him and to Saint Theodore. And the blessed Theodore told the brethren about him and said, 'Never in the whole desert of the East have I seen or heard of such a worthy servant of God'. And in his turn the just man from the East said to the disciples accompanying him concerning the holy Bishop Theodore, 'I had never met such a holy man up to now; for God declared the facts about him to me'. And his disciples when they had heard this took bits from the hem of Theodore's garments for a blessing. When the brethren of the monastery went to meet him to do obeisance Antiochus was indignant and with the interpreter's help he stopped them saying, 'As you have such a shining light and holy apostle of Christ why do you come to do obeisance to me who am like a

[1] Cf. Mark v. 43.

wild beast and imperfect and of no account? Pay attention to him and award honour to this holy man who is worthy of praise and admirable who conducts himself in the world in a manner pleasing to God and treads its pleasures underfoot and by his teaching turns many souls to God'.

74

Evening came and after reciting the holy liturgy they sat down together to eat their short accustomed meal; and after this the Saint wished according to his custom to wash the African's feet, but he would not allow that but they washed each other's hands. In the morning the servant of God was in a hurry to depart so as to accomplish the journey which lay before him. But Saint Theodore, having learnt by revelation that the other's death was near and wishing this to take place in his monastery begged him to stay for a time and rest from the weariness of the journey. But the other besought him to let him go saying, 'My departure from my body is at hand and I am hastening, if I possibly can, to reach my own cell'. So Saint Theodore went out and accompanied him to Anastasiou-polis, and he set before him the difficulties and worries which beset him in his episcopal work, and the break it had made in his rule of life and the slackness in his monasteries which was due to his absence and asked him what he thought was the best thing for him to do in the circumstances and whether according to his own desire he should relinquish the office of a bishop and be free to return to the company of his monks. The African advised him that the latter course would be right and that he should do it quickly that he might be innocent in the eyes of God. Theodore then gave him for his use the horse on which he himself used to ride and one brother to accompany him as long as he wished and thus sped him on his way from Anas-tasioupolis. They kissed and embraced each other and then separated. The blessed man returned to the bishop's house and said of the other that he would not be able to reach his own place as he would very shortly be leaving his body and so it happened. For a few days later report was brought of his falling asleep while he was still on the highroad.

75

The writer explains that Theodore's desire to resign his bishopric arose from the fear of neglecting his contemplation of heavenly matters if he were too much involved in earthly business. The villages belonging to the Church were a constant source of trouble.

76

For Theodore used to entrust the administration and the governance of the properties belonging to the church to men of the city and injustice was done to the peasants; in one case for instance he had entrusted them to a leading citizen (protiktor) of Anastasioupolis, Theodosius, by name; and he continually acted unjustly and defrauded the peasants. So they came to the servant of Christ and met him in tears, and he, moved with sympathy, grieved over them, for his holy and sensitive soul could not bear to see any one in trouble. He summoned Theodosius and with many admonitions besought him to cease his acts of injustice against the peasants. But Theodosius again invented some pretexts against the villagers and continued in his unjust treatment, whereupon in one of the villages, called Eucraous, when he was proceeding to his usual acts of injustice, the peasants of the village were roused to uncontrollable anger; they all gathered together with a common purpose, armed themselves with divers weapons and swords and catapults, and took up their stand outside the village to meet him, and threatened him with death if he did not turn back and leave them. When he saw them all prepared in this way for battle and surmising that he would get the worst of it, he left them and returned to Anastasioupolis as if with the intention of coming to attack them in greater force.

But when the holy man heard what had happened, he spent that day in much weeping and groaning, bearing in mind that, if this rising should by chance come to a head and many be killed, he himself would incur unforgettable dishonour as having been the cause of such a calamity, while it would be no easy task to clear himself from responsibility for the souls that he had endangered. So he fell to the ground on his face and worshipped and thanked the Lord for having prevented this outbreak of anger from coming to a fatal end. And he summoned Theodosius and informed him that in future he could not retain the administration of the villages lest some disturbance should arise in their midst.

Theodosius, however, asserted that it was at his, Theodore's, instigation that the rising of the peasants against him had taken place; then he barked out various insulting remarks at him and shouted a perfectly unjustified accusation of prodigality at him and finally kicked the chair on which he was sitting so that Theodore fell on his back on the floor of the council-chamber in front of them all. Thereupon the Saint got up and in a very gentle voice solemnly declared to them that he would not continue as bishop among them, but would return to his own monastery. Not satisfied even with this Theodosius still attacked him, threatening him with the fine of two pounds of gold which it had been stipulated should be paid by either party who did not abide by his contract, alleging that through Theodore he was being ousted from the villages before the time which had been fixed in the agreement. But his wife remonstrated with him and said, 'Let there be no quarrel between you and this holy man lest instead of a blessing and a prayer, which we have not had from him, we may get a curse and be doomed'. But he would not stop to listen to her, and again one day he went up to the bishop's house to vex him and to summon him to court on the matter. But when the porter had gone in to announce him to the Saint, suddenly great dread fell upon him as he stood waiting, and there appeared to him a young man of terrifying aspect and brilliantly clad, who threatened him angrily and who said, without wasting words, 'You villain, is it thus you oppose the great man and never cease causing him constant annoyance and sorrow? — here and now I forewarn you, that if you do not submit to him, great wrath will come upon you and you will end your life most miserably'. And with these words he vanished. Theodosius remained speechless for a considerable time and when he had recovered a little the Saint summoned him, and he went in and fell at his feet weeping, beseeching the bishop to forgive him for the many annoyances he had often caused him, and agreeing never to trouble him again about the fine of two pounds.

77

It happened that once, I do not know how, the Saint was poisoned by some men of Anastasioupolis, and he lay in his cell in the bishop's house speechless and immovable for three days, so that the report spread that he was dead. But after the third day our Lady the Holy Mother of God, Mary, appeared to him pronouncing, 'Woe' upon the wicked men and condemning them; and made known to him the reason of his illness and the names of the conspirators. Then she took three pills out of a napkin and gave them to him saying, 'Eat these and after that you will have no pain'. He thought he took them and then immediately awoke from sleep and arose glorifying his Saviour Christ and His Immaculate and Holy Mother. And he published the reason of his illness but forebore to mention those who had caused it, but on the contrary prayed to God to forgive them.

78

(*Summary*) Murmurs now arose that Theodore by his constant giving of alms was wasting the substance of the church, although out of the 365 'nomismata' allotted to him for his household expenses he only used 40 in the whole year and gave all the rest to the Church. And at times when he stood reading the portion of the Psalms appointed for the day, he was interrupted and was forced to break off in the midst of his prayers to settle questions of administration. While he was troubled by these distractions he found that the brothers in his monasteries were leading a careless and barren life through his absence and considering whether they should not move elsewhere. He reflected that he would have to render account concerning his monks in the day of judgment and was much troubled and thought long over all these difficulties.

He therefore laid the matter of his resignation before St. George in prayer and besought God that he might without condemnation deliver up his bishopric. He received assurance that his request was granted. So he summoned a meeting of the clergy and landowners of the town. They had refused to listen to his protests, he said, and had persisted in making him their bishop, though he knew that he was unfitted for the government of the church. 'And now this is the eleventh year that I have troubled you and been troubled by you, I beseech you, therefore, choose for yourselves a shepherd in whom you may find satisfaction, one who can take charge of your affairs.' As for himself, henceforth he was no longer their bishop, but as a humble monk he was returning to the monastery in which he had vowed to serve his Lord all the days of his life. Bidding them farewell he set out for the capital of the province, Ancyra, taking with him John, the archdeacon of his monastery.

And that night a man of the city saw, in a dream, how a bright and radiant star, casting its light over the city and standing above the church, moved away and was taken from them and then could scarcely be seen far away in the distance. When he saw this, he understood that it had its fulfilment in the holy man's departure from the city.

79

The servant of God journeyed to the metropolis, Ancyra, and there he met with the most blessed metropolitan, Paul, and begged him to accept his resignation; however, Paul asserted that he could not let a man of such virtue resign. After much argument one with the other finally they both decided to refer the matter to Kyriakus, the most blessed Patriarch of Constantinople, and to abide by whatever order he should send. So they both wrote; the blessed Theodore sent his requests to the Emperor Maurice of pious memory as well as to the most blessed Patriarch, Kyriakus, advising them to accept his resignation; but the metropolitan expressed his annoyance at this request to the most holy Patriarch and said he would await his commands.

And the most blessed Patriarch Kyriakus wrote to the metropolitan to grant Theodore's request — for the Emperor had ordered him to do this — and at the same time to bestow upon him the bishop's 'Omophorion'[1] so that he would retain his rank, because he was a holy man and it was through no fault of his that he was resigning his bishopric. On receiving this order the metropolitan relieved the blessed Theodore of his bishopric; and when the latter brought his petition of discharge, he bestowed the episcopal 'Omophorion' upon him and

---

[1] A wide band of embroidered stuff, corresponding to the Western pallium.

advised him to keep away from the neighbourhood* of Anastasioupolis until another bishop had been appointed in his stead. Theodore therefore left the metropolis of Ancyra and came to the region of the town of Heliopolis and hid himself in the oratory of the Archangel at Acrena, quite close to Pidrum.*

80

One day when he was celebrating the Eucharist in that same oratory of the Archangel, his countenance became bright and a joy to behold, shining with great glory and grace. One of the brothers present, a pious priest, Julianus by name, who had noticed the brightness and joy of his countenance, fell at his feet in private saying, 'One question I want to ask of you, father, and for the Lord's sake I beg you satisfy me on the point'. After the Saint had given him his blessing and persuaded him to rise promising to answer his question, Julian began, 'When you are offering the oblation, father, some days no change takes place in your face, but on most days we see your face shining brightly with great glory and filled with such deep delight that each one of us shares in the gladness which springs from your great rejoicing; so it was to-day when we looked at you. Do tell me, for the Lord's sake, what the cause of it is.' But the servant of the Lord tried to evade any explanation. However, the other adjured him earnestly and implored him to tell him about it. Then Theodore said to him, 'If you will promise me never to relate it to anybody, I will tell you the reason'. After the priest had taken an oath never to divulge the secret to anyone before the death of the Saint,* the blessed man said to him, 'When you see me rejoicing during the oblation, know that I am rejoicing because of a vision; for I see a very bright veil as if it were actually descending upon the Holy gifts while I offer them, and whenever I see that I rejoice and exult, and because I do not always see it, therefore my face is not always cheerful. And when I do not see it at the usual time, I lengthen the prayer of oblation while waiting for this vision which to-day also I was deemed worthy to behold'. The priest Julianus kept what he had heard secret and told no man of it until after the Saint's death. On hearing that a bishop had been appointed in Anastasioupolis the blessed man returned to his monastery rejoicing and glorifying God and by divine grace he worked many miracles on the sick that came to him.

81

(Shortened.) Among the sick who came to him was a certain priest called Paul who was brought on a horse from a monastery in Lycaonia. His right hip was dislocated and his head was bent down towards his left foot — so that he could neither stand nor could he lie down flat on a bed — he was a piteous sight. He had tried many baths and medicaments but all to no purpose. The blessed Theodore ordered him to stay three days in the monastery; and then when he had learnt the facts about him, he said to him, 'If you wish to be restored to health go back to your own country and be reconciled with him who has a grievance against you, and return before winter and God will give you health'. Paul however denied and said he had no difference whatever with anyone, then the holy man stopped him very sharply and said, 'Come, do not tell lies; you are at enmity with your abbot and have failed to obey him'. (And in fact Paul had engaged in great strife with him.) Paul then confessed the truth and begged Theodore to relieve him of his continuous pain before he started on his journey back. This the Saint did by ordering him to have his clothes removed; then he rubbed his limbs, which were diseased, praying over him and anointing his whole body with a salve made of wax. But the crookedness still remained; his attendants lifted him on to his horse and he returned to his own country. There he was reconciled to his abbot and came back to the monastery in the winter. The Saint was enclosed in a very narrow cell in the monastery of the holy Mother of God and through his prayers Paul was led back to health* and loosed from the malady which bound him. He was told to take a walk each day near the monastery, supporting himself on a staff which Theodore gave him and coming daily for a blessing. Later he was given a longer staff, and after Easter Theodore gave him yet another with these words: 'Hold this in your hand and go back whence you came; for very soon you will be deemed worthy of perfect health. But when this staff falls from your hand do not trouble to pick it up again.' After receiving a blessing the priest departed to his home, and one day while he was walking the stick fell from his hand; remembering the Saint's words he made no effort to recover it. He was completely restored to health and spoke to everybody of the miracle. Through the Saint's influence he was appointed priest to the oratory of the Mother of God in Sycae, in Constantinople, in the quarter of Galatius* (as the district was called), and later he became bishop of a town in Isauria.

<h2 style="text-align:center">82</h2>

About that time the holy servant of Christ received letters both from the Christ-loving Emperor Maurice and from the blessed Patriarch, Kyriakus, and from the magnates urging him to come up to Constantinople, the imperial city, and give them his blessing. Consequently, being thus compelled, he travelled to the divinely protected city, and after greeting the most blessed Patriarch, Kyriakus, and the Emperor and the senate and pronouncing a suitable blessing in each case, he sat down to table with them. The Emperor and the Empress and all the officers of the bedchamber shewed a tender regard for him and accorded him much honour. Further, by their sacred decree they bestowed upon his monasteries the right of sanctuary and transferred the appointment of abbots in them to the apostolic throne of the most holy great church of God in the imperial city so that they should not be subject to any other bishopric. Thus through this regulation by the dispensation of God and by the co-operation of the holy martyr George those who had renounced this world in these monasteries and those who celebrated the liturgy in them all alike received encouragement. During the short time Theodore stayed in the capital God through him performed great miracles in the city.

[We have thought it unnecessary to translate in full chapters 83 to 96, which describe the miracles performed by Saint Theodore while in Constantinople, but since there is in them material which may well be of interest to students of magic and of healings of the possessed we give a brief summary.]

83

A woman living near Saint Theodore in the quarter of Sporacius brought her blind child of four years old to the Saint who was lodging in the quarter of Varanas (or according to another reading, ch. 93, Euarane). He made the sign of the Cross over her eyes and blessed some water: with that she was to bathe her eyes every morning. This was done for three days and on the fourth day the child saw clearly. Her mother had previously been paralysed, lying on her bed for seven months, but was cured by the Saint's prayer.

84

The slave girl of a magnate had been possessed secretly by a demon for twenty-eight years so that she was always ill and did not know what caused the malady. Her master brought her to the Saint praying that either by death or a restoration to health she might be liberated from her sickness. Saint Theodore took hold of her head and prayed that the cause of her illness might be made known and driven away. Immediately the demon in her was disturbed and tore her, shouting: 'You are burning me, iron-eater, spare me, strangler of demons, I adjure you by the God who gives you power against me.' Theodore bade the demon be silent and told the girl to return in a week's time. On the following Wednesday she came and once more the demon in her became excited and abusive: 'Oh this violence that I suffer from this harlot's child! Twenty-eight years I have possessed this girl* and none of the saints found me out, and now this harlot's son has come and has made me manifest and handed me over to dread punishment. Cursed be the day on which you were born and the day that brought you here!' Theodore rebuked the demon with the sign of the Cross: 'Even if I am the harlot's son, nevertheless to the glory of our Lord Jesus Christ the Son of God I bid you in His name leave the girl* and never take possession of her again.' The demon shouted in reply: 'I do your bidding and go out of her, but after three days she will die.' The Saint answered: 'Come forth and the will of the Lord be done. For a God-fearing man may not trust you, since your words are vain and false.' The demon tore the girl, threw her down at the Saint's feet and went out of her. And she, coming to herself, said: 'It is through your holy prayers, father, that I have been healed, for I saw the demon coming out of my mouth like a foul crawling thing.' Theodore prayed over her and dismissed her, bidding her remain in the church for seven days. And the word of the demon proved to be false, for after some days the girl and her master returned to the Saint giving glory to God.

85

A woman who was paralysed was brought to the Saint by her attendants: he bade them put her on the ground: he seized hold of her head with his left hand, and stretching out his right hand to the East, he prayed to the God Who gives healing and had cured the paralytic. He anointed her with oil, made the sign of the Cross over her, raised her up and straightway she began to walk.

86

One Peter, a merchant's son, was smitten by a demon and 'was devoured in his heart'; he did not know the cause of his sickness. His father brought him to the Saint who recognized the cause of his trouble and took him to his cell. He made the sign of the Cross over his face and struck him over his heart saying: 'Do not hide yourself, unclean spirit, for your working is disclosed. The Lord Jesus Christ Who knoweth secret things bids you come out of him.' And forthwith the demon was set in motion and shouted: 'I am coming out, iron-eater: I will not disobey you, for I cannot bear your threats. I cannot bear the fire which proceeds from your mouth and scorches me.' This and much more the demon said, and then, loudly wailing, left the sufferer who, coming to himself, said to the Saint, 'I saw the demon, as he freed himself from me, in the form of a black woman and he was chased by you through the window howling at the top of his voice.' Theodore told the boy to wait for a day and on the morrow he restored him to his father cured of his malady.

87

A sailor had been put under a spell by someone and was troubled by an unclean spirit: his limbs trembled and he suffered from many other symptoms so that he was reduced to penury. The Saint prayed over him and blessed oil with which he was to anoint himself and dismissed him. After some days the sailor returned cured to the Saint: his affairs were prospering and 'by way of fruit-bearing and as a memento' he brought the tackle of his boat to Theodore who was only induced to accept it after much insistence.

88

A wrestler, wrought upon by an unclean spirit, suffered terribly in his head and all his limbs and came to the Saint for healing. Theodore prayed over him and gave him wine and oil: 'Go, my son,' he said, 'to your home and when you lie down to sleep on your bed in the evening anoint yourself with the wine and oil and whatever you see in a dream come and tell me.' The next day the wrestler returned and said that in his sleep he had seen a young man wearing a cloak and 'coming to me, as it seemed, from your holiness: he seized me by the hair of my head and drew me to himself and immediately all the pain was drawn off from my joints and bones and from all my limbs and through my hair there came forth, as it were, a violent wind'. The man was cured and Theodore explained to him that the young man whom he had seen in his sleep was Christ's glorious martyr, George.

89

Mannas, one of the leading guardsmen of the Court, suffered from a terrible, secret, internal malady caused by the working of the Devil. He came several times to the Saint, but was ashamed to tell him of his illness. So on one of his visits the Saint took him aside privately and brought him to his cell and with a smile he said: 'Many times, my son, you have come to me in order to pluck up courage and tell me some secret and you have checked yourself. Why do you do this, my son? Can't you just once pluck up courage and tell me secretly what the matter is?' Mannas then told him everything, begged for healing and implored the Saint to come and bless all those of his household. The Saint fixed a day for the visit and dismissed him. Theodore paid his visit, and that night the

silentiary, as usual, was sorely troubled and the Saint prayed
that he might be delivered from his malady. And on that same
night after the psalms for the day had been sung, one of his
disciples named Julianus saw in a dream the Saint standing by
the sea shore and there came to him the silentiary carrying in
his arms a great three-headed wild goose which was screeching
loudly, and he brought it to the Saint. Theodore grasped it
and it became a kitten* and was thrown by him into the depths
of the sea. The next day after the morning service they were
sitting at breakfast when the Saint said to the silentiary:
'Courage! my son: give glory to God, for I believe that in His
goodness He has driven away from you your malady: from
to-day it will trouble you no more.' Then the disciple remembered and recounted his dream. The guardsman was cured, and
the Saint blessed him, his wife, who was a fervent Christian,
and all his household and then returned to his cell.

90

The guardsman's wife, Theodora, besought the Saint on behalf of herself and her husband to tell her which of them would
die first. It was with great difficulty that the Saint was persuaded to do as she wished; he prayed to God and received a
revelation that her husband 'would be shortlived in comparison
with her'. Day after day with many tears she besought Theodore to pray to God that He would quickly transport her from
this present life. At last the Saint was persuaded and prayed
to his master Christ, Who has a ready ear, to grant her desire.
And assured by a divine revelation, he said to her: 'God has
granted your request; now look to yourself, for it will not be
many days before you die.' With great joy she set her affairs
in order, and after forty days she departed from human life.

91

Eutychius, the doorkeeper of Theodore, who was known as
Monosandalus, while he was asleep by the roadside was smitten
by a demon in his hand and all up his arm: his hand was
swollen and in a sling.* And as his custom was, he came to
the Saint to be blessed; Theodore asked him what was the
matter with his hand, and Eutychius replied that when he
awoke from sleep he had found his hand quite numb and after

that it had swelled up. The Saint took off the bandage and as
he felt the hand he prayed. The demon whose work the swel-
ling was began to run about in the man's arm, so the Saint
made the sign of the Cross on the man's shoulder lest the
demon should run up and kill him. The doorkeeper's hand
now began to be moved from side to side by the demon;
despite his embarrassment he could not keep his hand still.
But when the Saint seized it and rebuked the unclean spirit,
the movement stopped at once. Eutychius took home with him
oil that the Saint had blessed and, after anointing himself, in
three days he was healed.

92

A mistress brought her slave to the Saint: the demon who
had taken possession of the slave immediately grew violent and
refused to leave him. The Saint rebuked him and walked
round a limited space confining the demon within it and
condemning him to merciless punishments: 'Blessed be the
Lord', he said, 'the body of which you have taken possession*
shall not leave this house until you have gone out of it.' He
left the demon and went into his cell to recite the psalms for
the day. For many hours the demon within the sufferer was
tortured and then squatting down, because he had to remain
in the circumscribed space, he began to cry out in a piteous
voice: 'Servant of God, I am coming out, for I cannot bear this
punishment. Come and release me and I will come out. Don't
torture me more.' But the Saint came from his cell: 'Foul
spirit,' he said, 'It is not my wish that you come out now.' But
the demon shouted: 'Woe is me in my misery! It was an evil
day when I met with you. I beg you, loose me from this
circumscribed space. I have been punished enough. When do
you want me to come out?' The Saint said to him: 'I want you
to come out at midnight. You are freed from the circumscribed place: now restore the mind of the possessed.'* Then
the demon yielded. That night, when the Saint was awakened
in order to celebrate the midnight service, the slave leapt up
driven by the demon and began to suffer, while the demon
within him shouted out: 'The hour has come, come forth,
iron-eater, and bid me go out.' An hour later the servant of
God rebuked the demon in the name of Christ and ordered

him to come out. And the demon hurled the slave down at the Saint's feet and came out, and the slave was cured.

A slave-woman who had had a secret demon for thirteen years came to Theodore: he looked upon her with a severe expression and said the prayer used in the case of the demon-possessed and she was cured.

93

Three men possessed by demons came to the Saint. At that moment the Patriarch Kyriakus sent for Theodore, as he was accustomed to do. To two of the sufferers he gave relief at once, but the third he left to suffer terribly, for he was possessed by a demon who refused to yield. Theodore said to the demon: 'Since our most holy Patriarch has sent for me and I am not free to deal with you at the moment, stand in the same place while you are being tortured and don't move from it until I come back.' The Saint then went to the Patriarch and was with him for some hours. Sergius, deacon of the cathedral and attendant on the Patriarch, had a daughter who had been married for three years but was still childless. So Sergius placed his daughter and her husband by the winding stairway of the crypt — the so-called 'Side-Door' — and he besought the Saint's attendant, the sub-deacon John, who was in the office of Thomas, the treasurer, to bring Theodore down that way when he was leaving the Patriarch. This was done, and Sergius brought husband and wife within the gates and all three knelt at his feet and begged him to give them a child. But he said to them: 'Do not come to me, children, but to God and He will grant your request.' But since they still remained beseeching him, he took the girdles of both of them and put one on one side of him and the other on the other and kneeling between them he made his prayer and gave them the girdles to wear. And by the grace of Christ a boy was born to them nine months later. And the Saint having left by the so-called 'Side-Door', reached his lodging in the quarter of Euarane.* John the sub-deacon came with him to see if the demon had kept within the limit laid down for him. They found that he had not only kept the limit but was hanging above the ground. The demon swore by the Most-High that he would go out — only let the Saint spare him. But the Saint lashed him on the chest saying: 'Many a time have you agreed to this and have played me false. I will not give way to you.' But the demon with many oaths promised to go out that same night when the wood was struck* for service in the cathedral. And having received alleviation of his punishment, at the hour agreed upon the demon left the man and in the same way the other two sufferers having waited for three days with the Saint were cured at the hour of the midnight service.

94

A slave-girl named Theodora belonging to Theodore, deacon of the Church of the Virgin named after Orbikius and Notarius the treasurer, is made dumb by a demon and is cured by Theodore.

95

A girl eight years old, who had taken the monastic habit in the convent attached to the Cathedral, had remained dumb for three years. Her teacher brought her to the Saint imploring his help with tears. After prayers he told the teacher that she was to bring the child to him every morning and every evening so that he might pray over her. This was done, and one day he told the girl to open her mouth; he took hold of her tongue and over it he made the sign of the Cross and blew upon it three times, and bade her take a good drink. And immediately by the grace of God she spoke out loud exclaiming, 'I have drunk, master!' The crowd for a long time continued to shout the 'Kyrie eleeson' (Lord, have mercy!) and the girl went back with her teacher completely cured.

96

A woman who had suffered for ten years from an issue of blood came for the Saint's blessing, bringing an alabaster box with myrrh in it. Round Theodore she saw a great press of people and secretly mixed with the throng hoping to pour the myrrh on his feet. Knowing this, the Saint gathered his feet up underneath him and called out to her: 'Cease, woman; what do you intend to do? This is a grievous thing which you have planned to do to me', and in fear the woman gave him the myrrh and besought him to pray for her. And he prayed and said to her, 'The Lord Jesus Christ, Who knoweth secrets, will give effect to the mediation of the holy martyr George according to your faith and He will fulfil your request'. And immediately through God's grace the flow of blood was stayed and, declaring to all the miracle, she glorified God.

97

It happened that one of the children of the Emperor Maurice fell ill of an incurable disease (for many sores had broken out on the child's body, so that it seemed to be a case of elephantiasis, a disease which some call 'Paulakis', and others 'Kleopatra') and, although the physicians had tried many remedies, nothing had done the child any good.

So the Emperor sent for the holy man and had him fetched from the city to the palace at Hiereia* (for thither the Emperor had made a progress and there the child was lying); the servant of God said a prayer over the child and blessed some water; he bathed the child with it and left the rest for a further treatment; and through his holy prayer the child was cured of the disease and was restored to health. And at the invitation of the Emperor and the Augusta he dined with them and then he took his leave of them after giving them his blessing, and went his way, journeying to his own country, and thus reached his monastery.

98

A certain householder in the village of Alectoria had a savage ox that would not submit to the yoke, so he led it to the monastery, fell at the Saint's feet and begged him to make the sign of the Cross over it so that by his prayers the savageness should be driven out of it. The Saint went out to the ox, who was tossing its head wildly from one side to the other, and snorting, and took hold of its horns and prayed that the savageness might be expelled from it and that it might become docile; then he made the sign of the Cross upon it and said, 'I bid you in the name of Christ, cease your raging and submit to the yoke quietly, for God appointed you to that, and be obedient to your master'. As the Saint spoke, the beast ceased to rage, and the man led it back from the monastery to the village where his wagon was, and yoked it to it and it submitted to the yoke with great docility and the man was rejoiced thereat.

99

(*Summary*)   Similarly a woman's wild mule is rendered docile to drive or ride. Theodore did the same thing in the case of horses and various animals.

100

The blessed man greatly longed to find some relics of the glorious and victorious martyr George, and prayed to the latter to satisfy this longing. Now Aemilianus, the very holy bishop of Germia, had a piece of the martyr's head and one finger of a hand and one of his teeth and another small piece. So the martyr appeared to the bishop and exhorted him to give these relics to his servant Theodore for the church that the latter had built in his honour. The bishop sent to the monastery to the servant of God and invited him to come and offer up prayers in the venerable church of the Archangel in order that he might welcome him and give him the much-desired relics of the martyr. Theodore was filled with joy by this promise and left the monastery and went to the town of Germia and offered up prayer in the church of the Archangel. The very holy bishop, Aemilianus, welcomed him warmly, and then conducted him to the monastery of the Mother of God, called of Aligete.

101

At that time there was a great drought in the metropolis of Pessinus and the fruits of the trees and crops were withering. Consequently when the men of that metropolis heard that the servant of God, Theodore, was the guest of the Bishop Aemilianus in the monastery of Aligete, they hastened to him. Their headmen (domestikoi) and the clergy and a goodly number of the people came to this monastery of the Mother of God — a distance of some fifteen miles — and after receiving permission from the Bishop Aemilianus they took the servant of Christ and led him to their own city in order that they, too, might entertain him and that by his prayers their country might obtain rain from heaven. Now there was a garden about six miles from their city, and in this garden was a swarm of locusts which were ruining all the young vegetables. When the owner of the garden heard of the inspired man's approach he ran a distance of three miles from his garden to meet him, and falling at his feet, told him of the damage which the locusts had done to his garden. Theodore said to him, 'Go, son, and bring me some water in a pot'. So the man ran and fetched some water from the river close at hand and brought it to him. After the servant of God had blessed the water, he gave it to him, saying, 'Go back and water the four corners of your garden with this and the Lord will fulfil thy desire'. The man returned to his garden with all speed, and did this; and when he returned to the spot which he had watered first, he did not find a single locust. He went out again in the evening and found in the same way that all the locusts had vanished, so he filled his hands with all kinds of vegetables and went out in great haste to find Theodore whom he recognized as in very truth a worker of miracles.

Now the procession from the city had met Theodore some three miles beyond the city walls. Whilst he was entering the city with the procession, the owner of the garden came up and fell at his feet and offered him the vegetables he was carrying proclaiming the wonder worked for him. When the Saint had entered the city the most blessed metropolitan George went to greet him and received him with joy; and Theodore, the servant of Christ, bade him announce a religious procession for the morrow. When the morning came the whole town was gathered together in the principal Catholic church of the Holy Wisdom. After offering up prayer the blessed Theodore and the metropolitan George with all the people marched in procession, singing a litany, to the venerable church of the Holy Hosts of Angels outside the walls. And there they read the Gospel and returned again in procession, singing a litany, to the church of the Holy Wisdom. The saintly man at the desire of the metropolitan celebrated Communion, at the same time beseeching the merciful God to send down rain upon their country. After all had partaken and had sat down to a feast, the sky became overcast and that same day rain fell so heavily over the whole of their land that for two or three days there were streams of water and the land to the west of the town was impassable owing to the flooding of the river; and they all rejoiced and glorified God Who shewed kindness to His creatures at the request of His servants. And so, escorted by the metropolitan and the citizens, the holy and blessed Theodore left the city and went back to the Bishop Aemilianus; from him he received the relics of the holy martyr George, which had endured much suffering, and after embracing him and taking his leave he quickly reached his holy monastery with great joy.

102

In those days Stephen, the Bishop of Cadossia* (which is under the jurisdiction of Nicomedia) came in a litter; for he suffered from gout in his hands and was paralysed in all his limbs and could not even convey his food to his mouth with his own hands, but his attendants had to supply his every need. He was carried thus into the church of the Archangel and fell at the blessed Theodore's feet crying and saying, 'Have pity upon me, servant of the most high God and amongst all the others grant that I, too, may have my share in your miracles; for I know that God will give you whatsoever you ask'. When the servant of Christ heard that he was a bishop, he was grieved at his act of obeisance and implored him to rise; then standing in prayer he besought God to dispel the bishop's diseases. After the prayer he ordered him to be laid on the right hand side of the church of the holy martyr George, that is, in the adjoining oratory of the holy martyr Plato (where Theodore's own cage stood), and he said to the bishop, 'Be of good courage, my lord, for I trust to the goodness of God to release you from this sickness shortly'. He also blessed and gave to him some oil for anointing himself and in two weeks the bishop was restored to health and after he had received the blessing of Theodore he left the monastery 'walking and leaping and praising God'.[1]

103

(*Summary*) A cleric, Solomon, and his wife, of Heliopolis, both troubled by evil spirits, were healed after a short stay, and in gratitude for their cure the man presented a picture for

[1] Acts iii. 8.

the oratory of the church of the Archangel where he used to sleep. Another man from the village of Salmania, afflicted by a violent and uncontrollable demon, came to the Saint who had him put in the stocks. By the Saint's daily prayer over him the demon was burnt out and disappeared, and in a fortnight the man was completely cured and returned home.

104

It was about this period that a severe famine prevailed at one and the same time throughout the whole country; the brothers in the monasteries, together with the guests entertained there, came to the end of all their provisions. This happened in Lent when the blessed man was keeping his retreat in the monastery of the Mother of God. Two days therefore before Palm Sunday, Dionysius the cellarer went to him and told him: 'We have no supply of wheat', said he, 'either for our own use or for the reception of the crowd.' For on Palm Sunday Theodore was wont to come out of his cell and a great crowd gathered during those two days. The blessed Theodore said to him: 'Go to the store-room and sponge out the wheat-bins; put what you find on a clean dish and bring it here.' When it was brought, he bent his head and besought God the Provider, Who readily hears men's prayers, to grant him a supply of food for the monasteries; and after the prayer he said to the brother, 'Go in and place this wheat together with the dish under the altar of the all-holy Mother of God, and the Lord will send us food'. This was done and on the morrow some true lovers of Christ from a great distance came and brought him thirty large measures of wheat.

One day it happened that half the dough failed to ferment sufficiently, either because the flour could not be ground properly, or because the amount of wheat was insufficient; so the man honoured by God came to the kneading-troughs and blessed the dough that was fermenting in them, and through his holy prayer the troughs were filled with the leavened dough and it even overflowed from them. . . . (The chapter ends with the statement that influenced by Theodore's miracles of mercy many retired from the turmoil of life and entered both his and other monasteries.)

105

(*Summary*) Saint Theodore had much bodily suffering. From this we should learn not to be discouraged if we have to endure great pain or illness; it is God's way of profiting our souls; thus we should not pray for deliverance from weaknesses of the body. Like Saint Paul, Theodore had 'a thorn in the flesh'[1] — a wound which, as no attention was paid to it, grew worse, and, since it was rubbed by his rough hair-tunic, bled profusely. This wound Theodore said was God's benediction; it would until his last prayer be with him, and for it he continued to give thanks.

106

In addition to this he was afflicted every year by a painful affection of the eyes which lasted about a month and a half in the summer season; for this suffering, too, he was thankful beyond measure, but it made him unfit for receiving crowds. On account of this affection he was inspired by God to travel to the church of Our Lady, the Mother of God, which is in Sozopolis.* For he had had the desire for a long time to have sight of the divine bounty manifested there; and it certainly was fitting that witness should be borne to him by the divine power displayed there, and that he should save some folk from dangers on his journey.

As he was approaching the bridge called Tautaendia, Pherentinus, the innkeeper there, heard that he would be passing, so he sent a messenger to meet him imploring him to enter the inn and leave with him his blessing, as he had been lying half-dead for a long time and his face was twisted right round to the back.

So the holy Theodore went in to him and asked how this thing had happened. The innkeeper replied, 'I was standing outside my inn, sir, when a black dog came up and stood in front of me and yawned, which made me quite against my will yawn in the same way, and forthwith the dog disappeared from my sight! Directly afterwards I was seized with fever, I took to my bed and my face was turned round backwards. Oh servant of God, help me if you are able to! For at the time when my beasts were all dying, after you had said a prayer

---

[1] 2 Cor. xii. 7.

over them I did not lose a single one'. When he had finished speaking, the blessed man prayed over him and blew three times into his mouth, and after blessing some water he gave it to him saying, 'Drink some of this and rub yourself with it; for the thing you saw which cast a spell upon you was a demon; but in the name of Christ I hope we shall find you well when we return from our pilgrimage.' And he left the inn and continued his journey.

107

(*Summary*) As Theodore approached Amorion a child with crooked feet who could not walk was brought to him and healed. In Amorion the son of the 'illustris' John, a youth eighteen years old, who had been paralysed for three years, was carried into Theodore's presence. He had been hare-hunting with his father and at the second cast* his spear had stuck into him and the paralysis had followed. Theodore directed that the youth should be taken outside the city walls to the house of the 'illustris' Anastasius and laid in the oratory there, dedicated to the Virgin, where Theodore intended to lodge.

A procession met Theodore and prayers were said through the streets of the city until the cathedral was reached. Here the bishop, who through illness could not take part in the procession, asked Theodore to celebrate the Communion. On his return to the house of Anastasius, Theodore took oil and anointed the face, hands, feet and all the paralysed limbs of the youth; he then bade him stand up; 'Know', he said, 'that you are well, that your father may not be pained on your account.' The youth nodded his head and the Saint gave him his hand and raised him up and he was cured.

108

And leaving Amorion he came to Eucarpolis, and as he was on the point of entering the church of the Mother of God, behold! there lay a man stricken of palsy by a demon, for the unclean spirit had lain concealed in him for several years and had not shown itself, for the ever-Virgin Mother of God was reserving this great miracle for her servant. At that minute the paralytic suddenly leapt up and began to be tormented and met Theodore with these cries, 'Oh violence, why have you come here, iron-eater, with George the Cappadocian to my open shame? I have lain hidden so many years, and now through you I am found out!' and all who saw it were filled with amazement. But the blessed man rebuked the unclean spirit by prayer and by the sign of the Cross and cured him who had been paralysed.

Then he entered the venerable church of the all-holy Virgin Mary, the Mother of God, where the God-given myrrh flows, and stretched out his arms, and standing thus in the shape of a cross, he prayed and steadfastly gazed at the miraculous* 'Icon of the myrrh' opposite him. By divine working, the myrrh gathered into a bubble and then rained down plentifully upon his eyes and anointed his whole face so that all who witnessed this divine testimony said, 'Verily he is a worthy servant of God'.

109

(*Summary*) On his way home after a stay of forty days in Sozopolis, where he lodged in the house of the bishop Zoilos, he passed through Amorion and stayed in the house of John whose paralysed son he had cured; he went to Germia to visit the bishop, Aemilianus, and on leaving him passed the inn by the bridge Tautaendia over the river Sagaris where the grateful innkeeper Pherentinus gave him a horse out of his stud as thank-offering for his complete recovery.

110

(*Summary*) Two ladies of senatorial rank belonging to the aristocracy of Ephesus came to Theodore's monastery; they were carried in litters with a large train of servants. They brought their children to the Saint to be healed; the one had a son Andreas, a young man of twenty who was dumb, and the other had a little girl of eight, who was paralysed. Theodore ordered them to stay a few days. One morning about the third hour he went out after the psalm-singing to bless and dismiss the crowd, as his custom was, and found the little girl lying in the church, so he went to her and signed her with the Cross and prayed over her. After dismissing the crowd he called to the little girl to come to him, and she arose and came. He also made the sign of the Cross over the young man and told his mother that he would begin to speak on their journey home. Some time later an acquaintance of the ladies came to the monastery from Ephesus and reported that the young man had spoken.

III

(*Summary*) Theodore cures the nephew of Florentius, the chief elder of the village of Sandos. He suffered from an incurable malady—the so-called 'phugadaina'*—which had attacked the corner of his mouth and begun to eat away his flesh.

Florentius takes his nephew with him on horseback to the Saint. Theodore rubbed with his hand the part afflicted, blew three times into his mouth and gave him water which he had blessed, and he was then restored to health.

112

Every year on the Saturday after the Ascension of our Lord Jesus Christ a public procession regularly came to the monastery from all the neighbouring villages. Once when at this festival great crowds had poured in from the countryside a cauldron of hot water happened to be standing at the foot of the slope in a ditch at the side of the road and it had a fire under it. After the service was over and the crowds had finished their meal and were getting ready to leave the monastery, a boy came out of the church of St. George and ran to put his belongings into safe-keeping.* As his path lay close to the cauldron, through the Devil's operation he fell, as he ran, into the boiling cauldron.

His parents who were behind him ran and seized him by the feet and pulled him out and carried him to the church of St. George where the Saint was still blessing the people; they threw the child down at his feet half-dead and broke out into lamentations over the accident which threatened their boy's life.* The servant of the Lord laid the child near the sacred altar and bending his head, began to pray for him. After anointing the child with oil from the 'sleepless' lamp he raised him up by the grace of God and after leading him three times* round the altar he gave him back to his parents with his flesh whole and the skin uninjured.

113

Now Anicetus, the abbot of the monastery of the holy martyr Theodore of Briania, came with the folk in the procession. When he had heard of the boy's accident and seen him well with his skin unhurt, he thought that the water in the cauldron was in fact cold; as he wished to test the miracle, forthwith as he passed by with the procession he put his hand into the cauldron to see whether it would be burned or not; he was burnt immediately and badly hurt. The Saint had joined the procession below the monastery and was dismissing the crowds when the abbot Anicetus came to him and shewed him his hand and asked him to sign it with the Cross, saying that it had been burnt by the man in charge of the cauldron. But the Saint smiled and said, 'Oh no, brother! you thrust it into the cauldron yourself; nevertheless, we may pray that the Lord may heal it', and after Theodore had made the sign of the Cross upon it, the abbot was relieved of the burning and felt no pain and went home marvelling at the things he had seen and heard.

114

In the village of Sandos in the district of Protomeria a certain householder, Eutolmius by name, wanted to enlarge his threshing-floor because of the rich abundance of crops that had been given him and because the floor could not take a double yoke of oxen; close to it was a hillock in which there were many demons. Now as he dug and was levelling the ground in a circle round his floor he happened to dig into the neighbouring hillock and remove a stone out of it. And unclean spirits came forth and entered into the animals in the village and made them savage, and later began to work their mischief also upon the villagers.

After some of them, both men and women, had been tormented the spirits which were in them cried out that these disasters were happening to them because of the digging into the hillock. When the villagers saw the distress of their own people and thought that Eutolmius had dug in order to get money out of the hill, when they heard also that the governor of the province, Euphrantas, was preparing to take action against them in the matter for having brought the charge

against Eutolmius, they grew mad against the householder
and rushed to burn down him and his household as being
responsible for their ill-fortune. But as this attempt was foiled
by those who held the highest positions in the village and
wished to restore peace, they sent to the monastery begging
the Saint and servant of Christ, Theodore, to come to the
village and free them from the evils which had befallen them.
The Saint came back with them and standing on the place
which had been dug, he said to them, 'Believe me, children,
nothing has happened in this spot according to your sus-
picions; but in order that you may be more fully satisfied, make
the hole much deeper'. When this was done, they found
nothing whatever suspicious. So as they were fully satisfied,
on the morrow he made arrangements for a procession and in
company with them he led the procession with prayer round
the village — and the persons who were being tormented
followed him, too — and came to the hillock which had been
dug open; as he bent his head and prayed, all the spirits which
had come out of it and worked mischief among the beasts and
in various places were quickly collected to that spot. The
Saint then turned to the afflicted and rebuked the unclean
spirits that were in them, and by invocation to his master,
Christ, he cast them out, and by the power of his prayer to
God and by the visitation of the Holy Spirit he shut them all
up there. After putting back the stone which had been thrown
out and filling up the trench with earth, he placed above it a
model of the Holy Cross and stayed there sleepless the whole
night, singing and praying to God.

115

The next day he had read the liturgy and was on the point
of going back to his monastery, when the chief men of the
village of Permctaia came there and fell at his feet beseeching
him with tears to come to their village, too, because there
through a slab of stone having been removed from a certain
spot many demons came out and afflicted six men and eight
women of the village. So the Saint and servant of Christ,
Theodore, came out and went away with them together with
the chief men of the village of Sandos. As they drew near the

village of Aiantoi, by the working of those unclean demons because of whom he was travelling, the animal on which he was sitting fell in a heap and slipping down, he fell on the hinder parts of the beast; when it tried to get up the two boards which had formed the seat came backwards and landed under the Saint's stomach and crushed him, and owing to the great pressure they cut through his hair-garments and were driven a good way into his flesh. Much blood flowed out, so he took a linen rag, applied it to the wound in his body, and mounting his beast again, journeyed on with his companions and said with a smile, 'Truly, children, God's help protects me; for the unclean demons attacked me to injure me'. On arrival at the village his companions thought he would fall into some illness through the horrible wound he had received, but, mightily strengthened by the grace of the Holy Spirit, he stood like an iron statue through that night and without sleeping continued in praise to God.

On the morrow after praying he led a procession with prayer round the village and after ordering the slab to be replaced to its former position he went himself to the spot with the procession and after praying for a brief space of time and calling upon the name of the holy, consubstantial and life-giving Trinity, he cast out the spirits that were in people, and as they came out he drove them together and confined them in that place and for the future they did no harm to anybody. For in these cases he had also working with him the holy great martyr George, who had followed him closely from his earliest years. After marking the spot with the sign of the holy Cross, together with those who had come with him from the village of Sandos, he departed and regained his monastery. He also sent a letter to Euphrantas, the governor, and stopped him from proceeding against them by satisfying him that the digging in the hillock was not done for the sake of treasure but at the instigation of Satan. And thus he dismissed to their homes the householders of the village of Sandos who had come with him.

And at another time, when the vines of the same village of Sandos were devoured by a plague of locusts, and the vines of the men of the village of Permetaia were being eaten up by worms, through Theodore's presence and prayers in both these places all the pests were smitten dead at once, lying about in heaps to the glory of Christ our God, Who gave Theodore such grace.

116

Again, in the village of Eukraae in Lagantine there was a farmer, Timotheus by name, who happened to dig into the side of a hill, which bordered his land, whether in order to improve the adjoining property which belonged to him or in order to carry off some treasure I cannot say. For the report spread abroad that he had done it in search of money. Thereupon the great army of unclean spirits who dwelt in it came out and attached themselves to the persons of that village and most of the men with their wives and children were grievously tormented; and the spirits caused such disorders and such breakages that Euphrantas, the then governor of the metropolis of Ancyra, hearing of this, decided to send and arrest the aforesaid farmer, Timotheus, and subject him to a heavy fine for having broken open a grave. And through the working of the spirits in the possessed the governor seized some of the sufferers on account of the disorders caused by them, and inflicted many strokes with an oxhide whip on their naked bodies, thinking by these means to reduce them to quietness. But the men who were beaten, instead of weeping and asking for greater leniency, were on the contrary seized with uncontrollable laughter, begging that more strokes should be inflicted on them, and when released they went off madly to commit still more villainies and disorders. For first of all they went in a body and burnt down the granaries belonging to Timotheus, the cause of their being possessed by the demons, and him they tried to catch and kill, but he had fled. Then in the same way they went round and burnt down the other granaries in the village, and roaming round they would enter all their own houses and put up all they could find and they spoiled and smashed up all the furniture and wrought much havoc in their own homes, and if any spoke to them wishing to stop them they rained blows upon them. Such things as these were done not only in the case of men through their being possessed by the demons, but they further killed some of the animals, others they made savage, and they became

unmanageable and smashed things up and the spirits hovered
about the confines of their land and raised apparitions causing
great harm to the passers-by, and so there was an accumulation
of distress in that village and its borders. A few of the householders of the village, however, were free from the demons,
and they with their clergy came to the monastery to the Saint
and fell down and clasped his feet beseeching him with many
strong oaths to take pity on their populous village which was
in the throes of great misery. So the Saint yielded and went
with them; all the people of the village met him, both the
healthy and the possessed, while the unclean spirits roundly
cursed him. On reaching their church of the holy Archangel,
he remained the whole night in hymns and prayers begging
the merciful God to drive away the army of demons both from
man and beast and all the neighbourhood and to drive them
all back again to the place from which they came out and to
shut them all up there. At dawn all the inhabitants of the
village came to him in a body; the spirits in those who were
possessed called out that they were suffering violence at his
hands, since he had come out against them and was making
intercession to God. But the God-inspired man, strong in the
divine grace bestowed upon him, rebuked them as if they were
cheap little boys destined to slavery, and commanded them to
go away to the hill from which they had come and to enter it
again and stay there, harming no one.

117

Owing to illness he deputes one of his elders, named
Julianus, to go to the hill in his place and take the service and
reimprison the demons. After some demur Julianus obeys and
is successful.

118

Another time a similar thing happened in the same village.
For a marble sarcophagus stood at a certain spot on their
boundary and it contained the skeletons of some Greeks (i.e.
pagans) of ancient times which were guarded by demons; by
the latters' suggestion the following idea occurred to some of
the householders of the village; they came and opened the said

chest and took off the covering, or lid, and carried it to their village and placed it there to serve as a water-trough. Because of this many of the inhabitants of the village were again vexed by demons, and their beasts and properties were likewise injured.

So again they went and fetched the servant of God and by his prayers to God he healed all those who had been bewitched by the unclean spirits and freed the beasts and the district from the harm wrought by them and bound them down in the place where they had been before. Nor did he allow the lid of the sarcophagus to be given back to the spirits as they desired, asking that it should be restored to its former position; but he left it in the village as it was useful for the water-supply, and it is there to this day as witness of his marvellous works.

In the villages nearest to Eukraae, called Buna, Peae* and Hynia, a huge swarm of beetles appeared in the cornfields and ate up their summer crops; so the men of these three villages implored the Saint to come. He went with them to their plain, and as soon as he had offered a prayer, the whole swarm of beetles vanished and was never seen again.

119

Many similar wondrous works were done by him in various places to the glory of our Saviour, Christ our God, Who gave him these signs of His grace. One day before the murder of the Emperor Maurice[1] when the Saint was in the monastery of the Mother of God and was reciting the proper psalms for the day in the newly-built sanctuary, the 'sleepless' lamp went out. He made a sign to one of the brothers and had it lighted, and at once it went out; again the brother came and with many a prayer re-lighted it, but it went out immediately.

The blessed Saint found fault with him for his clumsiness, and went and himself lighted the lamp. Directly he had moved away, it went out again, as before. Then he gathered together the brothers who were there and spoke to them very solemnly as follows: 'I assure you, brothers, this sign has not been given us without cause or to no purpose. Therefore

[1] A.D. 602.

examine yourselves and consider what you have done, and confess your sin before God; for even if you wish to hide it, the Lord wills to make it known.' And when in response to this appeal the brothers declared that they were not conscious of any sin, he stood in prayer beseeching God to reveal to him the meaning of this sign. And God granted him a revelation, and he became very cast down and groaned and said, 'Very truly didst thou picture the nature of man, blessed Isaiah, for "Every man", it is written, "is grass and all the glory of man is as the flower of grass; the grass has withered and its flower has fallen." '[1] When he had said these words the brothers came and asked him to tell them what had been revealed to him. After enjoining them not to speak of it to anyone, he announced to them the manner of death by which the Emperor Maurice should die. They said, 'He deserves his fate for he has in many things governed ill, especially in the things which he is doing now'. The Saint replied, 'This man, children, will shortly be removed, and after him worse things shall happen, such as this generation does not expect'.

120

After a few days the Emperor Maurice was assassinated and Phocas usurped the throne. Domnitziolus, his nephew, was made a patrician and 'curopalates' and dispatched to the East by the Emperor to take over the army and make a stand against the Persian nation, which was invading and lording it over our country.* When this famous man arrived at Heliopolis, and heard of the raid of the Lazi* into Cappadocia and of the conspiracy of the patrician Sergius,* the Emperor's father-in-law, against him, he was in great distress and fear as he did not dare to proceed with his journey as he had been bidden. He had heard about the servant of God, so he came to him in the monastery and falling at his feet besought his prayers and begged him to give him good advice, as he was at a loss and did not know what he ought to do. He told him of the orders given to him by the Emperor and of the difficulty created by the invasion of the Lazi; the servant of God said to him, 'Go straight along thy way, son, in the name of God; you

[1] Is. xl. 7.

need have no fear of them, they will not hinder you, but you will reach your army in safety. However, in your war with the Persians things must take their appointed course*; you are going to experience great trials and conflicts, but I commend you to God and to his holy martyr George to keep you free from harm. When these dangers beset you, you will remember my prayer and God will rescue you from your great peril.' When he had told him of these and other things which were to come, he prayed over him and dismissed him on his journey. And according to Theodore's prophecy he accomplished his journey without hindrance through the grace of God, as the Lazi had retreated; and he found that all things happened exactly as the Saint had foretold.

In the war against the Persians he fell into an ambush; great slaughter was wrought on his army, and he himself was in sore straits. Then he remembered what had been foretold to him by the inspired man, and he called upon his prayers to come to his aid. Fleeing on foot to a bed of reeds, he hid himself there and by God's assistance he escaped from danger and got back into the Roman camp and reassembled his army.

On his journey back to the Emperor he visited the blessed man and falling at his feet in deep devotion he rendered thanks to God and acknowledged the help which the Saint's prayers had brought to him — how they had saved him from great perils — and he confessed that all things had happened to him just as Theodore had foretold.

Afterwards, when this distinguished man had been blessed by the Saint and had celebrated a feast-day, he went on his way to the imperial city. From that time forth he cherished a deep affection and trust for the servant of God, and for the holy monastery, and whenever he passed through the village by the imperial post on his way to the capital from the East, he used to go up on foot to visit the Saint in the monastery and would prostrate himself before him. He gave such bountiful alms to the oratories of the monastery that from them leaden tiles were made for the church of the holy martyr George and many precious things were acquired. He also used to distribute much money to the poor who happened to be there; and owing to his reverence for the Saint he always granted the requests of those who desired audiences from him.*

121

(*Summary*)   Relates the cure from severe gastric trouble of
Phocas, an imperial secretary, coming from the capital. The
cure is effected on the homeward journey at the bridge over
the river Siberis.

122

(*Summary.*) A blind cleric, a treasurer of one of the towns
in the neighbourhood of Sebasteia,* crawls to Theodore's feet
and begs him to cure him. However, he is bidden to rest two
days and then go home again. He obeys reluctantly, spends
the night at Arania (five miles from Sykeon), and on washing
next morning his sight is restored to him. He wished to return
to the Saint but did not venture to do so without his consent.
So he sent a messenger to report that he was healed and to ask
if he should come. Theodore told him to continue his journey
giving glory to God.

123

(*Summary*)   A sea captain from Kalleoi in Pontus, by name
Theodoulus, was afflicted with a demon under his skin, which
appeared in the shape of a mouse.* When the Saint put his
hand on the man's body he felt the demon running about as
though trying to escape. He confined it to the captain's arms
and after prayer he made the sign of the Cross over the arm,
and the demon disappeared and the man was cured.

124

One day the headman, Antipatrus by name, from the village
of Aiantoi, the priest Demetrius, dear unto God, of the village
of Silindoucomis, and Aetius, the headman from the village of
Alectoria, honourable men, came to the Saint when he was in
the nunnery of Saint Christopher; at dinner time he invited
them to dine with him. Now it happened that the stewing-pot
had been left uncovered and, by the machinations of the
wicked one, a green lizard fell into the vegetables that were
being boiled and got boiled with them; when the servant
placed the dish on the table, he kept back some of the vegetables in which the creeping thing still remained. When the
Saint had given thanks, they ate the vegetables placed before

them, and then he told the servant to set what remained before them, so he emptied out the rest and served it to them. As they ate, the green lizard was discovered, and on recognizing it they cried out saying, 'Oh holy father, we are dead men, we are dead men! what shall we do? for this creature is the venomous green lizard'. While they were lamenting and commiserating themselves — since they would never, they exclaimed, see their children and wives again — the servant of God said to them, 'Do not fear, children, for if you trust God and believe me, the humble Theodore, you will take no harm at all; for the God invoked by Elisha the prophet when the gourd fell into the pot[1] is still the same true God Who said, "If you drink any deadly thing it shall in no wise hurt you." '[2] After preparing a draught and blessing the cup, he gave it to them to drink and not one of them suffered any ill. On the morrow he dismissed them while they glorified God.

125

Again, a man called George, a Cappadocian, was passing along the public road, bound with chains about his neck, hands and feet, and in the custody of a strong contingent of the imperial guard and soldiers. He was charged, they said, with making insurrection against the Emperor Phocas. This man eagerly desired to go up to the Saint and be deemed worthy of his prayers, and as his guard had the same wish, they ascended to the monastery with him, and after praying in the oratories of the saints, they also went to the cell in which the Saint was. After doing reverence to him they received his blessing. The guards besought him to advise the captive to behave himself reasonably on the journey and not to harbour any evil designs against himself or against one of them, so that they themselves might not run the risk of punishment at the Emperor's hands. And this the Saint did, admonishing the prisoner from the Holy Scriptures, saying, 'Things here are temporal, son, but things there are eternal; and it is good that one who has suffered violence from another should die like just Abel, and God's blameless priest, Zacharias, and the holy John the Baptist, and Christ's holy apostles and martyrs,

[1] 2 Kings iv. 38-41.　　[2] Mark xvi. 18.

rather than meditate injury to himself and become subject to eternal condemnation. For think of this, son; if you undergo death either for the crime of which you are now accused or for any other reason, accept it willingly as thereby taking your punishment in this world and going away guiltless to the next life. But if you are innocent of any crime and are to suffer death unjustly here, you will receive a crown from God like his saints who were violently put to death.' With these and many other words from the sacred Scriptures the man's despair was cured and he then asked to be allowed to partake of the Holy Mysteries. The Saint said to the soldiers who held him, 'Shew honour, my sons, to our Master's Holy Mystery, and loose this man from his chains until he has partaken; for it is not right that a faithful man should be in bonds to receive the Christ Who suffered for us and loosed us from the bonds of Hades'. But they said he must excuse them, as they did not dare to do it because the man was brave, and if perchance he were to commit any folly, they would no longer be able to restrain him. The inspired man then took the holy cup of the Communion to give to him and looking up to heaven groaned, whereupon the captive's fetters were immediately loosened and the chains which bound him fell to the ground with a clatter. The guards were alarmed and ran to the doors and bolted them to prevent his running out and escaping from them, but the Saint said to them, 'Do not be afraid of him at all, for I know the man's mind and he will not commit any folly'. After administering the Holy Mysteries to him he arranged for him to have a meal together with his guards; after that his chains were put on again and they went their way.

126

On the sixteenth of July, when the festival of the holy martyr and athlete for Christ, Antiochus, was being celebrated in his oratory, the Saint was officiating. When he took the paten according to the custom of the country to raise the holy bread on high, and was beginning to chant the 'Holy things to the Holy', the consecrated bread began to manifest openly in the sight of all present that the offering of the celebrant was acceptable, for it made the motions of one that skipped for joy by rising high above the paten and coming down with a little thump on to the paten. This was heard and seen by all, for the bread ascended and descended regularly so that all we who stood there and saw it were amazed and terrified at this mighty wonder, and the Saint himself, filled with exceeding joy, though weeping from contrition, joined with us in glorifying our God's unsurpassable goodness.

127

One day the true lover of Christ, Photius (a well-known patrician who afterwards became exarch of Rome and whose son Gregory the Saint himself received at the holy font) came to him and stayed for the sacred Liturgy. Whilst the God-inspired man was making the oblation in the church of the holy great-martyr George, Photius observed that the holy bread of oblation was stale wheaten-bread, yet he noticed that much steam seemed to be rising from it and he concluded that the bread must be fresh and for this reason was steaming. At the moment of the administration of the sacrament when he went up to partake of the elements he found that the piece of bread given to him was exceedingly stale and he marvelled. After the dismissal of the congregation he approached the Saint, told him what he had seen and begged him to give him an explanation of it. The Saint replied, 'This sign has been shown to you, son, because you are worthy; for the grace of the saints is being collected and ascends from us into the heavens on account of our unworthiness and our sins in order that on earth our State may have experience of many afflictions and dangers; but let us pray to the God of pity that whatever He ordains, may be done in mercy'. When the distinguished patrician heard these words he wept, and after receiving the Saint's blessing he left the monastery and went his way.

When the folk of the towns and villages round about went in procession singing their litanies the little crosses that they carried in the procession began to jump about and make a rattle; it was a terrible and piteous sight to see. And when men asked the God-inspired man what it might mean, he said, 'Pray, my children, since great afflictions and disasters are threatening the world'.

128

(*Summary*) Domnitziolus sent to the Saint a gold cross for processions and worship; in its central boss Thomas (who had succeeded Kyriakus as Patriarch of Constantinople*) had the following relics inserted — a piece of the Holy Cross and a piece of the stone of Golgotha and a piece of the holy tomb of our Saviour God, and the hem of the Holy Virgin's tippet. Thomas asked the deacon Epiphanius, Theodore's 'apocrisiarius' whom he had sent to Constantinople to fetch the Cross, whether the story about the crosses in the religious processions in Galatia (ch. 127) was true, and on being assured that it was, he was terrified at this strange phenomenon, and wrote to Theodore, bidding him come up forthwith to the capital.

129

(*Summary*) The Saint restores to his senses Theodore, an imperial groom, who had come to him from Upper Pylae;* his mind had been deranged by the demons inhabiting his house. Theodore promises when on his way to the capital to pass through Pylae to bring salvation to his house.

130

(*Summary*) Philoumenus, the abbot of the monastery, dies and the priest, John, though against his will, consents to be appointed his successor. (He wanted to retire to the East but Theodore threatened that if he did not obey he would in future have no part with him.) Theodore starts for the capital and visits Dorylleon* on his way thus answering the prayers of the inhabitants and the monks and of his former disciples, Photius and Kerykus, the heads of the monastery of St. George called 'the Monastery of the Fountains'.

131

Near the monastery of the all-holy Mother of God at Katharae, Theodore, the imperial groom, met him (the one who had been a supplicant of the Saint's before) and conducted him to the port of Pylae where he worked various miracles. He also took him to his own house in Upper Pylae to free it from the great distress caused by the demons (see ch. 129). For both his servants and his beasts were bewitched by the unclean spirits, and when the members of the household were at breakfast or dinner, stones would be thrown at the tables, causing fear and great dismay; they also broke the women's looms. The whole house, too, was filled with mice and snakes which terrified the inhabitants and in fact made it quite uninhabitable. The servant of God entered into the house and stayed the night there, supplicating God by psalm-singing and prayers; and after he had blessed some water and sprinkled the whole house with it, he freed the owners from the demons' malignity.

132

(*Summary*) Theodore drives out the demon from a fellow-traveller in the boat when crossing from Pylae to Constantinople; the demon had been secretly active in the man for many years and during the crossing violently abused the Saint. The other passengers, not knowing that the man was possessed, told him to hold his peace and not malign the Saint in this scandalous and drunken fashion. Theodore beat upon the man's chest and making the sign of the Cross compelled the hidden demon to go out. The demon was seen by those in the boat to leave the man's mouth in the form of a mouse.

133

When Theodore disembarked at the imperial city the most blessed Patriarch, Thomas, received him and they embraced each other with much joy. Theodore also introduced to him his disciple John, whom he wished to be ordained abbot, bearing witness to his virtuous life. The Patriarch immediately agreed thereto, invested him with the pallium and appointed him abbot, escorting him to their own monasteries in the countryside.

The Emperor Phocas heard of the Saint's visit, and requested to see him (for he was confined to his bed with gout in his hands and feet). Theodore came to him and after he had laid his hand upon him and prayed over him, the Emperor was relieved of his disease. But when the Emperor asked him to pray for him and for his rule, the servant of Christ began to admonish him and said that if he wished to be always held in remembrance by him and wanted the Saint's prayers on his behalf to be effective, he must cease his killing of men and shedding of blood. If he were successful in this, 'then my prayers for you,' said Theodore, 'will be answered by God'. But if the Emperor persisted in his murderous ways, he foretold to him the woes that would come upon him through God's wrath; at these words the Emperor became very incensed against him.

134

When he had left the palace, the most blessed Patriarch, Thomas, would give Theodore no peace, for he held him in great respect and had such full confidence in him that after many entreaties he persuaded him to adopt him as a brother, and Theodore promised to ask of God that in the future life, too, they might not be separated from each other.

Next he asked him whether the tale about the extraordinary jumping of the little crosses during processional litanies was really true; and on learning from the Saint that the story told him about them was true, he began privately to beg him to explain to him what such a sign meant. However, Theodore, pleading his own insignificance and calling himself an abject sinner, asserted that he did not know how to answer the question. Then Thomas fell at his feet and held them and protested that he would not get up from the ground unless he consented to satisfy him on this point, saying, 'I know and am convinced that you understand not only this sign, but many others as well; for you cannot have been content up till now to consider this as of no account and not to seek an explanation of it; if, however, it has been concealed from you till this moment and you have not been anxious to learn about it, yet now if you ask God, He will certainly reveal it to you'. Then the servant of Christ, having consented to satisfy him, made him get up and weeping bitterly said to him, 'I did not wish you to be troubled, for it is not to your profit to learn these things. But since you insist, the shaking of the crosses portends many painful and dangerous things for us — it means instability in our faith and apostasy, and the inroads of many barbarous peoples, and the shedding of much blood, and destruction and captivity throughout the world, the desolation of the holy churches, the cessation of the divine service of praise, the fall and perturbation of the Empire and perplexity and critical times for the State; and further it foreshadows that the coming of the Adversary is at hand. Therefore do you, as governor of the Church and shepherd of the people, implore God continuously, as far as in you lies, to spare His people and to order these things with pity and with mercy'. At these words the most blessed Patriarch was seized with an agony of fear and began with tears to beg Theodore to pray God to take away his life and not let him be overtaken by any of the disasters he had foretold.

And from that time forth the Patriarch continually lived in retirement in his palace and poured out confessions to Theodore and besought him with tears saying, 'Since you have with your whole heart deigned to accept me as your brother and are thus so closely bound to me and to my welfare, pray to God on my behalf that He may take my spirit and that I may not see the dangers which are to come upon us. My courage fails me and I have not the strength to see these things come — and live'.

135

(*Summary*) The Patriarch Thomas earnestly prays Theodore to spend his yearly period of seclusion in the capital, as the city will soon need his presence. There was a fear that Constantinople might fall. He agrees thereto and after Christmas he shuts himself up in the diakonikon of the winter church of the monastery of St. Stephen or monastery of the Romans near the Petrion.* The Patriarch implores Theodore to pray to God to grant him a speedy release from the troubles threatening the Empire. After some resistance Theodore complies and God grants the prayer: the death of the Patriarch soon follows.

136

(*Summary*) Sergius is appointed patriarch and shows the same respect towards Theodore as Thomas had done: he pleads that he is young for his high office and needs Theodore's prayers. Theodore replies that his youth will give him courage to face the perils which threatened the Empire and promises him a long and worthy tenure of the patriarchate. Sergius constantly appeals to Theodore for advice.

137
(*Summary*) Many in Constantinople especially those in high
places were accustomed to go to the baths after communicating.
Theodore condemns the practice. A number of the cathedral
clergy come to Theodore and ask him whether this condemnation has support in scripture or is based on a special revelation.
Theodore replies that God had revealed to him that those who
take a bath after receiving the Eucharist through wantonness
and for bodily enjoyment commit a sin, 'For no one who has
anointed himself with myrrh and perfumes washes off the
pleasant scent thereof and no one who has lunched with the
Emperor straightway runs to the baths'.

138
(*Summary*) While in the monastery of the Romans Theodore
heals many sufferers amongst the crowds which resort to him
there. Zoilus, abbot of the monastery, witnesses the cure of a
demoniac.

139
(*Summary*) The monks together with the abbot Christo-
phorus wish to have a picture of Theodore as a permanent
memorial and to secure his blessing. They summon a painter
without Theodore's knowledge: he can only see the Saint
through a small aperture, but manages to produce a good likeness. Before Theodore left the monastery they asked him to
bless the portrait: he smiled at the bearer of the message: 'You
are a fine thief', he said, 'what are you doing here? We must
see to it that you don't run off with something!' Then he
blessed the painting, and dismissed the messenger.

140
(*Summary*) Domnitziolus, patrician and curopalates, asks
Theodore to visit him in Arcadianae. His wife Eirene has no
children: the saint blesses her and promises her three children
— and they will be boys. All the male and female slaves of the
household are brought to Theodore for his blessing. A slave
girl had long been ill, troubled by a hidden demon. He beats
on her breast and the demon declares itself. Then the Saint
laying her on the ground put his foot on her neck, turned his

eyes to the east and uttered a silent prayer. At the end of his
prayer he recited aloud the doxology of the Holy Trinity.
For some time the slave girl remained speechless and then was
completely cured. Later Eirene gave birth to three sons, as
the Saint had prophesied. The conception of her first son immediately followed the Saint's prayer. Emperor and Patriarch
say farewell to Theodore and he returns to his monastery.

141

(*Summary*) In the village of Skoudris near the monastery of
the Archangel there is a heavy hail-storm, the neighbouring
stream is in flood and destroys houses and crops, carrying men,
women, children and little babies in their cradles down into
the river Sagaris. The householders of the half of the village
which had not been ruined appeal to the Saint who comes to
the place, prays and sets up a cross, and thereafter even when
there were storms of snow and rain the stream was not flooded
and no one suffered damage.

142

About that time the inhuman consul Bonosus* was travelling
to the eastern parts of the Empire and as he passed near the
monastery he heard tell of the inspired man's holiness and felt
a reverence for it, violent and cruel though he was. So he sent
a messenger in advance to him beseeching him, if he could
endure the fatigue, to come down to the oratory of the holy
martyr Gemellus near the posting-station in order that he
might do reverence to him there and be deemed worthy of his
prayers, saying that he himself was unable to go up to the
monastery owing to the pressure of urgent affairs; so the Saint
went down and received him and whilst he was praying for
him the consul stood but did not bend his neck, so the Saint
took hold of the hair of his forehead and pulled it and in this
way bent his head down (virtue is wont to act thus with courage
and not fear human authority 'For the righteous', it is said, 'is
bold as a lion'[1].) We who were present were thunder-struck
and terrified at the just man's daring and imagined that the
consul would turn insolent and furious, for we knew well by
report that his savagery was like that of a wild beast. But he

[1] Prov. xxviii. 1.

readily accepted the prayer and the rebuke and showed honour to the Saint by kissing his hands, and then putting his hand on his own chest because of a pain which oppressed him he begged the Saint to pray that he might be freed from it. But the Saint gently tapped with his fingers on the consul's chest and said to him, 'You must first pray that your inward man may be reformed and grow healthy; for when that is healed, the outward man, too, will be restored to health; therefore I will pray for you and do you devote yourself to the good and fear God in order that my prayers may be effective. But if I pray and you neglect to amend your ways, my prayers will be unavailing. Be merciful then and pitiful to all Christian people and do not use harshly the authority entrusted to you, but while examining your own consciousness of sins, sympathize with those that go astray and never shed innocent blood. For if there is to be punishment for the mere insult of a spoken word — for calling another a "fool" — how much more will blood, shed unjustly, be avenged by God?' These counsels the Saint gave him like a man sowing seed in unfruitful ground, and the consul fetched out a few coins and offered them to him in token of gratitude. But as the Saint did not deign to accept them, he drew back his hand and took out some 'trimisia'* begging the Saint at least to accept those and to give one to every brother in the monastery. But before looking at them Theodore said, 'There are only fifty and not sufficient for giving one to each, however, they can be changed into smaller money and then distributed equally'. But the consul marvelled at his discerning words, as being God-inspired and answered, 'Yes, reverend father, by thy holy prayers, there are only fifty as your holy mouth has said; however, I will send as many more at once as are needed to make up the number'. This he did, for after being dismissed by the Saint he went to his baggage and sent what he had promised.

Thus the virtue of the righteous knows how to correct the violent and the savage, and by persuasion makes them yield to those who practise it.

143

The community of the village of Apoukoumis slaughtered an ox and were eating its flesh. But it happened that all those who partook of it fell down like dead men and the meat that was over turned black and gave forth a horrible stench. Some of the villagers who had not eaten of the meat went to the Saint to report the disaster which had occurred in their village. And he told them that the meat had been rendered so harmful by a troop of demons that had passed through the pot, and as he could not go with them himself because of the visit of a high official, he blessed some water and sent it by one of the brothers for sprinkling the sick and giving it to them to drink. When this was done, they all arose as if from sleep and one only died. For the headman John had not waited for the Saint's prayer to help his brother, but ran to a woman who used enchantments and, taking an amulet from her, hung it on to his brother, who immediately died.

144

(*Summary*) A heavy hailstorm does great damage in Apoukoumis at the time of the vintage. The Saint prayed and erected a cross and thereafter storm clouds passed over the village and no such damage occurred again. In gratitude the villagers presented a vineyard to the monastery.

145

In other villages, too, he worked similar wonders in the case of beetles or locusts or worms or dormice which were devouring the crops or the vines. Wherever anything of the kind occurred the people at once ran to the Saint and either took him back with them or carried away water blessed by his hand for sprinkling over the places which had been damaged, and immediately they gained their desire.

Or again, if a cloud-burst had taken place in any village, or the rivers overflowed their ordinary bed and caused devastation, the sufferers from these calamities went to the holy man in all haste and carried him off to the spot or received a cross at his hands which he had blessed and after fixing it in the spot which had been devastated they never experienced a similar catastrophe again.

And in any case of mortality among oxen or other domesticated animals — I mean mares or any kind of beasts — or birds, or even men, they would in the same way fetch the Saint, or would ask his prayers and carry away with them some water which he had blessed, or the halters and bells of their cattle over which he had pronounced his benediction, and a cure would be sure to follow.

Or when a spell was cast on people by evil spirits, the sufferers were freed from injury if they gained his prayers.

Did husband and wife come to hate each other, they would go to him and he would pray over them and the hatred was dispelled.

If a couple had been childless from youth up to middle age, and he prayed over them and blessed their girdles, then in that same year they would have a child.

In the case of sick persons who were lying in their own homes their relations would bring back oil or water that had been blessed by him and received them back restored to health. Those who were afflicted with wounds or maladies of any kind obtained healing through his prayers.

Again if any required medical treatment for certain illnesses or surgery or a purging draught or hot-springs, this God-inspired man would prescribe the best thing for each, for even in technical matters he had become an experienced doctor. He might recommend one to have recourse to surgery and he would always state clearly which doctor they should employ.

146

In other cases he would dissuade those who wished to undergo an operation or take some other medical treatment and would recommend them rather to go to hot-springs, and would name the springs to which they should go.

Or he would prevent those who wished to go to the hot-springs at Dablioi or to take the waters, say, at Apsoda, and would advise them rather to drink a purging draught instead under a doctor whom he would name.

Others again he would not allow to do that but sent them away to drink hot waters or to some other hot-springs. Others who had been wounded or had abscesses and might perhaps wish for an operation he would send to hot springs or he would advise them to use plasters of which he himself gave them the name.

In a word, as the very best of physicians and as a disciple of the true master-physician, Christ our God, to each one of those who came for treatment he gave exactly the suitable advise that each man's case demanded, and of those who carried out his instructions not one failed to regain his health; and thus in him was fulfilled the thanksgiving sung by David to God, 'Oh, Lord, Thou shalt preserve men and beasts'.[1] However, if perchance one of those who had been advised by him neglected, or made a change in, his orders, either by consulting another doctor, not the one the Saint had named, or by using other plasters, or different treatment, or other hot-springs that person's illness became incurable until he reverted to the treatment the Saint had prescribed and to the hot-springs he had named and to the doctor chosen by him.

147

And to those who exposed to him the doubts and the hidden diseases of their heart he gave appropriate and healing counsel; and to those who had transgressed in various ways he ordained a certain period for repentance, and cleansed them by fastings, prayers and acts of charity. Whereas if any concealed from him the wounds of their souls, he would tell them openly some of the things they had done, and advise and warn them to accept discipline. And those who were convicted of much swearing and blasphemy he would regard sternly and adjure them earnestly to abstain from such a habit and to propitiate God for such transgression of the law by many tears and supplications and good works and would cite the testimony of the psalmist: 'If the Lord shall destroy those that only speak falsehood[2] how much rather shall He visit with His sharp wrath and condemn to perpetual punishment those that add thereto oaths and pile up perjury?' The divine voice testifies 'Thou shalt perform to the Lord thine oaths';[3] and again 'Every idle word that men shall speak, they shall give account thereof in the day of judgment';[4] and if we shall render account for an idle word, how shall we endure God's threat against our many oaths and evil deeds?

[1] Ps. xxxvi. 6.　　　[2] Ps. v. 6.
[3] Matt. v. 33.　　　[4] Matt. xii. 36.

When men were at enmity with each other or had a grievance one against another he reconciled them, and those who were engaged in law-suits he sought to bring to a better mind counselling them not to wrong each other and to think nothing of temporal things but to prefer before all wealth the commandment of God which says: 'Thou shalt love thy neighbour as thyself'[1] for love, said he, worketh no ill to its neighbour and whosoever loveth his brother, loveth God. He exhorted all to be hospitable and to give alms for by such works they would gain redemption from their sins and lay up a store beforehand for the future.

The blessed Saint was very sympathetic and pitiful to all; if anyone was oppressed by an official or a tax-collector or by anybody else he came to the Saint and laid the matter before him. And the blessed man acted according to the Scripture which says 'Deliver the poor and needy; rid them out of the hand of the wicked'.[2] He further desired to imitate the just dealing of Job, who said, 'I delivered the poor out of the hand of the mighty'[3] [here there is a lacuna in the MS.]. . . .

148

All these things I have set forth by God's help, I His sinful and unworthy servant, Eleusius, who was also called George by the Saint, and I to a greater degree than others had a full share of his kindly deeds. For my parents who were natives of the village of Adigermarae had been married several years yet had had no children, so they came to the Saint who prayed over them and blessed their girdles, and through that prayer I was conceived and born. As a child I was brought to him and reared in his holy monastery and was taught letters so far as was necessary by the abbot beloved of God and through the Saint's prayer my parents received another son, as a substitute for me, whom they named after the Saint. For twelve years I was a disciple of this saint and servant of Christ and during these years I was deemed worthy to be an eye-witness of many of his wondrous works. As for the events which occurred in his earliest years and those of his middle life I have diligently sought them out and learned of them from those who ministered

---

[1] Matt. xix. 19.   [2] Ps. lxxxii. 4.   [3] Job xxix. 12.

to him during those years and were eye-witnesses, and also from others who had actually been healed by him.

Of their many tales I have selected a few — some I forgot and others I shrank from recounting through my faint-heartedness. But if anyone wished to relate them all, I fancy the writer would not be strong enough for the task, and time, too, would fail him to tell the story.

This holy, thrice-blessed and saintly servant and faithful follower of Christ, Theodore, died in the third year[1] of the reign of our pious and Christ-loving Emperor,[2] Heraclius, and in the first year of the reign of his divinely-protected and divinely-crowned son Heraclius, the new Constantine, the eternal Augusti and Emperors, in the first indiction in the month of April at dawn of the twenty-second day, a Sunday, it being the first Sunday after Easter.[3]

May we find mercy at the judgment-seat of Christ our God through the prayers and intercession of this Saint, and may we be deemed worthy of the Kingdom of Heaven together with him and with all those who cherish his memory, to the glory of our Saviour Jesus Christ; with Whom to the Father and to the Holy Spirit be glory both now and for ever and world without end,[4] Amen!

[1] A.D. 613.
[2] A.D. 610-41.
[3] εἰς τὰ ἀπολούσια.
[4] Literally 'to the ages of the ages'.

Introd., p. 87   We have omitted from the translation the long-edifying preface. For the geography of the Vita see Sir W. M. Ramsay, *The Historical Geography of Asia Minor* (cited as Ramsay, *infra*), Royal Geographical Society, Supplementary Papers, vol. 4 (John Murray, London, 1890) (with map at p. 196), and J. G. C. Anderson, *Exploration in Galatia cis Halyn*, Journal of Hellenic Studies 19 (1899), pp. 34-134 (with map of Galatia cis Halym) — cited as Anderson *infra*.

ch. 3, p. 88   Sykeon: On Sykeon and Justinian's bridge over the Sibaris (the Ala Dagh Su) cf. Anderson, pp. 65-9; on Anastasioupolis (? at Mal-Tepe on the banks of the Bey-bazâr) and Langania, ibid., pp. 64-5. Ancyra was the capital of Galatia Prima.

3, p. 88   'The public highway': cf. Anderson on The Pilgrims' Route between Ancyra and Juliopolis, ibid., pp. 53 sqq.

3, p. 88   'a brilliant star': cf. ch. 58 and 78.

4, p. 88   Balgatia would be pronounced Valgatia: Anderson would identify Valgatia with Valcaton: cf. ibid., p. 71.

5, p. 89   St. George: one of the military saints: cf. H. Delehaye, *Les Légendes grecques des Saints militaires*, Picard, Paris, 1909, pp. 45-76; N. Nilles, *Kalendarium Manuale utriusque ecclesiae*, 1870, vol. 1, pp. 143-4.

6, p. 90   'boiled wheat': κόλλυβα: the word is derived from the dialect spoken in Euchaita. Stephen, it would seem, was following Anatolian ascetic tradition: Hilarius, who had been 'beaten up' by the clergy of his district, came to inner Pontus, and there for eighteen years he tasted no bread, but ate only plain vegetables and kolluba. Palladius, *Dialogus de Vita S. Joannis Chrysostomi*, ed. Coleman-Norton, Cambridge University Press, 1928, p. 127.

7, p. 91   We have adopted the emendation of this passage suggested by P. Nitikin: *O nyekatoruikh grecheskikh Tekstakh zhitii Svyatuikh*, Mémoires Imp. Acad. d. Sci., St. Petersburg, 8th Series, Classe historico-philol., vol. 1, No. 1, 1895, p. 59. For ἠναγκάσθην read ἠναγκάσθη, and for ἦν read ᾖ.

ch. 8, p. 91   'where the cross was set': ἐν τῷ σταυροδόχῳ. We are not sure if we have translated this rightly.

10, p. 93   St. Gemellus: a native of Paphlagonia and martyr under Julianus.

13, p. 95   St. Christopher: Reprebos, Aramaic Rabrąb, received on baptism the name of Christopher and suffered martyrdom in Lycia during the persecution of Decius: see H. Usener, *Acta S. Marinae et S. Christophori*. Festschrift for the fifth centenary of the University of Heidelberg, Bonn, 1886, pp. 56-76. For the adoption of the name of Christopher see p. 64. Cf. *Analecta Bollandiana* 1 (1882), pp. 122-48.

13, p. 96   St. Heuretus: we can find no particulars concerning this saint; he is not mentioned in the *Kalendarium* of Nilles.

13, p. 96   Iopolis. Should, it appears, be Juliopolis: 'Ιοπολιτῶν= 'Ιουλιοπολιτῶν, cf. Ramsay, pp. 244-6; Anderson, p.71.

14, p. 96   cf. Athanasius, *Vita Antonii*, ch. 4.

15, p. 97   ἀλλὰ μετὰ τὸ κατελθεῖν αὐτούς: we should prefer to read αὐτάς.

16, p. 98   It is because of this commemoration of the Baptism that the consecration of the holy water takes place on January 6th.

21, p. 101   'these four talents': this is mysterious, as only the ordination as lector, sub-deacon and priest are mentioned. Mr. H. St. L. B. Moss has suggested to us that the fourth talent is the ordination to the diaconate which the author of the Vita has omitted from his account. Cf. N. Milasch, *Das Kirchenrecht der morgenländischen Kirche*, 2nd ed., Mostar, 1905, pp. 238 sqq. We adopt this explanation.

22, p. 102   See ch. 148.

23, p. 103   We are not sure how κατὰ τὴν τοῦ Κυρίου ἐπαινετὴν προβολήν should be translated.

23, p. 103   Reading ἀνέμων for ἀνόμων.

24, p. 104   Cf. K. M. Koikulides, Τὰ κατὰ τὴν Λαύραν καὶ τὸν Χείμαρρον τοῦ Χουзιβα. Jerusalem, 1901.

28, p. 107   'Of triple mail': Professor Hugh Last has suggested that for τρίμυτον we should read τρίμιτον: it is the trilix lorica of Virgil, *Aen.* III, 467; V, 259; VII, 639. We gladly adopt this emendation.

28, p. 108   'Till the "Paralepsis" ': we feel that the Paralepsis should be a feast in the ecclesiastical year, but we are assured by Archbishop Germanos that there is no such

ch. 28, p. 108   festival in the calendar of the Orthodox Church to-day.
(cont.)   Professor Franz Dölger writes to us that it means simply 'bis er wieder hervorgeholt wurde': cf. ch. 104.

28, p. 108   For ὑποπιέζων we would read ὑπωπιάζων: cf. 1 Cor. ix. 27 and see F. Vanderstuyf, *Vie de Saint Luc le Stylite*=Patrologia Orientalis, Tome 11, Fasc. 2. Firmin-Didot, Paris (1914), p. 202 οὕτως οὖν διετέλεσεν ὑπωπιάζων βιαίως τὸ σῶμα.

30, p. 109   'It was through faith': we are not sure of the construction of πίστει γίνεται in this sentence.

35, p. 112   'Iron-eater', σιδηροφάγε cf. e.g. ch. 43, 46, 84, 86, 108. It is a singular term, but metals have often been used metaphorically — 'he is as hard as iron' — and if a grammarian can be styled by Suidas 'a man of brazen bowels' (see Liddell and Scott, s.v. Χαλκέντερος) a demon might attribute to a ruthless saint a digestion which could assimilate even iron.

39, p. 115   'as they did in that sacred icon'. Greek: Καθ'ὁμοίωσιν τῆς λατρείας ἐκείνης. SS. Cosmas and Damian had vowed never to take any money for their cures: they are therefore known as the 'Anarguroi'.

39, p. 116   Reading, on Nitikin's suggestion, ἀνιόντες for ἀνιέντες.

39, p. 116   'immediately regained his health and strength': Greek: διαφορὰν καὶ ἰσχὺν ἀναλαβών. This must, we think, be translated 'having recovered *health* and strength' (cf. ch. 81 καὶ ποιήσας αὐτῷ εὐχὴν εἰς διαφορὰν ἤγαγεν), though how διαφορά comes to have this meaning we are at a loss to explain.

40, p. 117   For διὰ λόγου we have adopted Nitikin's emendation, Mémoires, etc. (see note on ch. 7), p. 60, δι'ἄλλου; cf. δι'ἑτέρου, p. 416, l. 3, ch. 59.

40, p. 117   'the oratory . . . was small.' It is not easy to see how σεμνὸς comes to mean 'small' as it does in later Greek. There is no reason to emend to στενόν as Nitikin suggested.

40, p. 117   'and others', etc.: read καὶ⟨τοὺς⟩ εἰς εὐχὴν παραγινομένους.

42, p. 118   ὡς ὅταν ἀπέχων ἄργυρος ἐκ τῆς τοῦ καμίνου πυρᾶς μέλας ἐξέλθοι. For the meaning of ἀπέχων we can offer no suggestion: it looks as though it ought to mean 'impure' or 'counterfeit'.

42, p. 118   'the manager': Greek: ἀρμαρίτην: should this be ἀρμαρίτην derived from the Latin 'armarium'?. The modern Greek word ἄρμαρι is said to be derived from Turkish.

ch. 43, p. 119   'iron-eater': cf. note on ch. 35.

43, p. 119   'who had ordered a procession of supplication': ἐκβαλὼν λιτήν (so again in, e.g., ch. 51 and 52). 'To throw a procession' sounds strangely like modern colloquial English.

43, p. 120   ῥίψας sc. ὁ δαίμων cf. ch. 46 and 92.

44, p. 120   Herakleia Pontica = Eregli.

46, p. 122   'was raised from the ground': for this levitation cf. ch. 71 and 93.

49, p. 124   St. Autonomus: martyr in Bithynia during the persecution of Diocletian. See *Acta Sanctorum*, September, vol. 4, pp. 14-20.

49, p. 124   St. Theodore: which saint of this name? Probably St. Theodore Stratelates: see Nilles, *Kalendarium* (see note on ch. 5), p. 96; *Acta Sanctorum*, February, vol. 2, February 7th; Delehaye (see note on ch. 5), pp. 10-43 and Appendix.

51, p. 125   For ἐξαλλάσσουσαι στολαί cf. Genesis xlv, 22 (Septuagint).

55, p. 127   Plato was martyred at Ancyra in the last great persecution. Festival Day, November 18th.
SS. Sergius and Bacchus were soldier martyrs of Commagene. Festival Day, October 7th.

57, p. 129   We must obviously read ἐνθάδιος.

59, p. 130   δι'ἑτέρου cf. note on ch. 40.

60, p. 130   'a narrow platform': we are not sure of the translation of ἐν φατνείῳ. For the meaning 'platform' cf. Liddell and Scott, s.v. We owe this suggestion to Professor Hugh Last.

69, p. 134   To what passage in scripture does this quotation refer?

71, p. 135   For Germia = Colonia Julia Augusta Felix Germa: see Anderson, pp. 84-8. For the joint festival of the people of Eudoxias (Yürme) and Germia at Mousga see Anderson, pp. 8, 9, 'the actual site of Mousga was beside the ruined village called Arslanli close to the hot-springs', for Ramsay rightly pointed out that Mousga probably lay on the frontier of Germia and Eudoxias and that 'the Christian custom perpetuated an old religious connection of both cities with some holy spot between them', i.e. the fine hot springs (Hammam) some hours to the N.W. of Yürme.

ch. 71, p. 135	Levitation: cf. ch. 46 and 93.
78, p. 142	For the star cf. ch. 3 and 58.
79, p. 143	ἀπὸ τῆς ἐνορίας πόλεως ἐνορίαν: ἐνορίαν appears to be superfluous.
79, p. 143	'the oratory of the Archangel': on the widespread cult of the Archangel Michael in Galatia see Anderson, p. 72. Pidron: perhaps Tchardak: Anderson, pp. 74-5. Acrena (Akreina): cf. Anderson, pp. 71-4.
80, p. 143	ἕως τῆς κοιμήσεως ἑνὸς ὁποτέρου αὐτῶν. This text does not appear to make sense. We have given in our translation what we conceive to be the meaning of the sentence.
81, p. 144	'led back to health': see note on ch. 39.
81, p. 145	Sycae=Galata: for the communication between Sycae and the capital cf. A. van Millingen, Byzantine Constantinople, Murray, London, pp. 216-17.
84, p. 146	on the use of the word πλάσμα see note on ch. 92.
89, p. 149	Professor Mavrogordato has helped us in the translation of this section.
91, p. 149	his hand 'in a sling': Greek: καὶ ἐν τῷ τραχήλῳ αὐτοῦ συνδεδεμένην. With ch. 91, cf. ch. 123.
92, p. 150	We know no parallels to the use of πλάσμα in this chapter and in ch. 84; it apparently means the human body which the demon has chosen for its habitation. Are there other parallel passages?
93, p. 151	Cf. ch. 83.
93, p. 152	'the wood was struck': the wooden gong: the monasteries of the Orthodox Church do not make use of bells.
97, p. 153	Hiereia: on the palace of Hiereia at Fener Bagtchèssi on the bay of Moda near Kadikeui cf. Van Millingen (see note on ch. 81), p. 175 s.f.
102, p. 156	'Gallos, Lophoi and Kadosia were probably three places near each other on the road between Prousa and Nikaia on the upper waters of the river Gallos.' Ramsay, p. 182, and cf. p. 247.
106, p. 158	Sozopolis: Ramsay, pp. 246-7, 400-1.
107, p. 159	'at the second cast': Greek: ἐκ δευτέρου cf. in ch. 112, ἐκ τρίτου. And see A. Sigalas, Des Chrysippos von Jerusalem Enkomion auf den heiligen Theodoros Teron (=Byzantinisches Archiv. Heft 7) Leipzig, 1921, p. 62, ὡς δὲ καὶ ἐκ δευτέρου πάλιν ἐξέδραμε κ.τ.λ.
108, p. 160	Read παραδόξῳ.

ch. 111, p. 161   'the so-called "phugadaina" ': usually 'phagedaina'=a cancerous sore. A popular writer is quoting a technical term: hence τὸ λεγόμενον: cf. similarly Palladius, *Historia Lausiaca* 24 (p. 78, ed. Butler): κατελάβομεν αὐτὸν ἀρρωστίᾳ τοιαύτῃ περιπεσόντα κατ'αὐτοὺς τοὺς τόπους τῶν διδύμων κἀι τῆς βαλάνου ἕλκος ποιήσαντα τὸ λεγόμενον φαγέδαιναν [for ποιεῖν meaning 'to get' or 'acquire', cf. *Byz. Zeits.* 30 (1930), pp. 228-9].

112, p. 161   ἐπὶ τὴν ἀπόθεσιν τῶν πραγμάτων αὐτοῦ. We are not sure how these words should be translated. The picture as we conceive it is that the boy had been given some cakes, etc., and wanted to put them into safe keeping.

112, p. 161   ἐπὶ τῇ συμβάσει αὐτῷ θανατηφόρῳ ἀνάγκῃ: ?read συμβάσῃ.

112, p. 161   ἐκ τρίτου. Cf. note on ch. 107.

118, p. 167   In text Πεῶν: Peton in Latin translation: perhaps abbreviation of Petobriga: see Anderson, p. 64.

120, p. 168   Leontius after his defeat by the Persians was brought in chains to Constantinople and Domentziolus was appointed general in his place: see Theophanes, ed. De Boor, I, p. 292. We do not know of any other mention of this inroad of the Lazi, but since Maurice had liberated Lazica from the invading Persians, the Lazi may well have carried out a foray into the territory of the Empire under the pretext of avenging Maurice's murder. Of Sergius' plot we do not seem to have any information.

120, p. 169   'things must take their appointed course': δάτον ἔχει συμβῆναι. This is remarkable Greek; we hope that we have translated it aright: cf. Virgil, *Aen.* I, 382, data fata secutus.

120, p. 169   Read τὸ ἱκανόν: τὸ ἱκανὸν ποιεῖν=Latin satisfacere.

122, p. 170   Sebasteia: capital of the province of Armenia Prima on the upper course of the Halys.

123, p. 170   Cf. ch. 91.

128, p. 174   The dates of the Patriarchs of Constantinople at this time are: Kyriakus, A.D. 595-606; Thomas, A.D. 607-610; Sergius, A.D. 610-38.

129, p. 174   The classic discussion of the harbour of Pylae from which the Byzantines crossed from Asia to Europe, to which Heraclius came when he began his Persian campaign is that of G. L. T. Tafel, *Theophanis Chronographia*, Vienna, 1852, pp. 146 sqq. See also E.

ch. 129, p. 174   Honigmann, *Byzantion* 14 (1939), pp. 618-19,
   (cont.)   625-6.

130, p. 174   Dorylleon: more usually Dorylaion on the river
Tembris: the modern Schar-oejuk.

135, p. 177   Petrion: the district on the Golden Horn of which the
name is still preserved in the gate Petri Kapoussi at
the east end of the enclosure round the Patriarchal
Church: see Van Millingen (cf. note on ch. 81), p. 28.

142, p. 179   Bonosus: cf. A. J. Butler, *The Arab Conquest of
Egypt*, etc., Clarendon Press, Oxford, 1902, p. 14.

142, p. 180   'some trimisia': the tremissis=the third of a solidus:
cf. Warwick Wroth, *Catalogue of the Imperial Byzantine Coins in the British Museum*, London, 1908,
vol. 1, pp. lxxiv-v.

ST. JOHN THE ALMSGIVER

INTRODUCTION

THE first half of the seventh century was marked in the Eastern provinces of the Empire by great literary activity in hagiography and four outstanding figures in the writing of lives of the saints were intimately associated. Leontius bishop of Neapolis in Cyprus wrote a biography of St. John the Almsgiver, Patriarch of Alexandria. Both Leontius and the Patriarch were, it would seem, natives of Cyprus and the former probably lived in contact with St. John during his patriarchate. John Moschus, a Palestinian monk, was the author of the *Pratum Spirituale* — the 'Spiritual Meadow' or 'New Paradise' in which he gave an account of the lives of the solitaries whom he had visited in his wanderings. John Moschus twice went to Egypt accompanying the 'sophist' Sophronius who is perhaps to be identified with the Bishop of Jerusalem (633-7) of the same name. Both John Moschus and Sophronius were in Egypt during St. John the Almsgiver's patriarchate and gave him their loyal support. Later, working, it would seem, on material which John Moschus had collected but had not lived to publish, Sophronius wrote a Life of the Patriarch; this Life has not been preserved. Leontius not only wrote his biography of John the Almsgiver but also composed a Life of Spyridon, a Cyprian saint, which is lost and an immensely popular account of St. Simeon of Emesa, the Fool for Christ's sake. Finally the Patriarch, whose favourite reading was Lives of the Saints, wrote a panegyric in honour of St. Tychon, the patron saint of Amathus, the Cyprian town in which he himself was born and to which he returned to die. St. Tychon was the protector of the vinegrowers of the island and the Patriarch gives a vivid account of the Festival of the New Grape Harvest celebrated on the saint's anniversary.

There were thus two contemporary biographies of St. John the Almsgiver, one by Sophronius and John Moschus and another intended to serve as a supplement to this written by Leontius. The former, as we have seen, is no longer extant, but both it and the supplementary Life by Leontius were used by an editor and by him fused into a single story. The text of this conflation of the two biographies was published from a manuscript in Venice by Père Delehaye in 1927 and it was this version, and not the original texts of the two Lives, which was used by the Metaphrast in the second half of the tenth century for his biography of the Patriarch. Since we thus possess the source employed by the Metaphrast his text ceases to have any independent value. We have therefore translated the opening chapters of the text published by Père Delehaye which represent for us the Life written by Sophronius and John Moschus and have then turned to the original text of the biography of the Saint composed by Leontius on which the latter part of the document published by Père Delehaye was founded.

The eastern provinces of the Roman Empire had long been distracted by the religious discords which formed the aftermath of the Council of Chalcedon. Egypt, which ever since the days of Athanasius had played the part of the Conscientious Objector, consistently opposing the envoys of the monarch ruling from Constantinople, had defeated all efforts at conciliation. Eulogius, the Orthodox Patriarch of Alexandria (A.D. 580-607), had in his many writings fought for the creed of Chalcedon but with so little success that in 611 St. John the Almsgiver found that the Monophysites held not only the valley of the Nile: even in the Greek city of Alexandria no more than seven churches were left in the possession of those who supported the dogma of the Two Natures in the Incarnate Christ. That is the background which the reader of St. John's Life must keep in mind: as Patriarch he chose a better way — he would recommend Orthodoxy to Egypt by a sympathy and a charity which knew no limits. There is no reason to doubt that in large measure he was successful.

In A.D. 602 the Emperor Maurice had been dethroned and together with his family put to death by the rude soldier Phocas whose reign was a bloody tyranny. The cities of the Empire were thrown into confusion by the fights of the circus parties, the Blues and the Greens, while Jews seized the opportunity of these conflicts to kill off some of the hated Christians. There was no effective opposition to the armed forces of Sassanid Persia which had invaded East Roman territory.

From Carthage which Justinian had recovered from the Vandals Heraclius sailed to Constantinople to overthrow the tyrant (A.D. 610) while his relative Nicetas attacked Egypt and established himself in Alexandria. When Egypt had been won for the new emperor it was natural that Heraclius and Nicetas, now Augustal Praefect of Egypt, should desire to have on the patriarchal throne one who had played no part in the recent warfare. Their choice of a native of Cyprus can thus be easily explained, but it would appear from the biography of Sophronius and John Moschus (as represented by the text published by Père Delehaye) that there was a further reason: St. John was the adopted brother of Nicetas. He was, however, a simple layman; he had been married and of that marriage several children had been born. Now wife and children were all dead. Despite John's protests, the imperial will prevailed and the layman stepped directly into the proud position of Patriarch.

And the Almsgiver was fortunate in having for his biographer his countryman Leontius. That biography (written at some time after A.D. 641) Leontius composed in a simple, homely style that it might be read by simple folk; his aim was, as he tells us, that the humble Christian should learn that even in his own day the Christian faith could inspire men to sainthood. The portentous rhetoric, which often makes the reading of Byzantine hagiography a weariness of the flesh, is abandoned, and in the vocabulary of Leontius many words are borrowed from popular speech, words carefully removed when later purists used his biography as their source. In fullest sympathy with the aims of his sainted fellow-countrymen he recalls past scenes of many of which he had been an eye-witness; he writes with no hagiographic stencil: freshly and vividly he paints his picture and gives us a glimpse of life as it was lived in seventh-century Egypt.[1]

One of the outstanding features of early Byzantine asceticism is its passion for social justice and its championship of the poor and oppressed. The Life of John the Almsgiver serves to show the difficulties which beset one who, inspired by ascetic ideals,

[1] See note on p. 270 infra.

was yet seated on the throne of St. Mark. Surrounded by a hierarchy of ecclesiastical officials it was no easy matter for the Patriarch to establish direct contact with the common folk of the city. That contact, however, John established, and the vast resources of his see he spent, not on the erection of sumptuous churches but on buildings which should serve the needs of the poor and homeless — the *humiliores* on whom the East Roman world pressed so heavily. St. John exemplified that tradition of universal and unquestioning charity which under the early Empire had embraced pagan as well as Christian in its generous self-devotion. The law which governed the Archbishop's whole administration was the command of his Master: 'Give to him that asketh thee and from him that would borrow of thee turn not thou away.' And after a Cyril, after a Dioscoros how refreshing to discover a Patriarch possessed of the saving grace of humour!

It has sometimes been said that the ascetic ideal of the East Roman was a barren withdrawal from the world of his day; the biography of John the Almsgiver may suggest why it was that the Byzantine in his hour of need turned instinctively for aid and comfort to the ascete in the full assurance of his sympathy and succour.

THE LIFE OF OUR HOLY FATHER, JOHN THE ALMSGIVER

I

JOHN, the great servant of God and His faithful high-priest, who was named after 'almsgiving' and received that exceptional and glorious title from his exceeding goodness which took Christ for its model — this John, I say, invites us to the present banquet of praise, and as dainty and free fare he sets before us for our common feast most pleasing tales of his achievements and his triumphs.

And every soul that delights in instruction will revel and find joy in them, and in its love for God it will be aroused by a sacred passion to pious imitation.

And the Lord of glory will be signally glorified, for He is always glorified in His own servants, and those that glorify Him He glorifies splendidly in return.

Come then! let us, as best we may, begin our story, it cannot be complete but we shall be graciously guided towards the end which we have set before us by John's merciful co-operation and intercession.

2

This renowned light of the Church and great father among saints was the noble offspring and precious nursling of the island of the Cyprians, and was descended not from ignoble or ordinary ancestors, but from those of an illustrious family and of brilliant renown.

For John's father, Epiphanius* (=Conspicuous) by name, did so many 'conspicuous' and remarkable things in his life in accordance, we may say, with his name that he was chosen by the rulers of that time to be entrusted with the reins of government in the island of the Cyprians. And we may, I think, reasonably suppose that his wife, I mean the mother of our wonderful John, had like her husband her share of good fortune and distinction.

3

This noble lad was given a generous education by his noble parents and was brought up in the fear of the Lord. As he grew in age he developed in body and progressed in spirit until he was joined to a wife in the partnership of lawful wedlock; not however by his own wish but in obedience to his father's authority did he take upon himself the yoke of marriage. Nor was it so much that he yielded readily but rather that he was forced thereto by constraint. And in his love of purity even after assuming the bonds of marriage he gave a proof of his great passion for the unmarried state. For accepting the marriage-contract only in name and treating it as but a form, in his love for continence he abstained for a considerable time from intercourse with his wife. Finally his father-in-law noticed what was happening, became very angry and threatened to brand with guilt the purpose of his guiltless son-in-law.

At this the great-hearted man yielded, for in all things he was ready to make concessions and earnestly strove to give offence to none. He therefore went so far as to submit himself to the lawful intercourse of married life. From this intercourse he allowed himself even to beget children of whom he had a bountiful crop, becoming the father of sons according to the law of nature.

These all departed this life while they were still in the flower of their age, and his wife, too, met her end soon afterwards. He had now gained complete freedom from all worldly burdens and anxieties and gave himself up wholly and entirely without any other thought than how to please the Lord and, like the great apostle, to 'become all things to all men'[1] and 'not to seek his own profit only but the profit of many'[2] that they might have a prosperous course.

And indeed he was always on all occasions amiable to all, advising, encouraging, assisting, acting as peacemaker, doing a kindness, reconciling, and ever anxiously striving to display his love for the highest virtue in all its forms.

4

And by this conduct John became everywhere very famous and at the same time dearly beloved, not only by the subjects of the Empire and by private individuals, but even by the Emperors themselves and by the nobles and governors.

[1] 1 Cor. ix. 22.   [2] 1 Cor. x. 33.

Thus under strong pressure by the Emperor Heraclius and largely through the counsel of Nicetas, who at that time had been raised to the rank of 'patrician' and shared in the government of the Empire (he was also the adopted brother of the blessed man) and further with the approval of the whole body of Alexandrians* he was raised to the high-priestly throne as Patriarch.

5

With his mind filled by the inspiration of the Divine spirit John first of all suppressed the blasphemous addition, namely the innovation in the 'Trisagion', which Peter, nicknamed 'the Fuller',* in his profane babbling had recited, daring impiously to say: 'Holy, immortal, Thou Who was crucified for us'. For when John by divine decree received into his hands the reins of the high-priesthood, he found only seven churches maintaining the services of the Orthodox liturgy; and by much diligence he succeeded in increasing the number to seventy and in all these he authorized the celebration of the Immaculate Oblation.

He absolutely refused to receive presents or money or any kind of gift whatsoever, not only as a fee for ordination, but also on any other pretext or excuse, whether the matter were great or small, for he ever kept in mind the words of the writer of Proverbs, who says 'He that is greedy of gain destroys himself but he that hateth taking gifts shall live'.[1] Moreover from all those who were seeking ordination at his hands, whether as bishops or priests, he demanded a written declaration in order to safeguard the orthodox faith and to secure the observance of all the ordinances set forth in the Canons.

With regard to the decisions concerning ordinations and the testing of candidates he was so very scrupulous that once when the Emperor sent to him about a certain monk, who feigned great piety, asking John to ordain him bishop he examined the facts with care and recognizing that the monk was unworthy of the priesthood he confined him to one of the monasteries, bidding him remain there quietly.* The monk escaped soon afterwards and reported the whole matter to the Emperor, but John was not afraid nor did he take any account of the Em-

[1] Prov. xv. 27 (Septuagint).

peror's order; he sent the monk empty away telling him to return to him who had sent him.

The priests who abjured their heresy and gave written declarations of their repentance, confessing the doctrines of the orthodox faith, accepting the four holy Oecumenical Councils and anathematizing all the heresies and the heresiarchs, were willingly received by John who made them members of the Catholic church.

6

At that time the Persian armies invaded and laid waste the whole country of the Syrians,* and the inhabitants of all the towns there came in great numbers with bishops and other clergy and governors and sought refuge in Alexandria. In the greatness of his mind and the generosity of his purpose he supported them all liberally, supplying most abundantly each one's necessities.

When he learnt that some of the bishops staying in Alexandria were in need, he summoned the richer members amongst the leading clergy and when he had brought them together he exhorted them with many counsels and then laid down that they all, and he himself first of all, should pay one pound of gold a year to their poverty-stricken colleagues.

He made a similar arrangement for the needy priests and deacons and the rest of the clergy of the Church, freely granting to each* in every rank a certain sum of gold yearly corresponding to the particular labour of his own station so that his wants might be satisfied.

In addition to this he built a great many poorhouses and hostels for strangers, and he decreed that all the corn and all the necessary expenditure for the feeding of their inmates should be paid for from the revenues of the Church.

7

Once when a severe famine was oppressing the city and the holy man's stewards were, as usual, ceaselessly distributing money or some small gift to the needy, some destitute women overcome with hunger and but lately risen from child-bed were obliged to hasten to receive help from the distributors while they were still in the grip of abdominal pains, deadly pale, and suffering grievously; when the wondrous man was told of this, he built seven lying-in hospitals in different parts of the city, ordered forty beds to be kept ready in each and arranged that every woman should rest quietly in these for seven full days after her confinement and then receive the third of a nomisma and go home.

8

It was not only for those in bodily need that he showed care but he took special forethought for the salvation of those suffering from spiritual hunger. For instance, there was a lake in Alexandria, called Maria,* in which a great quantity of papyrus grew, and the inhabitants of that district had been in the habit of cutting it down and using it as fuel instead of wood. And the boys, whose work it was to cut down the papyrus together with the men dwelling there, practised the vice of sodomy unrestrainedly; and they had no house of prayer, no priest at all, they never heard the Scriptures nor partook of the Divine Mysteries. When the inspired Patriarch heard of these illegal doings and of this pollution, he ordered the boys to be brought away from that place and he built houses of prayer for its inhabitants and set apart certain priests whom he appointed to minister to them and to teach them.

9

After Rasmiozan* the governor, or rather the general-in-chief, of Chosroes, King of the Persians, had demolished all the holy places of Jerusalem, the news of this wickedness* came to the ears of the thrice blessed Patriarch. When he heard of this horrible insolence and learned that all the holy things had been committed to the flames, then just as though he had been an inhabitant of the places which had suffered thus he sat down and made lament. He mourned for their desolation, not merely for one or two days, or ten or twenty or even twice as many but for a whole year; wailing and groaning bitterly he strove by his lamentations to outdo Jeremiah who of old lamented over the capture of this same city, Jerusalem. And this lamentation he did not compose, as it were, without careful thought, leaving it to be forgotten, but he is said to have committed it to writing.

And on receiving the news of this disaster he sent a man, dearly loved of God, Ctesippus by name, and at that time in charge of the monasteries of the Ennaton,* to view the destruction of the holy places in Jerusalem. And by his hands he sent a large sum of money and an abundance of corn, wine, oil and pulse; also garments for laymen and for monks; and for the sick various kinds of eatables, and finally, a great many beasts of burden for the distribution of these necessaries. He not only took much thought for those who had been captured in the towns but he took measures with great care for those from the monasteries who had suffered a similar fate, and especially for the women from the convents. A number of the latter had been done to death by the Persians and about a thousand of the nuns were captured, so John sent a large sum of money to ransom them and then he restored them all, settling them in convents.

The Persian governors heard of John's surpassing liberality and boundless sympathy — for certainly he was most appropriately named 'the Almsgiver' — and therefore they were very eager to see him — for even an enemy respects a man's virtue* — and they offered money to Dion, who was governor at that time, if he would make it possible for them to see him.

Besides all this, John sent Theodore, bishop of Amathus,* to rescue those who had been taken prisoners by the Madienians,* and with him Anastasius, abbot of the mount of the great Antony,* and Gregory, bishop of Rhinocoroura;* by their help he effected the rescue of very many captives, both men and women, whom he redeemed by paying a large sum of gold.

10

But it was not only in the distribution of money and the ransoming of captives that he showed the generosity of his disposition, but also in the matter of his simple fare; for he had no hesitation in showing that his own humble style of living was to buy cheaply and be content with little. One day in the large church of the great martyr Menas* he took a cup of wine in his hand and, when he noticed its bouquet and pleasant taste, he asked the steward where it had been bought and for how much. The steward replied that the wine had been brought from Palestine and purchased at a very high price, so John refused to drink it, saying, 'Humble John does not drink such fragrant and excellent wine, bought, too, at so high a price; pour me out rather some Mareotic wine,* for its taste is nothing to boast of and its price is low'.

11

A certain John, at that time bishop of the town of Tiberias,* escaped the barbaric invasion of the Persians, fled for refuge to the great city of the Alexandrians and there reached the end of his life. He used to wear on his breast a gold cross inside which was a portion of the precious Cross, and this he bequeathed to his heir. Now John longed to possess this and asked the man to take double its price and give him what he desired. The man took the sum agreed upon, then changed the pectoral cross and gave the Patriarch another in place of it. Afterwards the rascal at dead of night saw a vision of angels calling him to account and questioning him and using terrible threats to him and saying that unless he gave the just Patriarch (Papas) the precious bit of wood which he had inherited, he should suffer most grievous ills and end his life in utter misery. So he did this at once and asked forgiveness for the crafty theft.

12

Some of the clergy had deserted their own towns owing to the invasions of the barbarians and had come to Alexandria and had no expectation of ever returning to their native towns; these John accepted and enrolled in the Church. As these men had no shepherds, he did not insist on their supplying 'letters of introduction', but he took written declarations from them to prove their confession of the orthodox faith and their observance of the ecclesiastical canons.

13

On hearing of the wholesale devastation of the Roman realm by the Persians John decided to go to the Emperor and open negotiations for peace. But, although he had drawn up his farewell speech and read it to all, the people of the city would not allow him to leave. After the Persian armies had utterly laid waste the whole of Syria, Phoenicia and Arabia and various cities besides, these sinners threatened to take even Alexandria itself. And then the holy man, having found out by God's help, that a murderous plot was being hatched against him, sailed away to his native country, Cyprus.

Now a general, one Aspagurius* by name, had been sent to Constantia in Cyprus but had not been admitted by the town; so he prepared himself for war against its citizens and they on their side were arming themselves against him. And they were just on the point of engaging in this slaughter of each other when the all-admirable John, the disciple of the God of Peace, intervened and induced both parties to seek reconciliation and succeeded in bringing them to terms.

14

John once received relics from Jerusalem of Stephen, the first martyr, and of James the brother of our Lord; so he built a chapel in the name of this first great martyr and having made a list of all his belongings he generously dedicated them to this chapel.

15

Isaac who was general at that time betrayed the city of the Alexandrians (to the Persians) and then fled for refuge to Cyprus. There he found the most holy Patriarch (Papas) and formed a murderous intrigue against him, intending to kill him on the Monday before Palm Sunday. The divine man was informed of this and therefore stayed at home and received nobody, and thus by God's providence he was miraculously saved from this deadly attack. But the author of this plot, the miserable Isaac, by the just judgment of the unsleeping providence of God was savagely set upon by some men and murdered on the very day on which he had planned death against the righteous Patriarch.

John, the all-holy Patriarch (Papas), when he had arrived at Constantia paid reverent worship to the relics of the saints there, namely, Barnabas, the all-praiseworthy apostle, and Epiphanius, the great miracle-worker, and afterwards went on to Amathus and it was from there that he departed to be with his beloved Lord.

A SUPPLEMENT

to the Life of John the Almsgiver, our saintly father
and Archbishop of Alexandria, written by Leontius,
Bishop of Neapolis in the island of Cyprus

Our purpose in writing this biography of the glorious
Patriarch is the same as that of the earnest and holy men who
wrote before me, and that is, that from the study of his life all
may gain spiritual profit and a desire to imitate his piety; and
that men may ascribe glory and magnificence to the Holy and
worshipful Trinity Which in this, as in all things, from
generation to generation exhibits Its own luminaries 'to give
light to those that sit in darkness and in the shadow of death'[1]
which is caused by sin.

Then again, my Christ-loving readers, we completely fail to
admire the men of our own generation, even if they have lived
lives well-pleasing unto God; but rather by the Devil's instigation we often say to each other that in former times the lawlessness of men was not so multiplied, but now, the Devil whispers,
it is as the Holy Scripture foretold: 'because lawlessness has
been multiplied, the love of many shall wax cold'[2] — hence we
grow feeble in virtue.

This is the second reason for my undertaking this incomplete story of the Saint's life — to prove that even nowadays
those who desire it and carry out their purpose by force have
shewn themselves more excellent than we and have trodden
'the strait and narrow path' and closed the mouth of those who
utter unrighteous and soul-destroying thoughts.

The others, who before us wrote about this wonderful man
and high priest, John, have composed their works in a beautiful
and lofty style, for they were powerful in word and deed — I
mean John and Sophronius* — men who feared God and loved
virtue, true champions of piety.

And yet, although they won so high a reputation, even they
failed to tell all about this man's virtue and were in the same
case as industrious husbandmen. They, when gathering in the
crop of a goodly and fruitful vineyard, even without wishing
it, will be sure to leave something from the blessing of the

[1] Luke i. 79.   [2] Matt. xxiv. 12.

207

harvest to the poor who follow in their footsteps and glean the grapes remaining on the vines; and of such gleaners we are indeed the least.

And, although all these holy men strove in their zeal for God with all their powers to gather in the produce of this fruitful olive-tree, for indeed the olives on it were very rich, since 'it was planted in the house of God' (as says the psalmist David)[1] yet the greater part of the fruit of the tree escaped their eye. This was by the Lord's dispensation Who was willing to accept also our modest and cold-hearted desire, just as He accepted the widow's two mites.

For it was not with the idea of belittling them, or as though we could imitate their God-given wisdom, that we were anxious to commence writing this just man's glorious achievements, but in the first place because we thought it not right to bury in silence things that would bring profit to those who heard them, lest we, too, should incur the condemnation which was pronounced on the servant who buried his talent in the earth. And furthermore because the achievements and pleasant tales collected in this account of ours were not included in the eulogies of that true Saint, the blessed John, written by the worthy men whose names we have mentioned. Lastly, since those historians were clever and skilful writers, they have drawn a picture of their subject in a clever and exalted manner, and this very fact spurred us on still more to undertake our present work, which relates John's life in a prosaic, unadorned and popular style so that even 'the unlearned and ignorant men'[2] can profit from our words.

I

I, all unworthy as I am, came up to Alexandria to revere the holy and victorious martyrs, Cyrus and John,* and to enjoy their succour, and while I was in Alexandria, I met with certain pious Christian men, and as we were conversing about biblical and other edifying narratives, a stranger came up to us asking alms, 'for,' said he, 'I have only just been rescued from my captivity under the Persians'.*

Now it chanced that not one of us sitting there had either a large coin or even any small change with us. A servant of

---

[1] Ps. lii. 8.   [2] Acts iv. 13.

one of our company happened to be with his master, he was a hot-water carrier at the baths, who received only three nomismata a year, and had a wife and two children. When the beggar was going away this man followed him quietly, took off a small silver cross he was wearing, and gave it to him, saying that besides that he had only a sixpence[1] in the world.

Thus by chance, or rather through the good purpose of the all-wise God, I was privileged to see what he did, and deeply moved, I forthwith recounted it to the man sitting next to me, one Menas by name, a virtuous, God-fearing man who was also treasurer* of the most Holy Church in the time of the glorious and ever-blessed Patriarch John.

He, seeing me astonished and full of praise for the man who had done this deed of charity, said to me: 'Do not be surprised, for he practises that virtue by tradition and from instruction.' On my replying, 'How so? for pity's sake enlighten me!' he answered: 'He was servant to our most saintly, thrice-blessed Patriarch John, and like a true son he has inherited his father's virtue. — For the holy man once said to him, "Humble Zacharias, be charitable, for then you have a promise from God through me, a miserable sinner, that neither during my lifetime, nor after my death, will God desert you". And this promise He keeps to the present day. For God sends him many blessings and of these he spends nothing save that which he distributes forthwith to the poor, almost reducing his own household to want. Men have often heard him say to God in exultation, "Verily, verily, let us see who surpasses the other — Thou in sending blessings or I in scattering them! For Thou, Lord, art clearly the source of our riches and the giver of our livelihood". And it sometimes happens that he has nothing to give at the moment to a beggar, and then in his distress he says to some merchant or tradesman, "Give me a crown,[2] and I will work for you for a month or two, as you wish, because my folk at home are very hungry", and when he gets it he gives it to the poor man and begs him not to tell anyone.'

Menas, that pious man, observing that I listened to him as if to the gospel, said to me with emotion: 'Are you amazed at this, sir? What would you think then if you had met the sainted Patriarch?'

---

[1] Sixpence—a keration. [2] A 'crown'—one tremissis, see p. 192 *supra*.

'What!' said I. 'Is there anything I would rather have seen?'

Then he replied, 'By the grace of God he made me a priest and treasurer to the most Holy Church, and, believe me, I have seen him do things which are almost supernatural, and if you will deign to honour us to-day with your presence, I will relate to you the glorious deeds which I have beheld him do with my own eyes'. At these words I took him by the hand and helped him to rise, and he led me to his God-guarded house. But when he wanted us to sit down to table at once, I said to him, 'It is not right, master, to neglect the soul's nourishment and to satisfy the body before the soul, let us rather first partake of the food which perisheth not, and afterwards attend to the wants of the body'.

Then he began to give a truthful account of the holy man's life; he said, 'His first and most remarkable achievement is that he never at any time used an oath'. I at once asked for ink and paper and wrote down all he said, word for word.

2

After John had been elected and was to be enthroned in the Christ-loving capital of Alexandria most certainly by the will of God and not 'from men neither through man'[1] this was the first glorious deed and victory which he shewed forth to all men — he immediately summoned the treasurers and the official who is styled 'the guardian of the peace',* and said to them in the hearing of all in the Patriarch's council-chamber, 'It is not right, brethren, that we should consider anyone in preference to Christ'. The whole assembly which had gathered together was deeply moved at his words, and agreed thereto, and then the holy man continued, 'Go therefore through the whole city, please, and make a list of all my masters down to the last'. But his hearers could not imagine who these could be, and besought him to tell them, as they were astonished that any could possibly be masters of the Patriarch; and he opened his angelic mouth again and said: 'Those whom you call poor and beggars, these I proclaim my masters and helpers. For they, and they only, are really able to help us and bestow upon us the kingdom of heaven.'

[1] Cf. Gal. i. 1.

The imitator of Christ saw that this command was carried out with all speed, and he then bade them apportion a daily sum to be paid by his private treasurer sufficient for the needs of these poor; and they were more than seven thousand and a half.

Then like a true shepherd and no hireling he went with his sacred flock and the concourse of saintly bishops to the holy church and was enthroned by the will of God.

3

And there is another good deed which it would not be right to overlook amongst his achievements.— For on the morrow he again sent through the whole city his God-loving treasurers, and the ushers, and with them those who were entrusted with the civil administration of the city and insisted that it should not be lawful to use at will different measures or scales, whether great or small, throughout the city, but that everything should be bought and sold according to a single standard and weight, whether the 'modius' or 'artaba'.[1] He sent out an edict signed by his own hand throughout the whole neighbourhood worded as follows: 'John, the humble servant and the least of all the servants of our Lord Jesus Christ, to all whose lot it is to be shepherded under our Poverty by the same Lord, our God. The inspired and blessed apostle, Paul, gave this command and law to all through Christ Who spoke in him: "Obey them that have the rule over you, and submit to them; for they watch in behalf of our souls, as they that shall give account."[2] I, who am nothing, am convinced that in obedience to these godly words you will receive our requests as from God and not from man. Therefore, knowing this I exhort you, beloved, since God hates "a large and a small balance", as the holy Scripture says,[3] never to allow such a transgression of law to be seen anywhere amongst you. But if, after the promulgation of this our edict, subscribed by us, anyone shall be proved to have rendered himself open to such a charge, he shall hand over all his possessions to the needy, whether he will or no, and receive no compensation.'

We were anxious to insert this story about his public edict as we considered it most worthy of record.

[1] Both dry measures. [2] Heb. xiii. 17. [3] Deut. xxv. 13.

4

Some persons once informed this Saint of godly wisdom that the stewards of his church, being corrupted by bribes, were become respecters of persons in their administration of justice.

Thereupon he convoked them without delay and without bringing any charge against them, he increased the salaries they had received hitherto, and at the same time made it an inflexible rule that they should never take a gift from anyone whatsoever, 'for', said he, 'Fire shall consume the houses of the receivers of bribes'.[1] Consequently by God's grace their households from that time on prospered so exceedingly that some of them did not take their additional pay.

5

On another occasion the thrice-blessed found out that some who had been wronged by those who had gone to law with them and wished to appeal to the Patriarch were prevented from so doing through fear of the ushers and the disciplinary officials and the rest of his retinue. So he devised the following plan which was pleasing unto God.

Every Wednesday and Friday he had a seat and two stools placed in the open in front of the church and there he sat in company with a few virtuous men, or with the gospel in his hands and allowed no member of his great retinue to approach him except one disciplinary official. He was anxious to give confidence and ready access to those who wished to consult him, and on their behalf he caused justice to be done immediately by the disciplinary officials, and he used to order the latter not to touch food until they had settled the matter.

And he said so that all could hear, 'If we men have confidence that we can at any time enter into God's house with our petitions and make our requests known to the Unapproachable, the Lord of all creation, and we are impatient for our prayer to be granted, and we importune Him not to delay; nay, rather we at once cry in the words of the prophet: "Let Thy tender mercies speedily prevent us, O Lord!"[2] is it not then our duty to fulfil the requests of our fellow-servants with

---

[1] Job. xv. 34.   [2] Ps. lxxix.8.

all speed, remembering the words of our Lord, "With what measure ye mete, it shall be measured unto you again",[1] and those of the prophet: "As thou hast done, so be it done unto thee!" [2]

6

One day the admirable man went out as usual and sat in his accustomed place until the fifth hour, and as nobody came to him he returned all tearful and cast down. No one ventured to ask the reason of his despondency until the Saint Sophronius, who chanced to be present, said to him in private, 'What is the cause, God-guarded master, of this melancholy which is weighing down your holy soul and has cast us all into sudden dismay?' John answered in his meek voice, 'To-day for the first time humble John did not get any wages from anyone, and this was the first time that he could not offer anything to Christ on behalf of his countless sins'.

Then, inspired by God, Sophronius replied to the hierarch (for he at once guessed the reason of the Patriarch's sorrow), 'To-day you ought rather to rejoice and be delighted, most blessed master, for you are truly blessed if you have brought such peace to the flock entrusted to you, that nobody has a quarrel or dispute with his neighbour, but they are like the angels, free from enmity and from lawsuits'. When the truly meek shepherd felt satisfied that Sophronius had spoken the truth he lifted his eyes to heaven and said: 'I thank thee, O God, Who hast allowed me, unworthy as I am, to be called Thy priest and, though the least of men and a sinner, to be the shepherd of a reasonable flock.' Then he immediately laid aside all his despondency and much joy was added to him in his humility.

Some men say that Constantine* who reigned after Heraclius (whose son he was) imitated John in this respect.

7

During the lifetime of this saintly Patriarch the Persians came up and laid waste Syria and took its inhabitants captive.* All who escaped from the hands of the godless Persians ran

---

[1] Matt. vii. 2.   [2] Obadiah i. 15.

to the person of the thrice-blessed as if to a waveless harbour, praying that they, too, might enjoy help and assistance from him; and the blessed man welcomed and consoled them, not as if they were prisoners of war, but as though they were in truth his natural brothers.

He accordingly gave immediate orders that the wounded and sick should be put to bed in hostels and hospitals which he himself had founded, and that they should receive care and medical treatment without payment and that then they should be free to leave as each of them should choose. To those who were well but destitute and came to the daily distribution he gave sixpence apiece[1] to the men and one shilling[2] apiece to the women and children as being weaker members. Now some of the women, who came begging for alms, wore ornaments and bracelets, and those who were entrusted with the distribution reported this to the Patriarch. Then he, who was really gentle and of a cheerful countenance, put on a grim look and a harsh voice and said: 'If you wish to be distributors for humble John, or rather for Christ, obey unquestioningly the divine command which says: "Give to every man that asks of thee."[3] But, if you vex by your inquiries those who come to receive alms, God has no need of mischievous servants nor has humble John. If indeed the money given were mine and had come into existence with me I might do well to be niggardly with my own possessions. But if the money given happens to be God's, where His property is in question He wishes His commands to be followed absolutely.

'But if, perhaps, because you have no faith or are of little faith, you fear that the amount given away may exceed the moneys which we receive, I myself refuse to share in your little faith. For if it is by God's good will that I, an unworthy servant, am the dispenser of His gifts, then were the whole world to be brought together in Alexandria and ask for alms they would not straiten the holy Church nor the inexhaustible treasures of God.'

When he had dismissed them after banishing the indolence and little faith which beset them he told the following story to his companions who were astonished at his God-bestowed sympathy.

[1] i.e. one keration.   [2] i.e. two keratia.   [3] Luke vi. 30.

8

When I was in Cyprus and was but a stripling of about fifteen years old, I saw one day in my sleep a certain maiden whose countenance outshone the sun and who was adorned beyond all human imagining, and she came and stood by my bed and touched me on the side. I woke up and saw her really standing there and I perceived that she was no woman. I crossed myself and said to her: 'Who are you, and how did you dare to come into my room while I was sleeping?' She had, too, a wreath of olive branches on her head. And then with a joyous countenance and a smile on her lips she said to me: 'I am the first of the daughters of the King.' On hearing this I at once did obeisance to her. And then she said to me: 'If you will have me as a friend, I will lead you into the presence of the King. For no one has as free access to Him as I have. For I caused Him to put on man's nature on earth and bring salvation to men.' With these words she disappeared.

When I came to myself I understood the vision and said, 'Verily she is either Sympathy or Charity, and for this reason she had a wreath of olive leaves on her head. For it was certainly sympathy with, and pity for mankind that made our Lord become incarnate in our flesh'.* I dressed quickly and without waking anyone in the house I made my way to the church. For it was already dawn. And on my way I met a brother shivering with cold, so I took off my goatskin and gave it to him, saying to myself, 'Now by this I shall know whether my vision was really a true one or sent by a demon'. And truth bore witness, for before I reached the church a man clad in white suddenly met me and handed me a bag with 100 nomismata in it saying, 'Take this, brother, and use it as you like'. In my joy I turned round directly I had taken it, wishing to give him back the bag as I was not in want, but I could not see anybody. Then I said: 'Certainly it was not my imagina-tion.'

From that time on I would often give an alms to a fellow-brother and would say to myself, 'Let me see whether God will repay me a hundredfold as He said'. In this way I tempted God, acting wrongly, and after I was fully satisfied by the facts themselves in various ways, I said: 'Leave off, wretched soul, tempting Him who cannot be tempted.' To think that when my humble soul has received such ample proofs from God these faithless folk should come to-day hoping to persuade me as well as themselves to shew a want of pity!

9

Whilst this same crowd of people was still in the city, one of the strangers, noticing John's remarkable sympathy, determined to try the blessed man; so he put on old clothes and approached him as he was on his way to visit the sick in the hospitals (for he did this two or three times a week) and said to him: 'Have mercy upon me for I am a prisoner of war.' John said to his purse-bearer: 'Give him six nomismata.' After the man had received these he went off, changed his clothes, met John again in another street, and falling at his feet said: 'Have pity upon me for I am in want.' The Patriarch again said to his purse-bearer: 'Give him six nomismata.' As he went away the purse-bearer whispered in the Patriarch's ear: 'By your prayers, master, this same man has had alms from you twice over!' But the Patriarch pretended not to understand. Soon the man came again for the third time to ask for money and the attendant, carrying the gold, nudged the Patriarch to let him know that it was the same man; whereupon the truly merciful and beloved of God said: 'Give him twelve nomismata, for perchance it is my Christ and He is making trial of me.'

10

There was a foreign captain who had fallen upon evil days, he came to the blessed man and with many tears besought him to show mercy to him as he did to all others. So John directed that he should be given five pounds of gold. With these the captain went and bought a cargo, and no sooner had he gone on board than straightway, as it chanced, he suffered shipwreck outside the Pharos,* but he did not lose his ship. Then trusting to John's good will he again applied to him saying, 'Have mercy upon me as God had mercy upon the world'. The Patriarch said to him, 'Believe me, brother, if you had not mixed your own remaining monies with the money of the

Church, you would not have been shipwrecked. For you had them from an evil source and thus the money coming from a good source was lost with it'. However he gave fresh instructions this time that ten pounds of gold were to be given him and he was not to mix other money with it. Again the captain bought a cargo and when he had sailed for one day a violent wind arose and he was hurled upon the land and lost everything, including the ship, and he and the crew barely escaped with their lives. After this from despair and destitution the captain decided to hang himself. But God, Who ever takes forethought for the salvation of men, revealed this to the most blessed Patriarch, who, hearing what had happened to the captain, sent him word to come to him without delay. The latter came before him with his head sprinkled with dust and his tunic torn and in disorder. When the Patriarch saw him in this guise he found fault with him and said, 'May the Lord be propitious unto you! Blessed be God! I believe His word that from to-day on you will not be wrecked again as long as you live. This disaster happened to you because you had acquired the ship itself, too, by unjust means'.

He immediately ordered that one of the ships belonging to the Holy Church of which he was head should be handed over to the captain, a swift sailer* laden with twenty thousand bushels of corn. The captain, when he had received the ship, sailed away from Alexandria, and on his return he made a solemn statement to the following effect: 'We sailed for twenty days and nights, and owing to a violent wind we were unable to tell in what direction we were going either by the stars or by the coast. But the only thing we knew was that the steersman saw the Patriarch by his side holding the tiller and saying to him: "Fear not! You are sailing quite right." Then after the twentieth day we caught sight of the islands of Britain, and when we had landed we found a great famine raging there. Accordingly when we told the chief man of the town that we were laden with corn, he said, "God has brought you at the right moment. Choose as you wish, either one 'nomisma' for each bushel or a return freight of tin". And we chose half of each.' Then the story goes on to tell of a matter which to those who are ignorant of God's free gifts is either hard to believe or quite incredible, but to those who have experienced His marvellous works it is both credible and acceptable. 'Then we set sail again,' said the captain, 'and joyfully made once more for Alexandria, putting in on our way at Pentapolis.'* The captain then took out some of the tin to sell — for he had an old business-friend there who asked for some — and he gave him a bag of about fifty pounds. The latter, wishing to sample it to see if it was of good quality, poured some into a brazier and found that it was silver of the finest quality. He thought that the captain was tempting him, so carried the bag to him and said, 'May God forgive you! Have you ever found me deceiving you that you tempt me by giving me silver instead of tin?' The captain was dumbfounded by his words and replied: 'Believe me, I thought it was tin! But if He who turned the water into wine has turned my tin into silver in answer to the Patriarch's prayers, that is nothing strange. However, that you may be satisfied, come down to the ship with me and look at the rest of the mass from which I gave you some.' So they went and discovered that the tin had been turned into the finest silver.

Mark ye, lovers of Christ, this miracle is not strange. For He Who multiplied the five loaves and at another time converted the waters of the Nile into blood, transformed a rod into a serpent, and changed fire into dew, easily accomplished this miracle, too, in order to enrich His servant and show mercy to the captain.

II

One Sunday when this saintly man was going down to his church there came to him one whose whole house had been despoiled by burglars; they had taken everything even down to his mattress. The sufferer was in great distress* but, as those who had robbed his house could not be found in spite of a strict search, he was finally obliged by his extreme want, very shamefacedly, to apply to the Saint and told him about his misfortune. The Saint was very sorry for him — for he was one of the prominent foreign residents — and whispered to the man in charge of the gold to give him fifteen pounds of gold. When the latter went out to give the money to the man he took counsel with the cashier and with the treasurer and at the

Devil's prompting they grudged him so large a sum and gave him only five pounds.

On the venerable Archbishop's return from the service, a widow woman, who had an only son, brought him news that she intended to give him five hundred pounds of gold. After he had received this message and dismissed his venerable council, he summoned the stewards and said to them, 'How many pounds did you give to my suppliant?' and they answered, 'Fifteen pounds, sir, as your Holiness commanded'. But by the grace residing in him he perceived that they were lying, so he sent for the recipient and asked him how much he had received. On his replying 'Five pounds', the Saint produced from his venerable hand the bond the woman had given him and said to them, 'God will demand the other ten hundred pounds from you, for, if you had given fifteen pounds as my humbleness ordered, she who has offered me five hundred pounds would have given fifteen, and to convince you of this I will send and ask the giver to come'. He dispatched two pious men to fetch the very pious woman who had given him the bond and to bring her to the baptistry; he sent her a message, 'Come to my humbleness and bring with you the offering which God put it into your heart to bring to Him'. She arose hurriedly and came into the presence of the Saint bringing the sum of money with her. After receiving her oblation and bestowing many blessings upon her and her son, the Patriarch said to her: 'I charge you by your prayers, mother, tell me, did you intend to give only this to Christ or a little more in addition?' As she perceived that the inspired man had guessed what she had done she fell to trembling and said: 'By your Reverence's holy prayers and by my patron-saint, Menas,* I had written fifteen hundred on the bond and an hour before I gave it to your Reverence as I was standing during the service, I opened it unthinkingly and read it; I, your unworthy servant, had written it with my own hand and yet I found that the "ten." had got wiped out of itself. Then in my amazement I said to myself, "Evidently it is God's will that I should not give more than five".' When the Patriarch had dismissed the pious woman, the stewards who had disobeyed him fell at his feet craving his forgiveness and assuring him that they would never transgress again.

12

Nicetas, the patrician,* had observed this virtuous man's great-mindedness and seen that his hand was open unsparingly and gave to all as if from an ever-flowing spring; at the suggestion of certain slanderers he visited the Saint and said to him: 'The Empire is in great straits and needs money. Therefore instead of spending so prodigally the money that comes in to you, give it into the public purse for the benefit of the Empire.'

The Saint remained unperturbed by these words and replied, 'To my mind, my lord, it is not right to give to an earthly king what is offered to the heavenly King. But even if your heart is set on some such plan, let me tell you that humble John will not give you a penny. But see, the money-chest of Christ is there under my lowly bed. Do as you will.'

The patrician got up at once and shouted to his own followers to carry off the treasure; he loaded them with all the money, only leaving the Patriarch one hundred pounds. As the men were going down carrying their burden others were coming up carrying small jars containing money sent to the Patriarch from Africa, labelled either 'Finest honey' or 'Unsmoked honey'.

The patrician read the labels as he went down and asked the Patriarch to send him some of this honey for his cellar, for he knew well that the Saint never bore malice.

When the man in charge of the jars came up and gave the Patriarch the documents he carried he announced to him that there was money instead of honey in the jars. Thereupon that truly gentle shepherd forthwith sent Nicetas a pot labelled 'Finest honey', and with it a tablet on which were written these words: 'Our Master who said "I will not fail thee nor forsake thee"[1] cannot lie and is a true God. Therefore corruptible man cannot straiten God Who gives life and food to all. Farewell.' He ordered the men who were going to carry the jar to Nicetas to open it in his presence and say to him, 'All the jars you saw being brought up are full of money instead of honey'.

Now it happened that the men bearing the jar as well as the Patriarch's note were brought to Nicetas as he sat at table;

[1] Heb. xiii. 5.

and when they came in and he saw only one jar he said, 'Tell him, "Surely you are angry with me, great lord, you have not in the past sent me only one jar".'

After handing him the tablet when they had unsealed the jar, the men straightway poured out all the contents, and informed him that the rest of the jars which he had seen were likewise all filled with money.

Then when he read the words, 'Corruptible man is unable to straiten God' he was pricked to the heart by the message and said, 'As the Lord liveth neither will Nicetas straiten Him, for he is but a sinful and corruptible man himself'. And straightway he left his lunch and taking with him all the money which he had carried off from the venerable father and the jar which he had sent, as well as three hundred pounds of his own, he made for the Patriarch's dwelling; he took none of his suite with him but came to him in deep self-abasement and besought him to implore God's forgiveness as he had been incited to his act by others slanderously. He also assured the Patriarch that, if he assigned him a penance, he would willingly accept and fulfil it. As the Patriarch marvelled at the man's swift transformation he did not upbraid him for what he had sought to do, but rather consoled him with comforting words. And from that day so strong a bond of affection was knit between the two men that the Patriarch became the godfather of the patrician's children.

13

He that tempted Abraham for our advantage that the whole world might know and imitate his faith which was known only to God also tempted this glorious John. Now the manner of his temptation has become an example for the benefit of God's holy churches, and this was the temptation. An indescribable number of fugitives from the Persians invaded Alexandria, as I have said before, and great scarcity of food prevailed because the river had not risen to its usual height; therefore after he had spent all the money he had, the holy Patriarch sent and borrowed about ten hundred pounds from divers good Christians. After these too had been spent in their turn the famine still prevailed and no one was willing to lend him any more as all feared the persistence of the famine; since the need of those who had come to look for his support was still urgent, the blessed man continued in much anxiety and prayer.

Now a certain land-owner who lived in the city noticed the straits, or rather the absolute poverty, to which the Saint had been reduced; now his wish was to become a deacon of the Holy Church, but he had married a second time.* So he hoped to persuade the holy man to ordain him by reason of the stress which encompassed him on every side and he sent a petition to him in the following terms — for he did not dare to utter such a request to his face — 'To the most holy and thrice-blessed father of fathers, John the deputy of Christ, the request and petition of Cosmas, an unworthy servant of the servants of thy Holiness. Having learnt, most holy Sir, of the shortage in food which oppresses thy honourable person by the per-mission of God, or rather in consequence of our sins, I, thy servant, do not consider it just to live at my ease whilst my master abides in continual need. Your unworthy servant has two hundred thousand bushels of corn, and one hundred and eighty pounds of gold; these I beg that I may offer to Christ through you, my lord. Only let me, unworthy though I am, enjoy the post of deacon under you, so that by standing beside my lord at the holy altar I may be cleansed from the profligacy of my sins. For, true herald of God, it has been said by the holy apostle Paul that "There is made of necessity a change also of the law".'[1]

After receiving this letter the wise man of God sent for the writer and said to him: 'Was it you who sent me the petition by your notary and son?' and on his answering 'Yes, master', the blessed man sent everybody out of the room as in his great sympathy he did not wish to humiliate Cosmas before them all. Then he turned to him and said: 'Your offering is a generous one and much needed at the present time but it has a blemish, and you know that in the law a sheep, be it large or small, was not accepted for an offering unless it were without blemish, and for this reason God would not take heed of Cain even when he offered his sacrifice. As to what you said, brother, that there is made of necessity a change also of the law, the apostle said that about the law of the old covenant. For what

[1] Heb. vii. 12.

is it that James, the Lord's brother, says, "For whosoever shall keep the whole law and yet stumble in one point, he is become guilty of all"?[1] But as regards my brethren, the poor, and the holy Church, the God Who fed them before you and I were born will Himself feed them also in our day, but only if we keep His commands inviolate. For He Who long ago multiplied the five loaves is able also to bless the ten bushels in my granary. Therefore I say to thee, my son, what is written in the Acts, "Thou hast neither part nor lot in this matter".'[2]

After he had dismissed this man who was sullen at not having achieved his purpose, news was brought that two of the Church's fast-sailing ships, which he had sent to Sicily for corn, had cast anchor in the harbour. At these tidings the blessed man knelt on the ground and gave thanks to Almighty God saying: 'I thank Thee, Master, that Thou didst not permit Thy servant to sell Thy grace for money; verily they that seek Thee, Lord, and keep the canons of Thy holy Church shall never want any good thing.'

14

On one occasion two of the clerics committed a sin, for they attacked each other, and in consequence the Patriarch suspended them from their duties for some days according to the Canons. One of them willingly suffered his punishment and acknowledged his sin; but the other, a man of bad character, hailed the punishment with joy, for the wretched fellow was seeking a pretext for not attending church and desired a long freedom for his lawless doings. And he was very wroth with the Patriarch and threatened to do him as much harm as he himself could purpose. Some even say that it was he who talked slanderously about the Church's money to Nicetas, the patrician, who carried it off high-handedly, as we have already recounted. This fellow's maliciousness and perverse purpose were reported to the blessed Patriarch, who, being a true shepherd, called to mind him who said, 'Who is weak and I am not weak?',[3] and again, 'You that are strong bear ye the infirmities of the weak!'[4] Accordingly he determined to send

---

[1] James ii. 10. [2] Acts viii. 21.
[3] 2 Cor. xi. 29. [4] Rom. xv. 1.

for him, exhort him fittingly, and release him from the suspension, for he saw that the wolf was trying to seize the sheep. But by God's dispensation in order that the Patriarch's forgiving spirit might be made known to all men, he forgot to send for the cleric and release him from his punishment.

When Easter Sunday came round and he was near the holy altar to offer the bloodless sacrifice, and the deacon had all but reached the close of the catholic prayer,* and the holy veil* was about to be lifted, he suddenly thought of the malicious cleric. And straightway he remembered the divine command which says: 'If therefore thou art offering thy gift at the altar, and there rememberest that thy brother hath aught against thee, leave there thy gift before the altar and go thy way, first be reconciled to thy brother and then come and offer thy gift',[1] so he instructed the deacon to begin the deacon's prayer over again, and when he had finished, to repeat it once again, until his Holiness returned. For he pretended that his stomach was troubling him. Then he went into the sacristy of the church and at once dispatched about twenty vergers to search for the evil-minded cleric, since the shepherd's intention was to snatch the sheep from the lion's mouth. And God, Who does the will of those who fear Him, caused the cleric to fall into their hands at once, and when he was brought in, the Patriarch first of all, so a witness testifies, threw himself down and said: 'Forgive me, brother!' Then through awe of the honourable Patriarch's high-priesthood and the presence of the onlookers, but still more through fear of condemnation and dread lest fire should come down from heaven at that very moment and destroy him as he looked at that venerable grey head lying on the ground, the cleric too threw himself on his knees begging for forgiveness and mercy. After the Patriarch had said: 'May God forgive us all!' they both arose and went into the church. And thus with great joy and delight the Patriarch stood before the holy altar with a clear conscience and was able to say to God: 'Forgive us our debts, as we forgive our debtors.' From that day the cleric who held the post of reader in the church was so chastened and filled with compunction that later he was accounted worthy to be ordained priest.

[1] Matt. v. 23-4.

15

Some of the inspired fathers of the Church say, 'It is characteristic of the angels never to fight at all, but to abide in complete and perpetual peace; of men to quarrel indeed, but to be reconciled immediately and without delay; of demons to fight and to remain unreconciled all day long'.

I write this, lovers of Christ, as an introduction to the following narrative.

It happened one day that this glorious Patriarch had a dispute with the afore-mentioned patrician, Nicetas, about a public matter. The cause of the quarrel must also be stated as it is edifying — this was the quarrel. The patrician on his side wanted to regulate the market so as to ensure a profit for the State, whereas the Patriarch could not tolerate this because he took thought for the welfare of the poor. They argued about this for a long time in the council-room, and, as they could not come to an agreement, they separated in anger and unreconciled to each other. It was then the fifth hour; the Patriarch's resistance and bitterness were in support of God's command, while the patrician's were for the sake of a financial profit. Yet a righteous man says: 'Man ought not to grow angry either for a reasonable, or unreasonable cause.' So at the eleventh hour the Patriarch sent this memorable message to the patrician by the hands of the chief elder accompanied by the clergy, 'Master, the sun is nigh setting'.

When Nicetas heard the message, he could not bear the fever in his heart but, as if pricked to the soul by the divine fire of the Saint's message, he suddenly dissolved into tears and rising, went to seek the blessed man. Directly the righteous man saw him he said: 'The son of the Church, ever obedient to her voice, has done well to come.' Next they both knelt down and embraced each other, then seating themselves, the Patriarch opened his wise mouth and said: 'Truly, master, had I not known that you were very disturbed about this matter, I should not have hesitated to come to your lordship. For our Lord and God, Jesus Christ, used to go round the towns and villages and houses Himself and visited individuals, too.' All present were edified and amazed by the Patriarch's humility, and the patrician answered, 'Really, father, my ears are no longer big enough to hold all the slanderous tales people come and tell me'. Thereupon the wise teacher said to him, 'Listen, son and brother. If we were prepared to believe all we hear, we should be responsible for many sins, especially at the present time when the majority of men hate one another. For I, too, was often led astray by persons who brought me information about public affairs, and often after I had inflicted punishment wrongfully I found I had been misdirected, for others would come later and tell me that I had been misinformed in giving my judgment. Therefore after this had happened to me two or three times I made it a rule for myself never to give effect to any decision except after hearing both parties and to assign to those who brought me information, if their information was false, the same punishment as that which was fitting for the man informed against. So from that day nobody ventures to come to me with information about anybody without danger to himself.

'Wherefore, my son, I adjure and advise your Excellency to do likewise. For those entrusted with authority have often been known to put innocent men to death, if they have been credulous and have decided cases that came before them without full inquiry.' And the patrician, as if warned by God, agreed to observe this rule inviolate.

16

The glorious man had a nephew named George. One day this nephew had a quarrel with one of the shopkeepers in the town and was grievously insulted by him. George was bitterly vexed, not only because he had been publicly dishonoured, but more because it had been at the hands of a mean fellow, and most of all because he was the nephew of the Patriarch; so he went to see the latter in his private room weeping bitterly. When the gentle Patriarch beheld him so distressed and tearful he inquired the reason for his state of misery, wishing to learn what had caused it.

George, however, could not himself give a clear statement because of the bitterness of soul which had overmastered him; accordingly his companions who had been present when this insult was put upon him by the shopkeeper began to explain the reason to the Patriarch. 'It is not right', they said, 'for your Holiness to be so despised that your relations and kinsfolk should be insulted by abandoned creatures.'

Then he who was indeed a true physician wished first to treat his nephew's inflammation, as it were with a soothing salve, and afterwards, by his wise words, to cut out and remove the source of pain as if by the knife. Accordingly he began to allay his suffering by these words: 'What, did someone actually dare to open his mouth and shout recriminations at you? Trust me, child, and I, your father, will do a thing to him today at which all Alexandria will be astonished.' When he saw that his nephew was calmed and had shaken off all his grief, for he imagined that the Patriarch would proceed against the man who had insulted him and have him scourged and paraded in public by the overseer of the market, he kissed his breast and said to him, 'Boy, if you are in reality the nephew of my humbleness, prepare yourself to be beaten and insulted by everybody; for true relationship is not declared through flesh and blood, but through the virtue of the soul'.

He immediately summoned the overseer of the shopkeepers and ordered him never in future to accept from that shopkeeper either his customary 'tip' or the public taxes or the rent for the shop,* for this shop, too, belonged to the Holy Church.

All were amazed at the man's unshaken magnanimity and understood that this was what he meant when he said, 'I will do a thing to him which will astonish all Alexandria', i.e. to show him favour instead of taking revenge on him.

17

The blessed Patriarch was once informed that a certain cleric harboured a grudge against another and was quite irreconcilable; he accordingly asked for the man's name and rank. And on the morrow, which was a Sunday, he learnt that he was a deacon, called Damianus. He therefore ordered the archdeacon to point Damianus out to him when he came into the church, but not to say anything to him. At the Sunday service the next morning this deacon was present with the others, and as soon as he saw him the archdeacon pointed him out to the Patriarch. The latter was present that day at the holy altar for this one purpose, but he had not confided to anyone what he intended doing. When, therefore, the deacon

Damianus came up in his turn to receive the Holy Communion from him, the Saint took his hand and said: 'Go first and be reconciled to thy brother and then come and partake worthily of the immaculate Mysteries of the forgiving Christ!' Damianus was too ashamed to contradict the Saint before such a number of clerics and especially in such a place and such an awful hour, so he agreed to do this, and afterwards the Saint administered the Holy Mysteries to him. From thenceforth all, both clerics and laymen, took care not to bear malice to each other for fear the Saint should make them contemptible and ashamed as he had made the deacon.

18

This saintly man had also a good knowledge of the holy Scriptures, not so much an accurate knowledge of the words through learning them by heart (which is but for vainglory), but by actually practising their precepts and keeping their commandments. If you looked in at his council-room any day, there was no idle word spoken — unless he was engaged in the settlement of some civic matter — but only stories of the holy fathers, or scriptural questions or dogmatic problems due to the multitude of unmentionable heretics* who swarmed in the country. If perchance someone began slanderous gossip, the Patriarch, like a wise man, would courteously turn him off it by starting another subject, but, if the gossiper persisted, he said nothing more at the time but would point him out to the doorkeeper and tell him never again to admit him with those that came to consult the Patriarch; in this way the others were taught through him to practise self-control.

19

We must not omit to mention another rule which the just man put into practice. He had heard that, when an emperor is crowned, first of all the members of the guild of tomb-builders* have access to the royal presence while the whole Senate and the army are in attendance; directly after the crowning the builders of the imperial tomb come in and bring with them four or five small pieces of marbles of different colours and say to him: 'Of which mineral does Your Majesty desire his tomb to be made?' thus suggesting to him that, as a corruptible mortal who soon passes away, he should take thought for his own soul, and govern his kingdom righteously. — The blessed man imitated this truly praiseworthy custom and gave orders for a tomb to be built for him in the place where the previous patriarchs were buried, but to leave it unfinished until his death so that on some great feast-day when the clergy were present, the zealous Christians,* as they are called, should come in and say to him, 'Your tomb, master, is still unfinished. Allow us, we pray, to finish it because you do not know at what hour the thief will come'. The Patriarch arranged this to be done in that wise in order to leave a good example to his successors.

20

The Lord allowed His churches in Jerusalem to be burnt down by the heathen Persians because of the multitude of our sins.* So when the saintly Patriarch learnt that the holy Modestus, Patriarch* of Jerusalem, was in great distress, he sent him towards the rebuilding and repairing of the churches 1000 nomismata, 1000 sacks of corn, and 1000 of pulse, 1000 lb. of iron, 1000 casks of dried fish called 'Maeno- mene',* 1000 jars* of wine and 1000 Egyptian workmen, with the following letter: 'Forgive me, true workman of Christ, for sending nothing worthy of Christ's churches. Rest assured, that if it were possible, I would come and work myself in the house of the Holy Resurrection of Christ our God. Further I beseech your venerable self not to inscribe the name of my unworthy self anywhere at all, but rather ask Christ to inscribe my name there where the inscription is truly blessed.'

21

Another good habit this Saint also adopted, namely sleeping on the cheapest of beds and using only very poor coverings in his own cell. One of the city's landowners once went into the Patriarch's room and saw that he was only covered with a torn and worn quilt, so he sent him a quilt costing 36 nomismata and besought him earnestly to cover himself with that in memory, he said, of the giver.

John took and used it for one night because of the giver's insistence, but throughout the night he kept saying to himself (for so his chamber-attendants related), 'Who shall say that humble John' — for he ever called himself that — 'was lying under a coverlet costing 36 nomismata whilst Christ's brethren are pinched with cold? How many are there at this minute grinding their teeth because of the cold? and how many have only a rough blanket half below and half above them so that they cannot stretch out their legs but lie shivering, rolled up like a ball of thread? How many are sleeping on the mountain without food or light, suffering twofold pangs from cold and hunger? How many would like to be filled with the outer leaves of the vegetables which are thrown away from my kitchen? How many would like to dip their bit of bread into the soup-water which my cooks throw away? How many would like even to have a sniff at the wine which is poured out in my wine-cellar? How many strangers are there at this hour in the city who have no lodging-place but lie about in the market-place, perhaps with the rain falling on them? How many are there who have not tasted oil for one month or even two? How many have no second garment either in summer or winter and so live in misery? And yet you, who hope to obtain everlasting bliss, both drink wine and eat large fishes and spend your time in bed, and now in addition to all those evils you are being kept warm by a coverlet worth 36 nomismata. Verily, if you live like that and pass your life in such ease, do not expect to enjoy the good things prepared for us on high; but you will certainly be told, as was that other rich man: "Thou in thy lifetime receivedst thy good things, but the poor evil things; and now they are comforted, but thou art in anguish?"[1] Blessed be God! You shall not cover humble John a second night. For it is right and acceptable to God that 144 of your brothers and masters should be covered rather than you, one miserable creature.' For four rough blankets could be bought for one nomisma. Early on the following morning, therefore, he sent it to be sold, but the man who had given it saw it and bought it for 36 nomismata and again brought it to the Patriarch. But when he saw it put up for sale again the next day he bought it once more and carried it to the Patriarch and implored him to use it. When he had done this for the third time the Saint said to him

[1] Luke xvi. 25.

jokingly, 'Let us see whether you or I will give up first!' For the man was exceedingly well-to-do, and the Saint took pleasure in getting money out of him, and he used to say that if with the object of giving to the poor anybody were able, without ill-will, to strip the rich right down to their shirts, he would not do wrong, more especially if they were heartless skinflints. For thereby he gets a two-fold profit, firstly he saves their souls, and secondly he himself will gain no small reward therefrom. And to confirm this saying he would adduce as trustworthy evidence the tale about St. Epiphanius and John the Patriarch of Jerusalem — to wit that the former would skilfully steal away the Patriarch John's silver and give it to the poor.*

22

[The story which is related in this chapter is omitted, as a similar legend is found in other sources and the story has no direct bearing on the life of John. — We give the last paragraph of the chapter.]

For John was able to give profitable instruction to a man, even against the latter's will, not only by stories from his own life but also by other true and God-pleasing tales. And he used always to say to those that heard them, 'If some men have not spared their own blood, but have given even that for the service of their brethren, or rather of Christ, how much more then ought not we with zeal and humility to give of our possessions to the poor and needy so that we may receive our recompense from the just rewarder, God, on that fearful and terrible day of vengeance, when he who sows sparingly will also reap sparingly, and he who sowed in blessings, that is generously and large-heartedly, will also reap very abundantly, that is, he will inherit those good things which pass all understanding'.

23

Our Saint who was adorned with so many good deeds was not wanting either in this respect, for he dearly loved reading the lives of the holy fathers, especially of those who practised almsgiving.

One day when reading the life of St. Serapion,* who was nicknamed Sindonius, he came across the following passage: 'Serapion once gave his cloak to a poor man and as he walked on and met another who was shivering, he gave that one his tunic, and then sat down naked, holding the holy Gospel, and on being asked, "Who has taken your clothes, father?" he pointed to the Gospel and said, "This is the robber". Another time he sold the Gospel to give an alms and when a disciple said to him, "Father, where is your Gospel?" he replied, "Son, believe me, it was the Gospel which said to me 'Sell all you have and give to the poor', so I sold it and gave to the poor that on the day of judgment we may have freer access to God".'

He also read: 'Another time a widow woman asked the same St. Serapion for alms because her children were hungry and as he had nothing whatever to give her, he obliged her to sell him to some pagan* actors, and these he converted to Christianity in a few days.'

After reading all this about St. Serapion he was so overcome and filled with admiration for his goodness that he burst into tears and then summoned all his own officials and read all these portions about St. Serapion to them and said: 'On my soul, you lovers of Christ, see how greatly a man is edified by reading the lives of the holy fathers. For, believe me, until today I really thought that I was doing a little something by giving away the monies which came to me, for I did not know that some, when overcome by pity, even sold themselves!'

24

Above all, this Saint ever honoured and reverenced the monkish habit and felt special sympathy for any monk who was hard pressed for his bodily needs. And he had this peculiarity which was not shared by many, that he would never listen to an accusation, either false or true, against any wearer of the monkish habit. For owing to the suggestion of some slanderers he once had the following experience:

A monk wandered round in the city, begging alms for several days, accompanied by a rather young girl; some persons who saw him were scandalized and imagined she was his wife, and therefore carried accusations against him to the Patriarch,

'Because, reverend father,' said they, 'he is turning the angelic robe of the monkish life into ridicule, by having a girl as wife'.

Accordingly the Patriarch thinking to prevent sins against God — Who had appointed him to this end — immediately gave orders for the woman to be beaten and separated from him, and for the monk to be scourged and to be imprisoned in solitary confinement. The Saint's order was carried out with all speed, and in the night the monk appeared to him in his dreams, showing him his back which was all torn to ribbons — for the church police-officers had scourged him pitilessly — and said to him: 'So it please you, my lord Patriarch, this once you have made a mistake as any other man might', and with these words he vanished.

In the morning the holy man recalled the dream which had come to him in the night and sat on his bed full of thought. Then quickly he sent and had the monk brought to him by his syncellus* from the place where he had been confined, for the blessed man kept wondering in his mind whether he would resemble the monk whom he had seen in his dream. So when the monk came in, walking with great difficulty — for he could hardly move because of the terrible flogging he had endured — and the Patriarch saw his face, he remained speechless and immovable and buried in thought, unable to utter a sound. Only with his hand he motioned to the monk to sit down near him on his couch. After he had regained his self-possession and signed himself with the Cross he begged the monk to gird a cloth round him and then to undress without shame so that he might see whether his back was in such a state as he had seen in his dream; with much reluctance the monk consented, girt on his own loin-cloth, and began to undress. Now, as he was undressing to show his back to the holy Patriarch, by the unexpected will of God the loin-cloth he had on got loose and dropped to the ground, and all there saw that he was a eunuch, which no one had noticed before as he was a very young man.

When the Patriarch and all who were with him had seen this and especially his horribly mutilated back, the Patriarch immediately sent and subjected to penance those who had slandered the monk without inquiry, while he made many apologies to the most holy monk, saying that it was through ignorance that he had sinned against him and against God. Further, the just man gave to the monk this counsel: 'It is not right, my son,' he said, 'that those who are clad in the holy and angelic robe as you are should wander about unguardedly in cities and, above all, they should not take a woman about with them to the scandal of the beholders.' Then the monk in deep humility made his defence to the holy Patriarch, saying: 'I assure you, master, I am not lying — I was in Gaza a few days ago and as I was coming out of the city to go and worship at the shrine of the holy abbot, Cyrus, this girl who has so skilfully hung herself on to me, met me — it was already evening — and falling at my feet she begged that she might journey with me; "For", said she, "I am a Jewess and wish to become a Christian." And then she began to invoke horrible curses upon me if I left her to perish. Therefore through fear of the judgment of God I took her, thinking that Satan does not send temptation to eunuchs; I did not realize that he does not spare anyone. So when we came to the church, your Holiness, and had finished our prayers, I baptized her there in the church of the holy abbot, Cyrus. And in simplicity of heart I travelled about with her asking a few alms in order that I might place her in a convent.'

When he heard this tale, the Patriarch said: 'Upon my soul, how many hidden servants God has, and we, simple ones, do not know them!'* Then he related to all those who were present the vision concerning the monk which he had had in the night, and afterwards taking 100 nomismata in his hand, offered them to the monk. But he, the God-loving man and true monk, would not hear of taking any sum worth mentioning,* but spoke these words to the Patriarch: 'I do not want these coins, master, for if a monk has faith, he does not need money; and if he does need money, he has not faith.' This remark more than anything else convinced his hearers that he was a servant of God. After kneeling before the Patriarch he went away in peace. From henceforth therefore the Patriarch showed special honour and hospitality to monks, both to the good and to those who were reputed to be evil, and he at once built a hostel entirely for them and called it 'The Monks' Inn'.

25

When the plague was at one time raging in the city, the just man used to go and watch the funerals for he said that this and the contemplation of graves were very edifying. Often too he would sit at the bedside of persons in their death-anguish, and would close their eyes with his own hands, wishing thereby to keep the thought of his own death in continual remembrance. He also enjoined prayers for the dying to be celebrated diligently and perpetually, and in support of this he told the following story: 'A short time ago,' he said, 'a man was captured by the Persians, and when taken to Persia was confined in the dungeon called Lethe.* Some other prisoners who escaped and reached Cyprus were asked by his parents whether they had seen him by any chance; to which they replied: "We buried him with our own hands." But that was not really the man about whom they were questioned, but another exactly like him. They also told the parents the month and the day of his death, and so the latter had prayers said three times a year for him whom they presumed to be dead.

'Four years later he escaped from the Persians and returned to Cyprus. Then his relatives said, "We heard for certain, brother, that you were dead and therefore we have held memorial services for you three times a year".

'On hearing that they did this for him three times a year he asked on what month and day the services were held, and they replied: "At Epiphany, at Easter, and on Whit-Sunday."

'Thereupon he said: "On those three feasts in the year a man in white raiment, like the sun, used to come and free me invisibly from my chains and from my cell and all that day I walked about and nobody recognized me. Yet on the morrow there I was in chains again!"'

The holy Patriarch used to say: 'We learn from this story that those who have fallen asleep obtain comfort from the prayers we make on their behalf.'

26

The effect produced by this sympathetic man's deeds was often the same as that which we hear followed the actions of the holy Apostles. For many who observed his constant and unquestioning pity for the needy were often moved to sell many of their possessions and to bring the money and offer it to this kindhearted servant of God. For instance, a man came one day bringing seven and a half pounds of gold and told the holy man that was all the gold he possessed; then he begged him with many a genuflection to pray to God to preserve his son (for he had an only boy about fifteen years old), and also to bring back his ship safely from Africa, to which country it had sailed.

The Patriarch took the money from his hand and marvelled at the man's magnanimity in bringing him all the money he possessed, then on the man's behalf he offered up a lengthy prayer in his presence and so dismissed him. Yet because of the man's great faith he placed the bag containing the money under the holy table in the oratory of his own bed-chamber and at once celebrated the whole liturgy over it, earnestly importuning God on behalf of the giver to save the latter's son and to bring back the ship safely, as the man had begged him to do.

Before thirty days had passed the son of him who had brought the seven and a half pounds to the Patriarch died, and three days after the boy's death the ship arrived from Africa, on which the man's own brother sailed as 'Master', but near the Pharos* it suffered shipwreck, all the cargo was lost and only the lives of the crew and the empty ship were saved.

When the ship-owner, the father of the boy, heard of this further catastrophe which had befallen him, then in the words of the Psalmist: 'His soul had almost dwelt in Hades.'[1] For before his grief for his son had been assuaged he was further thrown into despair by the loss of the ship.

All these occurrences were reported to the Patriarch who grieved almost more than the sufferer himself, especially over the loss of the man's only son. And as he did not know what to do, he besought God in His mercy to comfort the man through His boundless pity; for he was ashamed to send for the man and comfort him face to face; yet he did send him a message not to let his spirits fail, reminding him that 'God does nothing without judgment, but all is to our profit though we know it not'. To show him that he would not lose the

[1] Ps. xciv. 17 (Ps. xciii, 17 Septuagint).

reward for the seven and a half pounds and for the trust which
he had placed in the holy Patriarch — and further to teach us,
too, to remain untroubled and thankful to God in any trials
that may befall us after doing a good deed — this true lover of
Christ saw in a vision the following night a man in the likeness
of the most holy Patriarch saying to him: 'Why are you so
distressed and despondent, brother? Did you not ask me to
implore God to save your son? Well, he is saved! For had he
lived he would have turned out a most pernicious and unclean
fellow. Then, as regards the ship, had not God been touched
by your good deed and my unworthiness, since it had been
determined that the vessel, souls and all, should go to the
bottom, you would have lost your brother also. Rise and
glorify God Who has granted you his life and has kept your
son unspotted from this vain world.'

When the man awoke he felt his soul comforted and freed
from all sorrow; so he put on his clothes and went in haste to
the most venerable Patriarch and, throwing himself at his feet,
gave thanks to God and to him and related the vision which
he had seen. The just man heard his story and then said:
'Glory to Thee, oh merciful Lover of men, for listening to my
prayer, sinner though I be.' And turning to the ship-owner he
said, 'Do not by any means ascribe your blessings wholly to my
prayers but rather to God and your own faith, for this it is
which effected all'. For the Saint was exceedingly humble-
minded both in words and thought.

27

One day this blessed Patriarch went to visit the poor in the
quarter called Caesareum* — for there he had had some very
long vaulted buildings erected; the floor was covered with
wooden boards and mats and rough rugs were provided. Here
the poor could sleep during the winter months. Accompanying
the Patriarch was a certain bishop, a lover of money and of a
most unsympathetic disposition. To him the blessed Patriarch
said: 'Give Christ's brethren a little present, brother Troilus,'
for that was his name, for somebody had whispered to the
Patriarch that the bishop's attendant was carrying thirty
pounds of gold at that moment in order to buy a set of engraved

silver for the bishop's table. The bishop, reverencing the
Patriarch's word and more probably momentarily quickened
in soul thereby, ordered the man carrying the thirty pounds of
gold to give a nomisma to each of the brethren sitting there.
In this way the large quantity of gold was quickly spent.

  After the Patriarch and the bishop Troilus had both returned
to their own residences, the latter, who had performed this act
of charity, so to speak, against his will, was seized by unreason-
ing and soul-destroying anxiety over the money which had
been distributed, and as an outcome of his miserliness and
pitilessness and change of mind a fit of shivers came over him
accompanied by an unnatural feverishness. In consequence of
this unexpected illness he straightway took to his bed. When
the servant came from the most holy Patriarch inviting him to
lunch, he excused himself saying that from some cause or other
he had an attack of ague. On receipt of this message the
Patriarch at once recognized that it was owing to his having
given away those thirty pounds that the involuntary giver was
ill, for we have already said Troilus was extremely avaricious
and unsympathetic.

  John could not bear that he himself should be waited on at
table while the other lay in torments in his bed, so in his utter
want of arrogance he quickly went to him and with a smile on
his face said to him: 'You must forgive me, brother Troilus,
for you imagine that I was serious when I asked you to give
that large amount to our poor brethren, but let me tell you, I
only said it in jest. For I wanted to give each of them a nomisma
for the holy feast and as my purse-bearer had not a sufficient
sum with him, I borrowed it from you, and now see, here are
your thirty pounds!'

  Hardly had the bishop seen the money in the venerable hand
of this true physician and shepherd before the fever suddenly
disappeared and the shivering ceased, and his ordinary strength
and colour returned so that there was no concealing the fact
that the money was the cause of his sudden indisposition.

  When he had accepted the gold from the Patriarch's venerable hands without making the slightest objection, the Patriarch asked him to acknowledge in writing that he abandoned
any claim for interest on the thirty pounds of gold which had
been distributed.

This Troilus did with joy, and wrote as follows with his own hand: 'Oh God, pray give John the most blessed Patriarch of the city of Alexandria, the interest on the thirty pounds of gold which have been distributed in Thy name, as I have received my own back.' The Patriarch, having received this acknowledgment, took the bishop back to lunch with him, for as we have already said, the latter had suddenly recovered.

However God, the Rewarder, wishing to chasten him and also to arouse him to pity and sympathy for his fellow creatures, showed him in a dream that same day, when he was taking a nap after lunching with the Patriarch, how great a reward he had lost.

'I saw,' said he, 'a house whose beauty and size no human art could imitate, with a gateway all of gold and above the gateway an inscription painted on wood which ran thus: "The eternal home and resting-place of bishop Troilus."

'When I read this, I was overjoyed,' he continued, 'for I knew that the king had granted me the enjoyment of this house. But I had scarcely finished reading this inscription when behold, an imperial chamberlain appeared with others of the divine retinue, and as he drew near to the gateway of the radiant house he said to his servants: "Take down that inscription," and when they had taken it down he said again: "Change it and put up the one the King of the World has sent." So they took away the one and fixed up another while I was looking on, and on it was written: "The eternal home and resting-place of John, the Archbishop of Alexandria, bought for thirty pounds." When I saw that,' he said, 'I awoke and went and related to the great arch-shepherd what I had seen in my sleep.' And Troilus was benefited by the instruction, for from that time he became compassionate.

28

The Lord who once took away all Job's wealth did the same to this virtuous John. For the ships of the Church of which he was head met with such a violent storm in the Adriatic* that the crew were forced to jettison the whole cargo; and all the ships were there at the same time. And the weight of their freight was exceedingly heavy for they had waterproof garments* and silver and other valuable goods, so that the weight of what was lost was estimated at thirty-four hundredweight; for there were more than thirteen ships each carrying 10,000 artabas.

Directly they reached Alexandria and cast anchor, all the ship masters and the captains took refuge in the church; when the Saint heard of this and learned the reason of their plight he sent them a message written by his own hand and in these words: 'The Lord gave, brethren, and the Lord, as He willed, has also taken away. As it seemed good to the Lord so it has happened. Blessed be the name of the Lord. Come out freely, children, and do not be afraid because of this, for the Lord will again take thought for the morrow.'

The next day almost half the city came up to the council-chamber anxious to console the glorious Saint, but he anticipated them by saying to them all: 'My sons and brethren, do not be cast down at all by this mishap to the ships. For believe me, humble John is found to be the cause of it. For had I not been high-minded, I should not have met with this misfortune. But because I had lofty plans with regard to the things that are God's and thought I was doing great things by distributing what belonged to men, this has befallen me, and God allowed this to happen to bring me to my senses. For almsgiving often exalts the mind and makes the foolish man haughty, whereas an unexpected calamity humbles him who patiently endures it. The Holy Scripture says: "Poverty humbleth a man", and again David, recognizing this truth, said: "It is good for me that Thou hast humbled me that I might learn Thy statutes."[1]

'Thus I was the cause of two misfortunes, firstly, I lost the wherewithal to make distribution through vain glory; secondly, such large sums of money have been lost through my fault that now I have to bear the blame for the persons in distress. However, beloved, God is the same now as He was in the times of Job, the righteous, and not because of my poverty, but because of the need of those in want He will not desert us. He Himself has said, "I will in no wise fail thee, neither will I in any wise forsake thee";[2] and again, "Seek ye first the kingdom of God and all these things shall be added unto you".'[3] In this wise the citizens who were anxious to console him, as I have said, were in fact consoled by his Beatitude.

[1] Ps. cxix. 71.   [2] Heb. xiii. 5.   [3] Matt. vi. 33.

After a very short time God doubled our new Job's possessions and he was again the same magnanimous man in the
way of sympathy, and, if anything, he was even more to be
revered than formerly.

29

One day the Saint gave to one of his servants who had been
reduced to extreme poverty two pounds of gold with his own
hands so that no one might know of it. When his servant said,
'After this gift I shall no longer have the courage to look
you in the face, a face so dear, so like an angel's', he made this
wise and praiseworthy answer: 'I have not yet shed my blood
on your behalf, brother, as Christ, our God, my Master and the
Master of us all, commanded me.'

30

A man was harried by the tax-collectors and was unable to
pay — for the crops had failed through the Nile not having
risen as usual — so he went to a military commander, one of
the grandees, and besought him to lend him 50 pounds of
gold and offered to give security for double the value if
desired. The officer promised to give it him, but postponed
doing so at the time. But as the collectors pressed the man
hard, he, too, like the rest, steered his course to the all-receiving
harbour, I mean to the gentle and admirable Patriarch. Almost
before he had fully explained the circumstances, the Patriarch
said: 'Why, if necessary, my son, I will give you even this robe
I am wearing.' For amongst his other wonderful traits was
this one: he could not bear to see anyone weeping for misery
without mingling his own tears with his. And so now, without
a moment's hesitation, he fulfilled the request of the man who
asked for a loan.

The next night the officer saw himself standing near an
altar to which many brought offerings, and for every offering
which they laid down they received a hundredfold in exchange
from the altar. Now the Patriarch was there too, behind him.
And one offering was lying in front of them on a stool; and
somebody said to the officer: 'Come, sir, pick up that offering
and bring it to the altar and take in exchange for it a hundredfold.' As he hesitated, the Patriarch ran forward, although he

was behind him, and picked it up before he could do so and carried it to the altar and received, like the others, a hundred-fold in exchange. When he awoke he could not interpret the dream. But he sent and had the man brought to him who had requested a loan, in order that he might give him the money; and when he came, the officer said to him: 'Take the money!' The man, however, answered: 'The Patriarch has anticipated your service. For as your lordship kept putting me off, I was obliged to flee for help to him as to a harbour, because the tax-collectors were very insistent.' Directly he heard that, the officer remembered his dream and cried, 'You have said rightly that he has anticipated my service to you, for truly he has anticipated me, and woe be to him who wishes to do good and puts it off!' and then he related his dream to him and to many others.

31

One day the Saint was in the church* of the holy and victorious martyrs, Cyrus and John, whither he had gone for prayer on their glorious anniversary, and as he went out of the gate of the city a woman was waiting for him and fell at his feet, crying: 'Avenge me on my brother-in-law, for he is wronging me!' Some of his suite, who felt that they could speak for him, told her that he would attend to the matter on his return, whereupon the all-wise remarked: 'How will God receive my prayers if I put this woman off, and who will go security for me that I shall live till to-morrow? And I might go to Christ with no excuse to make about her.' He did not leave the place until he had caused justice to be done for her.

32

To help this glorious man towards attaining his purpose which was indeed wholly divine, the Lord sent him John and Sophronius,* who were wise in the things of God and worthy of perpetual remembrance. They were really honest counsellors, and the Patriarch gave unquestioning ear to them as though they were his fathers, and was grateful to them for being most brave and valiant soldiers in the cause of the true faith. For trusting in the might of the Holy Spirit they engaged in a war of dialectics, setting their own wisdom against that of the mad followers of Severus* and of the other unclean heretics who were scattered about the country; they delivered many villages, very many churches, and monasteries, too, like good shepherds saving the sheep from the jaws of these evil beasts, and for this reason above others the saintly Patriarch shewed special honour to these saintly men.

33

If by chance the blessed man heard of anybody being harsh and cruel to his slaves and given to striking them he would first send for him and then admonish him very gently, saying: 'Son, it has come to my sinful ears that by the prompting of our enemy you behave somewhat too harshly towards your household slaves. Now, I beseech you, do not give place to anger, for God has not given them to us to strike, but to be our servants, and perhaps not even for that, but rather for them to be supported by us from the riches God has bestowed on us. What price, tell me, must a man pay to purchase one who has been honoured by creation in the likeness and similitude of God? Or do you, the slave's master, possess anything more in your own body than he does? Say, a hand, or foot, or hearing, or a soul? Is he not in all things like unto you? Listen to what the great light, Paul, says: "For as many of you as were baptized into Christ did put on Christ. There can be neither Jew nor Greek, there can be neither bond nor free, for ye are all one man in Christ Jesus."[1] If then we are equal before Christ, let us become equal in our relations one with another; for Christ took upon himself the form of a servant thereby teaching us not to treat our fellow-servants with disdain. For there is one Master of all Who dwells in heaven and yet regards the things of low degree; it does not say "the rich things" but "things of low degree". We give so much gold in order to make a slave for ourselves of a man honoured and together with us bought by the blood of our God and Master. For him is the heaven, for him the earth, for him the stars, for him the sun, for him the sea and all that is in it; at times the angels serve him. For him Christ washed the feet of slaves, for him He was crucified and for him endured all His other sufferings.

[1] Gal. iii. 27, 28.

Yet you dishonour him who is honoured of God and you beat him mercilessly as if he were not of the same nature as yourself. 'Tell me, is this all you care for humble John? Would you like it if each time you sinned, God were immediately to punish you and take vengeance on your sin? Assuredly not. Tell me how in your daily prayers you can say "Forgive us our debts as we forgive our debtors"?'[1]

With such and similar arguments from the store within him would the blessed one admonish the man and then dismiss him. Unless he heard that the master had reformed his ways, he would arrange that the ill-treated slave should reach in secrecy a place of refuge; then he would ask that he might buy him, and directly the just man had purchased him he would immediately set him free.

34
This chapter is omitted as the story would seem to have been originally told of the Alexandrian Patriarch Apollinarius (A.D. 550-69) and has been taken from John Moschus and re-told of the Patriarch, John the Almsgiver.*

35
Another command which the admirable Patriarch consistently observed was 'From him that would borrow of thee turn not thou away';[2] he never refused anyone who begged for that kind of help from him.

A certain rascally impostor was aware of this and asked him to lend him 20 pounds of gold — he was a so-called 'adventurer'* — and then treating the Patriarch as ungratefully as he had done many others, kept saying, 'He gave me nothing'. The treasurers and administrators of the church-funds* accordingly demanded that he should be imprisoned and his goods confiscated. But the imitator of Him Who said: 'Be ye good and merciful even as your Father in heaven, Who maketh His sun to rise on the evil and the good and sendeth rain on the just and the unjust'[3] would not hear of their troubling the man at all. Still they were furious against him for having tricked the Patriarch and they said to the Saint: 'It is not just, master,

---

[1] Matt. vi. 12.   [2] Matt. v. 42.   [3] Luke vi. 36 and Matt. v. 45.

that this prodigal should get money which the poor ought to receive.' In answer to this the thrice-blessed said: 'Assuredly, brethren, if you ever take anything away from that man in opposition to my purpose, you will transgress two commandments and only fulfil one, even if what you take you give to the poor. For, firstly, you will have shewn yourselves impatient under loss and become a bad example to others; and secondly you will have disobeyed your God and Master Who said: 'Of him that taketh away thy goods, ask them not again.'[1] It is expedient, my children, that we should be an example of patience to all men, and so, too, says the apostle: 'Why not rather suffer wrong and be defrauded?'[2]

And though it is truly good to give to everyone that asks, yet it is nobler and more honourable to give to him who does not ask, and to him that taketh away our cloak against our will we should give our tunic also, and thus really imitate the angelic, or rather the divine, nature. For from our belongings our Lord commanded us to do good to our neighbour. 'Thou shalt do good unto thy brother,' He says, 'as far as thy hand has the means, but not from the things that have been taken from the wrongdoer by litigation and strife.'

36

This chapter is omitted as the story of Bitalius and his efforts to convert the prostitutes of Alexandria has little direct reference to the life of the Patriarch.

37

One day a man asked an alms of the Saint who directed that ten coppers[3] and no more should be given him. The beggar then violently abused the Patriarch to his face for not having given him as much as he wanted. But when his attendants were anxious to thrash him for his insolence, the Patriarch rebuked them severely, saying: 'Leave him alone, brothers. Here have I been insulting Christ for sixty years by my deeds, and can I not bear one insult from this fellow?' And he commanded his almoner* to open the money-bag and let the beggar take as large a sum as he wished.

---

[1] Luke vi. 30.   [2] 1 Cor. vi. 7.   [3] φόλλεις.

38

One day the all-wise heard of a generous giver and so he sent for him privately and said jokingly, 'How is it that you became so generous? Was it natural to you, or did you put constraint upon yourself?' Some to whom he put this same question stood shamefacedly before him and would not answer, whilst others would tell him their story. One man whom the Saint questioned answered as follows: 'As a fact, master, I neither give anything nor do any good; but the little I do give and do from that which comes to me through Christ and your prayers I came to do in this way. Formerly I was very hard-hearted and unsympathetic and one day I lost money and was reduced to poverty. Then my reason began to say to me: "Truly, if you had been charitable, God would not have forsaken you." And thereupon I decided to give five coppers[1] a day to the poor. But when I started giving them Satan immediately checked me by saying: 'Those coppers would really have been enough to buy a bath-ticket or vegetables for your family." Then I felt at once as if I were taking the money out of my children's mouth and so I gave nothing.

'But I noticed I was being mastered by this vice, so said to my slave: "I want you to steal five coppers daily without my noticing it, and give them in charity." For I am a money-changer, master.

'My slave, worthy fellow, began by stealing ten coppers, and occasionally even a shilling.[2] As he noticed that we were being blessed, he began to steal crowns,[3] too, and give them away.

'One day I was expressing my astonishment at God's blessings to us, I said to him: "Those five coppers, boy, have greatly benefited us. So now I want you to give ten." At that the slave said to me with a smile: "Yes, be thankful for my thefts, since but for them we should not even have bread to eat today. However if there can be a just thief, I am he!" And then he told me that he had given shillings and even crowns. So it was through his faith, master, that I grew accustomed to giving with all my heart.'

The holy Patriarch was much edified by this story and said: 'Truly I have read many stories in the lives of the fathers, but I have never heard anything like this!'

[1] φόλλεις.   [2] A shilling—κεράτιν.   [3] Crowns—τριμίσια.

39

One of the high officials bore a grudge against another; great John heard of this and admonished him several times, but could not persuade him to be reconciled with his enemy. One day therefore the Saint sent and had him fetched on the pretext of some public business, and as soon as he had come the Patriarch held a service in his oratory, no one else being present save his syncellus.* After the Patriarch had said the prayer of consecration and had pronounced the opening words of the Lord's Prayer, the three of them began to repeat the Prayer. When they got to the sentence: 'Forgive us our debts as we forgive our debtors' the Patriarch made a sign to the syncellus to stop, and he himself stopped, too, and the magistrate commenced saying all by himself 'Forgive us as we forgive'. At once the Saint turned towards him and said in a gentle voice: 'Consider in what an awful moment you are saying to God "As I forgive, do Thou also forgive me"!'

Immediately, as though tormented by fire, the magistrate fell on his face at the Saint's feet crying, 'Whatever you command, my lord, your servant will do'. And from that time he was reconciled to his enemy in all sincerity.

40

Then again, if the blessed man noticed that anyone was haughty he did not reprove him to his face, but if he noticed him sitting in his reception-room he would introduce some talk about humility in order that by such teaching he might gradually break the pride of the haughty man and chasten him by some such words as these: 'I am astonished, my masters, that my wretched soul does not remember the virtue of humility which the Son of God manifested when He appeared on earth; but I am puffed up and exalt myself over my brother if I am perhaps a little better looking or richer or more distinguished or hold some public office, and I forget the divine voice which said: "Learn of me; for I am meek and lowly in heart; and ye shall find rest unto your souls."[1]

'Nor do I reflect upon the words of the saints, of whom one called himself "dust and ashes",[2] another "a worm and no

---

[1] Matt. xi. 29.   [2] Ecclesiasticus xvii. 32.

man"[1] and yet another a "stammerer and slow of speech".[2] Isaiah, too, worthy to behold God so far as a man may, declared then that he had unclean lips.[3] For what am I, humble man as I am? Was I not fashioned from clay just as a brick is? And will not all the glory which I think I have wither like "the flower of the grass"?'[4]

With these and many more similar discourses this wise man, while pretending to talk about himself, would cauterize the man afflicted with haughtiness and self-conceit, and do good to his soul. For the patient understood that the Patriarch was referring indirectly to him.

41

This chapter contains a further discourse on 'Humility' which is omitted in some MSS. — We give the second half of the chapter.

The blessed man always used to talk much about the thought of death and the departure of the soul so that on several occasions those who went in to him with a haughty bearing and laughing face and bold eyes came out from his presence with humble demeanour and a contrite face and eyes filled with tears. He used to say: 'My humble opinion is that it suffices for our salvation to meditate continually and seriously about death and to think earnestly upon the fact that nobody will pity us in that hour nor will anyone travel with us out of this life except our good deeds. And when the angels come hastening down, in what a tumult will a soul then be if it is found unready! How it will beg that it may be allowed a further short span of life, only to hear the words: "What about the time you have lived, have you spent it well?" '

And again he used to say as though speaking of himself, 'Humble John, how will you have the strength to "pass the wild beasts of the brake",[5] when they meet you like tax-collectors? Woe is me, what fears and tremors will encompass the soul when it is called to account by so many keen and piti-less accountants?' And indeed the saintly man had especially noted that which was made known through revelation by St. Simeon, the stylite; the words were: 'When the soul goes forth

---

[1] Ps. xxii. 6.   [2] Exod. iv. 10.   [3] Is. vi. 5.   [4] 1 Peter i. 24.
[5] Ps. lxviii. 30 = Septuagint lxvii. 31, which reads ἐπιτίμησον τοῖς θηρίοις τοῦ καλάμου.

from the body, as it rises from the earth to heaven there meet it troops of demons, each in his own regiment. A band of demons of arrogance meet it, they feel it all over to see whether the soul possesses their works. A band of the spirits of slander meets it; they inspect it to see whether it has ever uttered slanders and not repented. Again higher up the demons of harlotry meet it; they investigate whether they can recognize their pursuits in it. And while the wretched soul is being brought to account on its way from earth to heaven the holy angels stand on one side and do not help it, only its own virtues can do that.'

Pondering on these things the glorious Patriarch would grow fearful and troubled about such an hour, for he also bore in mind the saying of St. Hilarion* who, as he was on the point of leaving this life, lost courage and said to his soul: 'For eighty years, O humble soul, you have been serving Christ and are you afraid to go forth? Go forth, for He is merciful.' And the Patriarch would say to himself: 'If he, after serving Christ for eighty years and raising men from the dead and doing signs and wonders, was yet afraid of that bitter hour, what can you, humble John, do or say when you come to face those cruel and pitiless exactors of taxes and tributes? To which will you have the strength to make your defence? To the demons of falsehood, to those of slander, to those of unmercifulness, to those of avarice, to those of malice, to those of hatred, to those of perjury?' and with new doubts rising in his mind he would say: 'Oh God, do Thou rebuke them, for the whole strength of man is of no avail against them; do Thou, Lord, give us as guides the holy angels who protect and pilot us. For great is the fury of the demons against us, great is the fear, great the trembling, great the peril of the voyage through this sea of air. For if, when travelling from city to city on this earth, we require a guide to lead us lest we fall into crevasses, or into the haunts of wild beasts, or into impassable rivers, or into pathless and inaccessible mountains, or into the hands of brigands, or into some boundless and waterless desert and be lost, how many strong guides and divine guardians do we not need when we start on this long journey which is everlasting, I mean the exodus from the body and the journey up to heaven?' These were the teachings, full of God's wisdom, that the blessed man gave to himself and to all; these were his daily thoughts and meditations.

42

He also gave a great deal of thought to the holy liturgy and spent much care upon it.

One day when he determined to stop so many people from leaving the church as soon as the Gospel had been read to spend their time in idle talk instead of in prayer, what did he do? — Directly after the Gospel had been read in the church, he slipped away and came out himself and sat down outside with the crowd. And when everybody was amazed, the just man said to them: 'Children, where the sheep are, there also the shepherd must be. Come inside and I will come in; or stay here and I will stay, too. For I come down to the Holy Church for your sakes, since I could hold the service for myself in the bishop's house.'

After repeating the same action a few times he sobered the people and greatly reformed their conduct in this matter, for they were afraid that the never-to-be-forgotten Patriarch might act in the same manner towards them as before.

He also forbade anyone to make an appointment to meet in the sanctuary, but in the presence of all he would force any such to leave saying, 'If you really came here to pray, then occupy your mind and mouth with that; but if you came merely to meet someone, it is written, "The house of God shall be called the house of prayer; do not turn it into a den of thieves".'[1]

Now the really remarkable thing in the life of the saintly Patriarch was this: although he had not practised the discipline of the monk, though he had not spent his time in church amongst the clergy, but had lived in lawful wedlock with his wife; despite the fact that he remained a layman until the hour when he was consecrated as Patriarch,* yet he so mastered the ordering of the church and he attained to such a height of virtue that he excelled many of those who had distinguished themselves in the asceticism of the desert.

As he wished to have a share in this good thing also, I mean to be numbered amongst those who lived the monastic life, he devised the following scheme. He collected two bodies of holy

[1] Matt. xxi. 13.

monks, arranged that all their needs should be supplied from the lands belonging to him in his native city,* built cells for them and appointed them to the two oratories, the one of our Lady, the holy Mother of God, and the other of St. John, which he had rebuilt from the foundations. Then he spoke to the monks beloved of God and said: 'I myself — after God — will take thought for your bodily needs, but you must make the salvation of my soul your care, so that your evening and night vigils may be set to my credit with God. But if you celebrate the liturgy in our cells, your own souls will gain the benefit.'* This he did as he wanted to make the God-beloved monks very zealous.

So his God-pleasing organization of the two bodies of monks was established, and through their means the life of the city under him was conducted almost after the fashion of a monastery, for hymns were sung to God continuously in various places throughout the night.

Another thing the blessed man taught and insisted upon with all was never on any occasion whatsoever to associate with heretics and, above all, never to take the Holy Communion with them, 'even if', the blessed man said, 'you remain without communicating all your life, if through stress of circumstances you cannot find a community of the Catholic Church. For if, having legally married a wife in this world of the flesh, we are forbidden by God and by the laws to desert her and be united to another woman, even though we have to spend a long time separated from her in a distant country, and shall incur punishment if we violate our vows, how then shall we, who have been joined to God through the orthodox faith and the Catholic Church — as the apostle says: "I espoused you to one husband that I might present you as a pure virgin to Christ"[1] — how shall we escape from sharing in that punishment which in the world to come awaits heretics, if we defile the orthodox and holy faith by adulterous communion with heretics?'

For 'communion' he said, 'has been so called because he who has "communion" has things in common and agrees with those with whom he has "communion". Therefore I implore you earnestly, children, never to go near the oratories of the heretics in order to communicate there.'

[1] 2 Cor. xi. 2.

43

Amongst his wonderful achievements the blessed man attained unto this also, I mean never to judge his neighbour without good reason, or to listen to those who condemned him. Here let me give his teaching on this point from which all may profit.

A young man eloped with a nun and fled to Constantinople. On hearing this the just man almost died of grief. But some time later when sitting in his sacristy with some of the clergy and enjoying a profitable conversation someone happened to speak of the young man who had carried off the nun. Those who were sitting with the Saint began cursing the youth for having destroyed two souls, his own and the nun's. But the blessed man interrupted and stopped them saying: 'No, my children, do not speak like that! For I can prove to you that you yourselves are committing two sins, one because you are transgressing the commandment of Him who said: "Judge not that ye be not judged",[1] and the second because you do not know for certain whether they are still living in sin, and have not repented.

'For I read the life of a father which has the following story. In a certain city two monks were starting on an errand, and as one of the two passed through a square a harlot called out to him: "Save me, father, as Christ saved the harlot." And he, without a thought of men's censure, said to her: "Follow me!" and taking her by the hand he went out of the city openly in full view of everyone. Thus the rumour spread that the abbot had taken the woman, Porphyria,* (for that was her name) to wife. As the two travelled on so that he might put her into a convent, the woman found a baby which had been exposed and was lying on the ground near a church and took it with her intending to bring it up. A year later some of the citizens came to the country where the abbot and Porphyria (she who had been a harlot) were staying, and seeing her with the child said to her, "You have certainly got a fine chick by the abbot", for she had not yet adopted the monastic robe. The men who had seen her spread abroad the report when they got back to Tyre (for that was the city from which the abbot had taken her) that Porphyria had had a fine son by the abbot. "We saw him with our own eyes," they said, "and he is like his father."

---

[1] Matt. vii. 1.

'Now when the abbot knew beforehand by revelation from God that he would shortly die, he said to the nun, Pelagia,* for so he named her when he gave her the holy habit of a nun, "Let us go to Tyre for I have business there and I want you to come with me." She did not like to refuse, so she followed him and they both came to Tyre with the boy who was now seven years old.

'When the abbot fell ill with a mortal sickness about a hundred people from the city came to visit him, and he said to them: "Bring hot coals!" When the censer arrived full of hot coals he took it and poured all the hot coals on to his robe and said: "Now be assured, brethren, that as God preserved the bush unburnt from the fire, and as the live coals have not even singed my robe, so, too, I have never committed sin with a woman from the day I was born." And all were struck dumb with amazement that his robe was not burnt by the fire and they glorified God who has such servants, though they are unrecognized by men.* From the example of the nun Pelagia who had once been a harlot several other harlots followed her and renounced the world and went with her into her convent. For after the monk, the servant of the Lord, who had received her profession, had fully satisfied everybody of his innocence, he surrendered his soul to the Lord in peace. For this reason', the Patriarch continued, 'I warn you, my children, not to be so ready to mock at, or judge, the acts of other people.

'For we have often seen the sin of the fornicator, but his repentance, which he made in secret, we did not see, and we may have seen somebody steal, but we know nothing of the groanings and tears which he has offered to God. We still think of him as we saw him, a thief, a fornicator or a perjuror, but in the sight of God his secret repentance and confession have been accepted, and in His eyes he is honourable.'

Thus all were astonished at the teaching of this virtuous shepherd and teacher.

44A

Two clerics were shoemakers* and worked near each other; the one had several children, a wife, and his father and mother, yet found time to attend church regularly, and it was he who, after God, supported them all by his handicraft. The other, in spite of being a more skilful workman, could not even support himself, because he found no time for church, at times working even on Sundays.

Consequently he was envious of his neighbour and one day, unable to bear his jealousy any longer, he said to him angrily: 'How is it that you have grown so rich? For I pay more attention to my work than you do and yet am losing money.' The other, wishing to make him find time for going to church, said: 'Whenever I go to church, I find a coin thrown on the ground and thus bit by bit I have grown rich. Now, if you like, I will always give you a call, then you come with me and if we find anything, you shall go halves with me.'

The other consented and accompanied him to church and for that reason God blessed him continuously and enriched him. Then his good counsellor said to him: 'You see how much good one lie for the sake of God has done both to your soul and to your finances. To tell you the truth, I never found anything in the shape of money lying on the ground as you thought, but since our Lord said: "Seek ye first the kingdom of God and His righteousness and all these things shall be added unto you,"[1] therefore I concocted my story to make you take the plunge, and see! I did not fail, for you have found and found abundantly.'

When this reached the ears of the holy Patriarch he ordained the good counsellor to the priesthood as he deserved; for he already was a 'reader'.

44B

Here ends the narration of the very God-fearing Menas, whom I mentioned at the beginning of my work, he who had been treasurer of the most Holy Church of the metropolis of the Alexandrians. For the rest of the work I, unworthy as I am, am myself responsible, though some of the stories have been told me by trustworthy informants.

In one of the former chapters I mentioned the strong bond of spiritual love which united our blessed Patriarch with the patrician Nicetas, and the present chapter will give sufficient

[1] Matt. vi. 33.

proof of the happy relation which bound them to each other.

When by God's permission, or rather because of our sins, Alexandria was on the point of being betrayed to the impious Persians,* the shepherd, recalling our Lord's words: 'When they drive you out of this city, flee into the next',[1] was going to flee to his native country, Cyprus, where was the city in which he was born. So the patrician, Nicetas, seizing upon this favourable opportunity said to the holy man: 'I beseech you, if I have found grace in your sight, deign to take the trouble of travelling to the Queen of Cities[2] and grant to our most pious sovereigns your acceptable prayers.' The Patriarch, yielding to his friend's great faith, agreed to his suggestion, for God wished to show His purpose and the great honour in which He held the blessed Patriarch.

Whilst the boat on which the Patriarch and the patrician were travelling was continually being battered by violent winds and seemed likely to be engulfed in the deep, the patrician of whom I have spoken so many times and the officers with him, during the night when the storm took place, saw the Patriarch running round all parts of the ship with the poor people, and at times raising his hands to heaven together with them and bringing down help from on high.

When continuing their course* they had reached Rhodes, the Saint whom God had called saw with his waking eyes a eunuch in gleaming apparel, a golden sceptre in his right hand, standing by him and saying: 'Come, I beg you, the King of Kings is asking for you!'* Without delay he forthwith sent for the patrician, Nicetas, and said to him with many tears: 'You, my master, called me to go to our earthly king, but the heavenly King has anticipated you and has summoned to Himself my humbleness.' He then related to him the vision which he had just seen of the eunuch, or rather of the angel.

The most glorious patrician heard his words with mixed sorrow and joy, but did not attempt to hinder the holy man, but, after receiving richly of his holy prayers, and having treasured them up for the Emperors, with great respect he encouraged him to return to Cyprus.

[1] Matt. x. 23.   [2] Constantinople.

45

As soon as he reached his own city, Amathus by name, he bade those who ministered to him to draw up his will with all speed. Quickly and without delay they provided paper and pen and then his holy mouth bade them write thus:

'John, a slave, but free through the office of the priesthood which was bestowed upon me by the grace of God, I thank Thee, O God, for listening to me, a miserable sinner, when I begged Thy goodness not to let me possess when I died more than one "trimision".[1]

'Hereby I inform all men that the property of humble John has never amounted to more than this one coin. When by God's permission* I was elected bishop of the most holy Church of the metropolis of the Alexandrians I found in the house of the bishop about 8000 pounds of gold, and as my revenues from Christ-loving persons almost exceed human calculation, I pondered over the matter and recognized that all this money belonged to the Lord of all things and therefore I took pains to render unto God the things that were God's, and now I have this one "trimision" left, and, as that, too, is God's, I direct that it, too, shall be given to those who are God's.' — Oh, what wonders are here! What kindness of heart there was in this Saint! He did not cling to things as if his own when they were not his, as many prosperous people do, who hoard the gifts of God, or even wealth scraped together by injustice, as if they were their own treasures and would still pass with them at death, and who never give generously to the needy. No, he always sought the things that abide for ever and are never spent, and for this reason he did not fail to win those true promises which bring to us God's assurance that 'I will glorify those that glorify Me!'[2] And in truth the Lord Who was ever being glorified by the Saint's achievements did indeed greatly glorify this Saint.

Again this glorious man could not bear the thought that righteous and commendable achievements should come to an end with his brief life, so what did he do? — He built from the foundations up hostels for strangers, asylums for the old, and monasteries, and he gathered together companies of holy

---

[1] i.e. a third of a solidus.   [2] 1 Sam. ii. 30.

monks and thus through the good works which are done therein he has won a memorial of his righteousness which shall never pass away.

Some men accomplish evil things and leave after their death successors in this life to carry on their evil doings, and of these the apostle Paul says: 'Some men's sins are evident going before unto judgment, and some men also they follow after.'[1] Just the contrary could be said of this blessed man, namely: 'Some men's just deeds are evident, going before unto the Kingdom of Heaven, some men also they follow after,' and of these latter he was one. And that what I say is not a fable or merely said in flattery can be proved to us very clearly by the marvel that happened immediately after his venerable falling asleep. After he had yielded up and commended his soul to the hand of the Lord — as the scripture says: 'The souls of the righteous are in the hand of the Lord'[2] — and commending it to Him as a sacrifice free from blemish, his revered body was to be laid to rest reverently and with fitting ecclesiastical rites in the oratory of the miracle-worker St. Tychon.* And then the following incredible sign took place! In the sarcophagus where the just man was to be laid there already lay the truly holy bodies of two holy bishops who had died before him, and these, which had been lying there, I suppose, up to this time in a lifeless state, now accorded the Saint as much honour as did the living. For when the body of the most blessed Patriarch was about to be laid in company with those two saints, these shepherds who honoured this arch-shepherd and respected and admired his great favour with God, moved aside their bodies — not so much of their own will but rather at the command of God, just as if they were alive — and took the Saint between them.

So these men at God's bidding shewed honour as to a man honoured of God, and at once made clear to all the glory and exceeding exaltation which in heaven had been awarded to him by God.

This very great and most extraordinary miracle was seen not only by one or ten or a hundred witnesses, but by the whole crowd which had gathered for his honoured funeral.

---

[1] 1 Tim. v. 24.   [2] Wisdom iii. 1.

46

Yet another more astonishing miracle I will now attempt to describe; he began it indeed while still living in the flesh but completed it after he had been translated to the Lord. — A certain woman belonging to the Saint's native town heard that he had come from Rhodes and that an angel had appeared to him there and had told him of his call to our common Master. She had on her conscience a very grievous sin which she affirmed must on no account come to the ears of men. She cherished an unwavering faith in the Saint, so she came speedily to him and seizing hold of his feet and weeping bitterly, said to the holy man in secret: 'O thrice-blessed, I have, alas, committed a sin which must not come to men's ears, and I know that if you are willing you can absolve me from it. For the Lord said about men such as you, "Whatsoever things ye shall loose on earth, shall be loosed in heaven, and whatsoever things ye shall bind on earth, shall be bound in heaven. And whosoever sins ye forgive, they are forgiven unto them; whosoever sins ye retain, they are retained".'[1]

When the Saint heard the woman quote these words, he was afraid that, if he refused her request, he might be the cause of her suffering eternal punishment, while she could be freed from her sin by the faith she had in him, so he said to her very humbly: 'If you really believe, woman, in God that by my unworthy intercession He will forgive you the crime of which you speak, confess it to me.' But she replied: 'O master, I cannot possibly say it, for no man could endure to hear it.' Thereupon the Saint said to her: 'If you are ashamed to speak of it, go home and write it down, if you know how to write, and bring it to me.' She again replied: 'I really cannot, master.' Then the Saint kept silent for a few minutes and afterwards said: 'Cannot you write it down and seal it and bring it to me?' To this she answered, 'Yes, master, I will do that, and I implore your honoured and angelic soul never to let my tablet be opened or found by anybody.' After receiving the promise of the God-honoured Patriarch that nobody should open and read her tablet, she wrote down her sin with her own hand and sealed it and brought it to the blessed man.

Five days after the holy man had received the tablet he

[1] Matt. xviii. 18; John xx. 23.

journeyed home to God without having mentioned or given instructions about the tablet to anybody.

By chance, or rather by God's dispensation, the woman was not in town the day the Patriarch was translated in peace from this present life to the life beyond, for in this case, too, God wished to show what favour the Patriarch had won with Him through his loyal service. But the day after, when the time for the deposition of his venerable body had come, she returned and, on hearing of his death, immediately she became so distressed in mind as almost to be beside herself, thinking that the tablet she had given him had been left lying in the episcopal house and that her sin would consequently become known to all. So she jumped up, regained in her soul her former unwavering confidence in the Saint, made her way to the coffin of the God-honoured man, and there in utter desperation she talked to him as if he really were still alive: 'O man of God, I was unable to recount my sin even to you because it was so excessively grievous, and now, alas, it has perhaps been bruited and buzzed about everywhere. How I wish I had not disclosed the matter to you! Woe is me! For I hoped to be relieved of my shame, and now I am shamed in the sight of all. Instead of healing I incurred disgrace! What need was there for me to disclose my soul's secret to you? However I shall not grow weary nor mistrust you, nor let my tears at your coffin cease until I receive full satisfaction concerning my request. For, holy man, you are not dead, but alive; for it is written: "The righteous live for ever".'[1]

Then she would begin again and repeat the same words: 'I ask nothing from you, O man of God, except satisfaction for my heart. What in the world has happened to the tablet I gave you?'

Then the God Who once said to the woman of Canaan, 'Thy faith hath saved thee!'[2] Himself gave to this woman, too, full satisfaction. For after she had spent three days at the Saint's tomb without touching any food or drink, in the third night, when she was again saying with tears the same harsh yet trusting words to the blessed Saint, lo and behold! the servant of God came out of his tomb plain to see together with the two bishops who were buried with him, one standing on

---

[1] Wisdom v. 15.   [2] Cf. Matt. xv. 28; Luke vii. 50.

either side, and said to her: 'Woman, how long are you going to disturb those who are buried here and not allow them to take their rest? For, see, our robes are wet through with your tears.' With these words he gave her her tablet with the seal unbroken and said to her: 'Take it, do you acknowledge it? Open it and look.' And when she awoke from her vision she saw those saints entering their resting-place again and herself holding her tablet. Then she examined it and saw the seal whole and untouched, and breaking it open found that her own writing was blotted out and beneath the place where her confession had stood these words were written: 'For the sake of My servant John your sin is blotted out.' Oh, friends and brethren, who can recount the mighty acts of our Lord? Who is so merciful and generous as He, doing the will of those that fear Him and glorifying those that glorify Him and magnifying them by wondrous works?

Not only in the actual spot where his blessed death took place was God's well-known pleasure in him made manifest, but in other far distant places.

For on the same day that this blessed man took his departure from this life to go to his Lord one of those who have practised the angelic way of living and follow the monastic discipline,* an admirable and virtuous man, Sabinus by name, living in Alexandria, fell, as it were, into an ecstasy and saw John, honoured of God, come out of his own palace with all the clergy, bearing candles and going to the king, as, said he, a eunuch chamberlain had summoned him; and Sabinus also saw a virgin, bright as the sun, and when John had passed beyond the gateway of his palace — which signified his departure from his body — she welcomed him and took him by the hand, and on her head she had placed a crown of olive.

From this the holy Sabinus at once realized that the Patriarch's departure to his Lord had taken place at that very hour. He and his friends noted down the month and the day — it was the feast-day of the victorious St. Menas.* And when some folk arrived from Cyprus, those living in Alexandria asked about the Saint's translation and found that the vision was true, as it had come at the very hour in which the blessed man died. The sign of the virgin holding his hand was a special confirmation for, as we said in the introduction to his life,* the Saint had received a promise from her: 'If you gain me for a friend, I will introduce you to the King', and this promise she faithfully fulfilled.

From other signs, too, all received the assurance that his charity and his sympathy with the needy had brought him into the Kingdom of Heaven; for instance, another God-fearing inhabitant of the city of Alexandria saw (the same night as Sabinus had his vision) all the poor and orphans and widows carrying olive-branches and escorting the Patriarch on his way to church. There are not only two or ten or a hundred proofs of this, they are so abundant that we know for a certainty that the glorious Patriarch was deemed worthy to be enrolled among the saints. And there is yet another fact which proves it even more clearly.

Some considerable time after the holy man's falling asleep the yearly service of song was being held in the church of St. Tychon (of whom I have previously spoken) where the revered body of the most blessed Patriarch John was laid to rest; it was the solemn all-night service of psalm-singing held yearly in remembrance of the miracle-working St. Tychon, and the Lord of marvels, wishing to show to all men the great honour in which He held His holy servant John, granted that a healing perfume of myrrh should issue from his revered corpse which all present enjoyed in gladness of heart and gave glory to the Father, the Son, and the Holy Spirit, our true God, Who glorifies His saints with unending glory.

And let not anyone of you, my Christ-loving readers, refuse to believe this great miracle, for even to the present day in this Christ-loving island of the Cyprians this wonderful grace of God can be seen at work in the bodies of various saints. For, as if from springs, the sweet perfume of myrrh issues from their revered corpses to the glory of God's goodness, to the honour of His saints and to awaken in us, the after-born, an eager desire and a holy passion that by modelling our lives in imitation of these saints we also may be judged worthy of the same honours by the just God, the Rewarder. So let us also, beloved, strive to imitate the achievements which I have described of this our saintly father John, and since we are 'strangers and pilgrims'[1] in this life let us lay up treasures for

[1] 1 Peter ii. 11.

the life to come by giving generously to the needy. For according to the divine apostle 'He that soweth with blessings shall reap also with blessings'[1] instead of corruptible things the incorruptible, instead of the temporal the eternal, instead of things felt and seen, 'things which eye saw not and ear heard not and which entered not into the heart of man, the things which God has prepared for them that love Him'.[2] And may it be granted to us all to obtain these things by the grace and loving-kindness of our Lord Jesus Christ to Whom, together with the Father and the Holy Spirit, be glory, honour and power now and always and unto the ages of ages. Amen.

[1] 2 Cor. ix. 6.   [2] 1 Cor. ii. 9.

NOTES

Introd., p. 195   Texts. Heinrich Gelzer, *Leontios' von Neapolis Leben des Heiligen Johannes des Barmherzigen Erzbishofs von Alexandrien.* (=Sammlung ausgewählter kirchen — und dogmengeschichtlicher Quellenschriften, Heft 5). Mohr, Freiburg and Leipzig, 1893; Hippolyte Delehaye, *Une Vie inédite de Saint Jean l'Aumonier*, Analecta Bollandiana 45 (1927), pp. 5-74. For the history of the period, *Cambridge Medieval History*, vol. 2 (1913), pp. 263-301; for Egypt: A. J. Butler, *The Arab Conquest of Egypt and the last thirty years of the Roman Dominion*, Oxford, Clarendon Press, 1902, pp. 1-92. For the relations between John Moschus, Sophronius and John the Almsgiver, Hermann Usener, *Der heilige Tychon*, Leipzig, Teubner, 1907, pp. 80-107. For the saints of Cyprus, H. Delehaye, *Les Saints de Chypre*, Analecta Bollandiana 26 (1907), pp. 161-301. For an epitome of the Patriarch's panegyric on St. Tychon (the text of the panegyric was published by Usener, see above), ibid., pp. 229-32: on Cypriote hagiography, ibid., pp. 244-6. For Neophytus hailing St. John the Almsgiver as 'the brightest star' which Christian Cyprus had produced, ibid., p. 294. For Leontius, H. Gelzer, *Ausgewählte kleine Schriften*, Teubner, Leipzig, 1907, pp. 1-56.

ch. 2, p. 199   Epiphanius. There is an epigram (*Anthologia Palatina*, vii, 679; *The Greek Anthology*, Loeb edition, vol. 2, pp. 360-1), attributed to Sophronius where St. John is called 'the son of noble Stephanus'. But the present Vita, representing in this part the Life of St. John composed by Sophronius and John Moschus, shows that the name of St. John's father was not Stephen, but Epiphanius. It would thus appear that the epigram is wrongly attributed to Sophronius: see Delehaye, *Analecta Bollandiana* 45 (1927), p. 17.

4, p. 201   Had St. John previously settled in Alexandria and thus become widely known in the city or does this general approval simply mean that the population of Alexandria concurred in the choice of the Emperor and Nicetas?

ch. 5, p. 201   For Peter the Fuller, Monophysite Patriarch of Antioch 471-88, see the article by Edmund Venables in the *Dictionary of Christian Biography* (ed. W. Smith and H. Wace, Murray, London, 1887), vol. 4, pp. 338-40, and cf. L. Duchesne, *Histoire ancienne de l'Église* (4th edition, Fontemoing, Paris, 1911), vol. 3, pp. 508-9.

5, p. 201   ἡσυχάζειν perhaps in the technical sense 'to devote himself to contemplation'.

6, p. 202   See the note on the Introduction, p. 263, and for the Persian invasion see *United Service Magazine* for May 1913, pp. 195-201.

6, p. 202   The text reads: Τὸ δ'αὐτὸ τοῦτο καὶ ἐπὶ τῶν πενομένων πρεσβυτέρων ... ἐποίησεν, φιλοφρονησάμενος ἕκαστος αὐτῶν ... ποσότητα χρυσίου ἐνιαύσιον λαμβάνειν κ.τ.λ.   This nominative absolute — an infrequent construction — appears to us awkward: we would read ἑκάστῳ, and translate 'freely granting to each'.

8, p. 203   The lake called Maria=the Mareotic Lake west of Alexandria: see map 7 in George Adam Smith, *Atlas of the Historical Geography of the Holy Land*, Hodder and Stoughton, London, 1915.

9, p. 203   Rasmiozan: a title; the general's name appears to have been Khorheam. See A. J. Butler, *The Arab Conquest of Egypt*, etc., Clarendon Press, Oxford, 1902, p. 59 note.

9, p. 203   The text reads τῆς τοιαύτης πονηρᾶς ἀγγελίας: we would prefer to read πονηρίας.

9, p. 204   The Ennaton. Probably the monastic settlement nine miles from Alexandria to the west of the city, not the monastery of that name within the city. Cf. Jean Maspero, *Histoire des Patriarches d'Alexandrie*, etc., Champion, Paris, 1923, pp. 48, 279 and Index under *Énaton près d'Alexandrie*.

9, p. 204   'Even an enemy', etc. Delehaye cites Gregory of Nazianus, Migne, *Patrologia Graeca* 36, col. 561.

9, p. 204   Amathus: St. John's birthplace. 'Many generations have passed away since Amathus was a city of living men, but the site is still pointed out, at the end of a ridge or spur of high ground, running southwards down to the sea, about six miles east of Limassol. The site, on which some ruins may yet be seen, is known to the native inhabitants as "Old Limassol". Time brings curious changes in its course, for in the days of St. John the Almsgiver Limassol was generally known as Neapolis — "Newtown" — in contradistinction to the "old town" of Amathus of which it was most probably an offshoot.' H. T. F. Duckworth, *St. John the Almsgiver Patriarch of Alexandria*, Blackwell, Oxford, 1901, p. 5 (this is a disappointing sketch). On Amathus see Sir George Hill, *A History of Cyprus*, vol. 1, Cambridge University Press, 1940, pp. 265-6.

ch. 9, p. 204   The Madienians=Midian. Cf. R. F. Burton, *The Gold Mines of Midian* (1878) and *The Land of Midian Revisited* (1879).

9, p. 204   The great Antony — this, of course, is St. Antony 'the first monk' whose biography is St. Athanasius' masterpiece.

9, p. 204   Rhinocoroura=Rhinocolura on the coast-road leading from Palestine to Egypt=el-'Arish. See map 8 of George Adam Smith's *Atlas* (cf. note on ch. 8 *supra*).

10, p. 204   St. Menas: St. Menas appears in Egypt as a military saint: cf. H. Delehaye, *Les Légendes grecques des Saints militaires*, Picard, Paris, 1909, p. 6. For the collection of his astonishing miracles see Delehaye, *Analecta Bollandiana* 29 (1910), pp. 117-50; id., *Les Recueils antiques de Miracles des Saints*, Brussels, 1925, pp. 46-9; id., *Les Légendes hagiographiques*, 3rd ed., Brussels, 1927, pp. 146-8. For the confusion between the different saints of the name of Menas see De Lacy O'Leary, *The Saints of Egypt*, Society for Promoting Christian Knowledge, London, 1937, pp. 194-9.

10, p. 205   Mareotic wine: see note on ch. 8 *supra*.

11, p. 205   Tiberias: on the west bank of the Lake of Gennesaret in Galilee.

13, p. 206   Aspagurius. This is a very perplexing incident. Sir George Hill writes: 'The context of this story and the name of the governor might suggest that he was sent by the Persians; but an expedition across the sea on their part would be unprecedented and we must assume that Aspagourios was the representative of Byzantium.' And in a note he adds: 'The wording of the passage suggests that he was a military officer, not an ordinary governor, sent against Constantia [ἐπὶ Κωνσταντίαν]. But if he was sent *against* Constantia, he cannot have expected to be peacefully received by the authorities of the city. Possibly therefore we must not press the

ch. 13, p. 206   wording. Was he leading an expedition, sent by the
(cont.)   Byzantine government, to Alexandria, and had he
stopped on the way? (N.H.B.)'. *A History of Cyprus*
(see note on ch. 9 *supra*), p. 282. For Constantia see
ibid., pp. 249-50.

NOTES ON SUPPLEMENT

Introd., p. 207   John and Sophronius: see the Introduction, p. 195.

ch. 1, p. 208   Cyrus and John: the 'national saints' of Egypt.

1, p. 208   For the Persian invasion and the capture of Jerusalem
see *United Service Magazine*, May 1913, pp. 195-201.

1, p. 209   'treasurer of the most holy church': the office was
important and distinguished: some treasurers later
became Patriarchs. For a note on the officials of the
Patriarchate see H. Gelzer, *Leontios' von Neapolis
Leben des Heiligen Johannes des Barmherzigen Erz-
bischofs von Alexandrien*, Mohr, Freiburg i. B. 1893,
pp. 120-3 (cited below: Gelzer).

2, p. 210   'The treasurers and the official who is styled "the
guardian of the peace",' i.e. those charged with the
financial administration of the different branches of
church activity, e.g. the relief of the poor, acting under
the head treasurer (see note on ch. 1) and the officer
ἐπὶ τῆς εἰρήνης.

6, p. 213   Heraclius novus Constantinus, eldest son of the Emperor Heraclius, reigned from February 13th to May
24th, 641.

7, p. 213   See the Introduction and note to p. 202 *supra*.

8, p. 215   For the vision of the Virgin and the promise cf.
ch. 46.

10, p. 216   The Pharos: the famous lighthouse at the entrance to
the harbour of Alexandria.

10, p. 217   'a swift sailer': δόρκων, so named from the fleet-footed
gazelle, δορκάς. For the trade of the ships belonging to
the Patriarchate cf. ch. 13, two ships, δόρκωνες, bringing corn from Sicily, and ch. 28, the whole fleet of
the Patriarchate undertake a trading-voyage to the
Adriatic.

10, p. 218   The Pentapolis, i.e. Cyrenaica; cf. Gelzer, op. cit.,
pp. 128-9.

11, p. 218   'in great distress'. Gelzer's text reads ἦν δὲ ἐν εὐπορίᾳ
πολλῇ. We prefer to read ἀπορίᾳ, and have so trans-
lated.

ch. 11, p. 219   Menas: see note p. 265.

12, p. 220   Nicetas, the patrician: see the Introduction, p. 197, and Gelzer, op. cit., pp. 129-31.

13, p. 222   A second marriage as a bar to ordination into the higher ranks of the clergy, see Nikodemus Milasch, *Kirchenrecht der morgenländischen Kirche*, 2nd ed. Mostar, 1905, p. 642.

14, p. 224   'the catholic prayer'. On the 'great collect' see Gelzer, op. cit., pp. 131-2; he concludes that in the orthodox Church of Alexandria the liturgy of St. James or of St. Gregory must have been in use; in the liturgy which goes under the name of St. Mark it is the priest who reads the 'great collect'.

14, p. 224   'the holy veil'. The Καταπέτασμα is the curtain over the door leading into the sanctuary; it hides from the congregation the altar and the clergy.

16, p. 227   'his customary "tip" ': the 'sportula' was universal (in the Greek text τὰς συνηθείας): paid to the tax-collector by the tax-payer, by the soldier to the officer, the monk to the abbot, the priest to the bishop; the rent for the shop: the ἐνοίκιον: the house was the property of the Church and the rent would naturally be paid to the ecclesiastical official; the public taxes: τὰ δημόσια. Here there is a difficulty: how did the Patriarch release the innkeeper from the payment of a State tax? Did he make himself personally liable for this?

18, p. 228   The 'unmentionable heretics' are the Monophysites: see ch. 32.

19, p. 228   There does not appear to be any other mention of this ceremony at imperial coronations. The μνημοράλιοι are clearly the members of the guild charged with the building of the Emperor's tomb-memorial.

19, p. 229   'the zealous Christians': Philoponoi, 'lovers of labours'. The Philoponoi, the Spoudaioi, i.e. the 'zealots', the 'Companions' formed 'une sorte de confrérie composée par chrétiens plus zélés, vivant au milieu du monde, mais y pratiquant une vie plus austère que le commun des fidèles'. They regularly attended the vigils held in the churches and other special services; they took action against paganism, they gave themselves to social service — they volunteered for nursing of the sick (cf. Usener in *Göttinger gelehrte Anzeigen*, 1892, at p. 1017), they tended the poor year after year in the deacons' quarters. We know

ch. 19, p. 229 (cont.)	of them from the fourth to the seventh century, particularly in Jerusalem, Antioch and Alexandria. The students from Alexandria who were members of these brotherhoods went to Beyrut for its law school and thus we hear of them there. It appears that many of these zealots later became monks. Cf. S. Petridès, *Spoudaei et Philopones*, Échos d'Orient 7 (1904), pp. 341-8.
20, p. 229	Persian capture of Jerusalem, see note, p. 264 *supra*.
20, p. 229	'Modestus, Patriarch of Jerusalem': not Patriarch, but rather the priest representing the Patriarch Zacharias who had been carried into Persia as a prisoner.
20, p. 229	Maenomene or maene: a cheap fish. See the note of Gelzer, op. cit., p. 138.
20, p. 229	'*jars* of wine': ἀσκαλώνια: the Latin translation of the Vita has 'vascula vini'. 'The word is otherwise known only for a special species of fig, Athenaeus iii, 78a.' Gelzer.
21, p. 231	Life of St. Epiphanius, ch. 44-5, ed. Dindorf, pp. 49-52.
23, p. 232	On St. Serapion cf. Palladius, *Lausiac History*, ch. 37; in Lowther Clarke's translation (S.P.C.K., 1918), pp. 127-32, and cf. Gelzer, op. cit., p. 140.
23, p. 232	'pagan actors': μίμους Ἕλληνας, the context shows that the word here means 'pagan'.
24, p. 233	'syncellus': literally 'cell-mate', and thus the Patriarch's confidential adviser: cf. ch. 39 and see Gelzer, op. cit., p. 121.
24, p. 234	Gelzer in his note (pp. 140-1) shows that this thought recurs in the Greek hagiographical literature. Cf. ch. 43 *infra*.
24, p. 234	'any sum worth mentioning': he would seem to have accepted a token gift so as not to wound the Patriarch's feelings — a pleasant touch.
25, p. 235	This famous dungeon is often mentioned by the Greek and Armenian historians. It was situated in Susiana and was located by Rawlinson at Gilgird.
26, p. 236	Pharos: see note on ch. 10.
27, p. 237	Caesareum: on the main harbour of Alexandria; see Gelzer, op. cit., p. 141.
28, p. 239	The fleet of the Patriarchate, see note on ch. 10.
28, p. 239	'waterproof garments': Greek ξηρόφορτα ἱμάτια. The translation is a guess proposed by Krumbacher.

ch. 31, p. 242 The church of St. Cyrus and St. John. It was begun under Theophilus as Patriarch (384-412) and finished in the patriarchate of Cyril (412-44). It was situated near Canopus (Gelzer).

32, p. 242 John and Sophronius: see Introduction, p. 195 supra.

32, p. 243 'followers of Severus'. Egypt, true to its tradition of hostility to the Imperial government in Constantinople, was strongly Monophysite. For Severus cf. J. Lebon, *Le Monophysisme Sévérien*, Van Linthout, Louvain, 1909. For Monophysitism: W. A. Wigram, *The Separation of the Monophysites*, Faith Press, London, 1923.

34, p. 244 Cf. Moschus, *Pratum Spirituale*, ch. 193, and see Gelzer, op. cit., pp. 143-4.

35, p. 244 'a so-called "adventurer" ': Gallodromos, i.e. a merchant who makes trading voyages to Gaul, and then, in a bad sense, of a fraudulent speculator.

35, p. 244 For the officials of the Patriarchate cf. Gelzer, op. cit., pp. 120-3. The Greek text here is οἱ τῆς ἐκκλησίας οἰκονόμοι καὶ διοικηταί.

37, p. 245 'almoner', διαδότης, i.e. the official charged with distributing the Patriarch's charity.

39, p. 247 'syncellus': see note on ch. 24.

41, p. 249 St. Jerome wrote the Life of St. Hilarion. Migne, *Patrologia Latina* 23, coll. 29-54.

42, p. 250 It will be remembered that John's wife had died before his consecration.

42, p. 251 'his native city', i.e. Amathus

42, p. 251 'your own souls will gain the benefit': apparently the celebration of the evening and night services will accrue to the credit of the Patriarch and advantage his soul, but the celebration by the monks of the Eucharist in the cells provided by the Patriarch would be counted to the credit of the monks and would advantage their souls.

43, p. 252-3 Porphyria: Pelagia. For the theory of the continuance of paganism in Christian legends based by Usener on the appearance of such names as Porphyria and Pelagia see, Hermann Usener, *Legenden der Pelagia* Festschrift für die XXXIV Versammlung deutscher Philologen und Schulmänner zu Trier, Georgi, Bonn, 1879; H. Delehaye, *Les Légendes hagiographiques*, 3rd ed., Brussels, 1927, pp. 186-96.

43, p. 253 Unrecognized servants of God: see note on ch. 24.

44A, p. 253 'two clerics were shoemakers': for the trades and employments permitted to the clergy see Gelzer,

ch. 44A, p. 253   op. cit., p. 150, and the full discussion in E. Herman,
(cont.)   Le Professioni vietate al Clero Bizantino, Orientalia
                Christiana Periodica 10 (1944), pp. 23–44.

44B, p. 255   Capture of Alexandria by the Persians: A.D. 619.
                John with the patrician Nicetas leaves Alexandria and
                dies in Amathus, November 11th, 619.

44B, p. 255   'continuing their course': Greek: ἀναβάλλοντες. We
                are not sure how this word should be translated; the
                Latin version of the Vita renders it by 'ascendentes'.

44B, p. 255   'the King of Kings is asking for you': Gelzer has
                pointed out that this formula is taken from the funeral
                ritual of the emperors. The Master of the Ceremonies
                at the Court says: 'Come forth, Emperor, the King of
                Kings and Lord of Lords is calling thee.' Constantine
                VII, De Ceremoniis I 60 (p. 275, Bonn edition). 'The
                prince of the Church is here granted, as it were, Im-
                perial honours' (Gelzer).

45, p. 256   We do not understand the meaning of κατ'ἐμέ in this
                sentence.

45, p. 257   St. Tychon: see H. Usener, Der heilige Tychon, Teub-
                ner, Leipzig, 1907, and see Introduction, p. 195.

46, p. 260   'and follow the monastic discipline': Greek: καὶ
                σχῆμα μοναχικὸν κατερχομένων. We are not sure
                how these words should be translated. Gelzer under-
                stands by σχῆμα μοναχικόν the monk's robe.

46, p. 260   Feast Day of St. Menas — November 11th.

46, p. 261   The vision of the virgin: see ch. 8 supra.

It will be noted that for events in Alexandria Leontius cites as his sole
authority the narrative of Menas, his own account begins with the return
of the Patriarch to Cyprus (ch. 44b). This is apparently a literary artifice.
Gelzer accepts as genuine and accurate an addition to the Preface of the
Vita which is lacking in many manuscripts and also in the Latin translation of the Life. In this addition the writer says that most of these high
achievements of the Patriarch 'I myself have seen, the others I have
described from the reports given to me by trustworthy and pious men
who have confirmed on oath the truth of their accounts and who once
belonged to the circle of those who followed the sainted Arch-shepherd'.
This passage might well have been omitted as inconsistent with the body
of the Vita. I have therefore followed Gelzer in his view (Ausgewählter
kleine Schriften, Teubner, Leipzig, 1907, pp. 7-8; the Greek text is
given on p. xiv of Gelzer's edition of the Vita) that Leontius must have
been present in Alexandria during St. John's patriarchate (see p. 197
supra).

INDEX

271